Coming S

COMING SLOWLY

•

A Kaleidoscope*

of life on, and around,

the Greek island of Poros

Anne Ibbotson

*Kaleidoscope (-lid-), N. Tube through which
are seen symmetrical figures, produced
by reflections of pieces of coloured
glass and varied by rotation of the
tube; (Fig.) constantly changing
group of bright objects. Hence
~scopic(ar)aa; ~scopically adv.
<f. GK. Kalos, Beautiful,
eidos, form and scope.

Ashgrove Publishing
London

This book is dedicated to the people of Poros,
to my friends in other parts of Greece
and to one very special Cretan!

CONTENTS

•

Chapter One
TO BEGIN AT THE BEGINNING
Page 9

Chapter Two
THE CAST LIST.
Page 41

Chapter Three
SNAPSHOTS
Page 51

Chapter Four
MILESTONES
Page 91

Chapter Five
TRIPS ON THE *ANNA II.*
Page 215

Chapter Six
FINALE
Page 253

MAPS
Page 254

ACKNOWLEDGEMENTS

My special thanks for all the love and the laughter to so many people, but especially to Spyros Spyridion, the Mayor of Poros, and to Mr Yiannis Maniyatis for all their help and encouragement; to Keren Eliot for always believing; to Ada and Ewart Reavey for always being there; to John Payne for a haven when the going got rough; to Sue Payne for being a true friend, and a delightful travelling companion; and to Brad Thompson for all his care and expertise in handling the mysteries of publication.

GREECE

This country where the light makes images the world but rarely sees.
This country where a love of life makes every day a joy.
Where laughter rings from crowded café tables,
And music flows throughout a nation's veins.

Here tragedy and comedy a mixture make, no time between,
And passions blaze with the noonday sun.
Here history stands on every ancient stone,
And every man a story – his to tell.

To stand within the ancient walls of Phaistos is to see the ghosts of yesterday,
Their lives still held within the pithari*,
Their shadows falling now across the echoes of lost lives.

To walk on Monemvasias' heights is to smell the malmsey wine,
To hear the shouts of long dead mariners, or pirates from some alien shore,
To glimpse the shores of Africa, and taste the spices of the Orient.

In Sparta stand the Mistra with rich icons and crusaders' swords,
In Delphi hawks swoop down across the barren rock, the hillsides rich
　with pine,
On Mount Olympus, here the gods still sit, frightening in their omnipotence.

So much in one small land, no one can know it all,
But every day in some new place, a sight, a glimpse of something more.
And every day the light to lift your heart and set you on a voyage of new
　discovery.
A life so full you cannot catch the days, here in this land, this patrida* that
　is Greece.

**Pithari:* The ancient jars for storing oil and wine.

**Patrida:* A Greek's word for his country, but includes everything that a Greek carries with
　him in his heart.

Chapter One

To Begin at the Beginning

•

Ever since I can remember there have been Greeks in or around the edges of my life, their influence sometimes waxing and sometimes waning, but always there. In my early teenage years, when we were living in a small village in Derbyshire I was awakened in the middle of a summer's night to the unlikely sound of gunshots. My bed was under the open window that faced down the main street and as I leaned excitedly out of it I heard shouts and the sound of running feet. I shivered in the moonlight and waited, but in vain. The sounds died away and nothing more was heard until the cockerel in the farmyard close by began its morning exultation.

A little while later I sauntered down to breakfast.

'What was all that shooting last night?' I enquired casually, as though we were living in the middle of a revolution where gunshots were the order of the day.

'Don't be silly,' replied my mother, 'gunshots in Hathersage?' and she returned to frying the bacon. I held my peace; I was almost sure I hadn't dreamed it all but even at that early age I had acquired a reputation for being 'dramatic' – something of a 'drama queen'.

It must have been the summer holidays for I remember returning to the house mid-morning after taking the dog for a walk and finding my mother nearly bursting with excitement.

'You were right,' she said, 'those were gun shots you heard.' And there followed an exotic account of how the wife of the local English teacher had 'become involved' with a Greek waiter who worked in the hotel at the bottom of the main street and how the husband had found out and chased him up the road with a shotgun. We spent the rest of the day agog, eager for the latest developments but we were to be disappointed. The waiter was long gone on the early bus to Sheffield and a curtain of silence fell over the whole episode. But over the weeks it was impossible not to notice how the teacher's wife pined alone and, romantic that I was, I harboured secret hopes that 'love would find a way.' Alas, it was not to be, but to this day the memory of it all stays vividly in my mind together with the very first hint of the passion which, I was to discover later, is an essential part of Greece and all the Greek people. It was a hint too of the existence of a country whose customs and people were to shape my life definitively for most of the years to come.

Inevitably, the years rolled by and I left the village to continue my education in London. There I added to my knowledge of Greece by experiencing *retsina* (resinated wine), *mousaka* (mince meat and aubergines) and the Parthenon (Elgin) Marbles – regrettably in that order, I have to say! After I had found my feet in London there came other experiences too, the Greek theatre productions at the famous little Unity Theatre in Kings Cross, Jimmy's in Soho with its huge plates of roughly chopped cabbage smothered in oil and lemon and the pieces of aromatic fried liver which left plenty of sauce on the plate to be mopped up with chunks of freshly baked bread – a practice which would have produced a torrent of protest back in Derbyshire. Then, walking back to the bus stop, past the other Greek restaurants too expensive for student grants, you would hear the strains of 'Greek music' – in fact the distinctive sound of the *bouzouki* – which became forever associated in my mind with the other memories of laughter, friendship and violent political argument that later would send me racing across London to find the obscure Arts Cinema which was playing '*Zorba the Greek* – for one week only!'

That night, I emerged from the cinema a completely different person, One who was to spend the next day searching the bookshop shelves for other Kazantzakis books, and in so doing come across Lawrence Durrell, Gerald Durrell, Henry Miller and Patrick Leigh Fermor, and then George Seferis and C.P. Cavafy – there seemed to be no end to the riches on offer.

My education finished, I went to Paris for a weekend – and stayed for a year. I made friends there, friends I still have today, and then, with other student friends, I began hitchhiking across Europe, staying in youth hostels and meeting people from all over the world, even a recent escapee from East Germany.

Graham Greene replaced Laurence Durrell and for a time Greece was pushed into the background. After France I wanted to carry on to Italy and then into the Balkans, but letters got lost and people were not at the end of telephones. Maybe fate was playing a bumpy hand but I gave up and went back to England. There I set about achieving another ambition – I was desperate to work in the Theatre. It took a while but eventually I wriggled in as that most vital of cogs – the assistant stage manager. I was over the moon. I simply couldn't believe that people were paying me to do all the things I had been dreaming of doing for years. In all truth they weren't paying me much, and half of that came on Saturday with the rest on the following Wednesday! But I was enthusiastic – goodness was I enthusiastic – and I slowly moved through weekly rep and then on to the Oxford Playhouse, run in those days by Frank Hauser. It was there that Greece came back into my life in the person of Minos Volanakis, who was a friend of Frank's and, that season, responsible for two productions at the Playhouse. I loved working with Minos and he completely reaffirmed my image of the Greek male compiled with such earnest research in my student days. Then Nikos Stefanou came from Athens to design the second production, and I advanced my studies even further. We worked hard and long on that production, lunch breaks were unheard of and it was rare to leave the theatre before midnight. We opened in Croydon, I remember, one of the early civic theatres conceived as a homage to concrete but for me it was a place bursting with excitement.

One morning, while I was making some prop or other, the

scalpel in my hand slipped and plunged into my knee. The scar is still there today and I have really only to look at it to have a string of vivid memories come swimming to the front of my mind. This was the time of the *Junta* – the right-wing military dictatorship – in Greece and we tried to persuade Nikos to stay but he wouldn't. He said that he could not work without Greece as his inspiration, for he was a painter too. I was impressed, but only much, much later did I realise that I had come across my first personal instance of *philopatrida*, the passion (that word again) that all Greeks have for Greece. To be deprived of their country can sometimes produce a homesickness that literally results in death.

The night before Nikos left we went out for a meal together and then I drove him back to where he was staying and returned home. As I put on the handbrake of the car, I looked down and saw his passport lying on the floor; I knew that it expired in thirty hours' time. We all wanted him to stay, there was design work for him and no one really knew how long the desperate situation would continue in Greece. By this time there were many ex-patriot Greeks in London too, some his friends. From our point of view it made so much sense for him to stay but he didn't want to. I looked hard and long at the passport but I knew it wasn't my decision to make and eventually I drove back to the house I had left only half an hour earlier and pushed the passport through the letterbox. I thought I would never see him again but I wasn't quite right about that!

I left the Oxford Playhouse but still stayed in touch with some of the ex-patriot Greeks living in London. I moved over into television, mainly out of curiosity, for my first love was still the theatre. Life was exciting and, although I still searched the bookshop shelves for books on Greece, I somehow didn't see myself going there just yet. But I was wrong again. Out of the blue a friend asked me to go with her to Crete. She had worked on the island as a holiday rep a few years before and a generous boyfriend, too busy to take time off from work, had offered to pay for both of us to go there for a two-week holiday. Somehow we got it all got sorted, even my Barney dog was found a luxurious second home on Kew Green where the four girls who shared the house promised to supply a twenty-four-hour dog sitting service. As we flew off one sunny morning I could hardly believe my luck. These were the early days of package tours and Iraklion's Airport runway was too small for the International jets, so we sat in Athens Airport waiting for the evening flight to Crete.

After Nikos had left London I had not heard from him, had not expected to, but he had given me his address and telephone number in Athens and my address book was with me in my hand luggage. I stood outside the airport building drinking in the heat and the noise and finding it all just as I had imagined. I half expected to see the Parthenon on the horizon, 'the whore of Athens' as Nikos had always called her, but she was too far away. On impulse, I walked back to the airport shop, bought a postcard, stamped it and sent it to the flat in Kolonaki, telling Nikos I was in Greece and giving him the phone number of the villa in Crete. I was sure he would not ring. They called the flight and the adventure began again.

Crete was everything I wanted it to be, though the pavements of the little town were packed with soldiers and the vehicles of the military crowded the roads. But we were tourists, welcome for our foreign currency and not to be interfered with unless it was absolutely necessary. There were people at that time who felt I should not have gone to Greece while the *Junta* was in power but I did not, and do not, agree with this stance. I feel it is essential to keep contact with a country that has thrown out democracy; people should go and see for themselves how it really is and by doing so give hope to the citizens of that country and help to keep a dialogue open. But that first night, if I am honest, I have to say that I did not have one political idea in my head. I fell asleep quickly full of good food, the local retsina and a final conscious thought that it was all a dream anyhow.

The next morning my friend and I went into Iraklion. As we crossed the main square in search of a cup of coffee, a taxi squealed to a halt in front of us and the driver fell out shouting. He swept J. off her feet and swung her round, then he opened the other doors of the car yelling, 'Out, out. My friend is back, I don't work today.' Three bewildered tourists got out of the cab and stood in the middle of the road surrounded by their luggage. Another cab came into the square and was stopped by the driver, words were spoken and the three foreigners were pushed into the second cab and driven off. The first driver turned back to us. 'Get in,' he said. 'Where do you want to go? We go for picnic.' This was my first taste of Cretan hospitality. By the end of the week I was practically overwhelmed.

The third day of our stay we spent walking and swimming and in the evening, after an early supper, we fell exhausted, into bed. The telephone started ringing in my dream and then turned itself into reality. I sat up in bed just as J. came in to get me. 'You go, she said. 'It's someone who speaks French.' I suppose I should have guessed but I didn't. It was Nikos phoning from Chania, along the coast. By one of those extraordinary coincidences that are so much a part of everyday life here, he had been walking in the White Mountains for several days. A member of his family had read my postcard and phoned to one of the *tavernas* (traditional Greek restaurant) where he had said he would stay but he had already left. Never mind, the message had been passed on along the route, the phone number intact, until it had finally caught up with him that evening. He said he was catching the morning bus from Chania and he would be in Iraklion late tomorrow afternoon. I gave him the name of the villa and we said good-night. Back in bed it all started to seem quite inevitable and I fell quickly back to sleep.

Nikos arrived and, rather to J's annoyance, he took me out to dinner. We went in a taxi out of Iraklion into a small village in the mountains. At the *taverna* they seemed to know Nikos very well and we were made so very welcome. I don't remember the food but the wine was special and there was music and dancing and I wanted the evening to go on for ever. The tables were emptying fast and it was getting very late but still we sat there, until finally they closed the shutters, and then the windows and the door, and on the record player they played the music from *Zorba the Greek* very, very quietly. The atmosphere in the *taverna* was electric and after the record had finished there was silence. I looked across at our hosts and saw that there were tears in their eyes; they were brave men indeed for at that time the music of Mikis Theodorakis was banned by the *Junta* – even the letter zed was forbidden by law and they could all have gone to prison. Nikos and I got up and left quietly, there was nothing more to say. We had ordered a taxi earlier and we set off along the road towards the town intending to stop it as it approached. The village was in darkness as we left, only a chink of light shone through the closed shutters of the *taverna*. I looked up into a sky thick with stars and I understood how men might choose to die fighting for freedom. We walked in silence; tears were very close just as they are now as I sit writing this. Eventually, the taxi appeared ahead of us and we were quickly in Iraklion. It had been an evening I shall never forget.

Next morning J. and I had arranged to go to Phaistos with a small group. Nikos was returning to Piraeus on the mid-morning ferry. I wanted to stay in Iraklion to see him off but he was adamant that I should go on the trip. It was important to see this very special site, he said, and anyhow, we were to spend a day together in Athens when J. and I were on our way back to London. He was quite right. Phaistos was extraordinary, more so because we had the place to ourselves. Not only was the setting memorable, but the atmosphere too, the sense that people from the distant past were moving all around you just out of conscious sight. This was my first serious Greek site and I was shaken by my reaction to it all. This was no mere pile of dead stones; here was history, mythology and the very beginning of story-telling. I have never been back but I can see the images of that day still clear in my mind. Two days later we went to Knossos. Interesting, I thought, like a film set, but somehow the stuffing had been knocked out of it by Sir Arthur Evan's archaeological zeal.

With Nikos gone, the Cretan hospitality that enveloped us was almost overwhelming in its intensity, and it was with great sadness that we moved on to Aghios Nikolaos for the second week of our holiday, leaving behind vows of everlasting friendship and promises to return.

Aghios Nikolaos in those days was little more than a fishing village, and one five-storey hotel was the only advance sign of the busy holiday resort it was soon to become. There too we were not short of friends. One day we were taken along the coast to Spinalonga, crossing to the little island and walking through the empty remains of the leper colony that had only recently been dispersed. It was eerie. Ghosts again, like Phaistos, but not happy ones. Easy to imagine the pain and the sickness, the buildings casting long shadows in opposition to the sun. We left quickly and found a waterside *taverna* on the mainland.

'Potato omelette or fish?' they asked.

'Two omelettes and the fish,' we replied and then watched as a small fishing boat put out to sea and returned a few minutes later with the fish.

The meal was delicious though we felt a little guilty for being so directly the fishes' executioners. We washed it all down with retsina and lemonade and afterwards, feeling sleepy, we stretched out in the shade to doze away the hours of *mesi meri*, (the hot, middle hours of the day). We drove back at sunset, the vivid red rays spreading across the sea until the sun fell below the horizon and the colours changed to the shades of night.

Another day we caught a bus up into the mountains and set off to walk. Coming to an isolated cottage, we found an elderly couple outside and asked for water. We were taken into their home and a tablecloth was produced, snowy white with beautiful lace at its edges. Two plates were brought, two glasses of crisply cold water, two olives each and a small piece of feta cheese. They watched anxiously as we sipped the water and ate the olives and cheese. We felt embarrassed then for we knew that there could not be a lot of food in that house. We wanted to give something in return but knew instinctively that it could not be money. Then I remembered my cigarettes and offered two to the old man. They both beamed with pleasure and I imagined him taking them to the *cafenion* (village café) that evening and telling of the two strange English girls. We walked back towards the village and the afternoon bus, I still savouring one of the great feasts of my life.

Thrilled with the success of our first venture away from the group, we set off in the bus again the next day, going high into the mountains until we drove into a large village and found ourselves in the middle of a village wedding. Within minutes of descending from the bus we had been pulled into a group sitting around a great plane tree. Food arrived from nowhere and glasses of wine.

'Stay,' they said. 'Wait till the evening; there will be dancing.'

We asked if there was a bus back to Aghios Nikolaos.

'Of course,' they said. ' But of course.'

But J. was more familiar with Greek logic than I and asked again. 'Today?'

'Ah, no,' came the reply, but tomorrow was no problem.

'Stay,' they said again. 'We have houses if you wish for a bed, or you can sleep under the stars. No one will sleep until dawn. You will be our honoured guests."

I longed to stay but I allowed myself to be dragged back on to the bus as it pulled out of the village – a decision I regret to this day. A Cretan wedding is not something you pass up on easily and the *kefi* (high spirits) was already starting to build.

The next morning we awoke to the realisation that our two weeks were nearly over. The thought of leaving this wonderful island was almost insupportable, only the knowledge that Nikos was waiting in Athens made getting on that early morning plane possible. Somehow we did it, leaving so early in the morning that our senses were still numbed by sleep.

After coffee on the plane we arrived at Athens Airport and stood staring across the runway at Hugh Hefner's black Playboy jet that stood there looking totally out of place. Of Nikos there was no sign so we waited, my travelling companion becoming tetchier by the second. Eventually, I phoned the Athens flat.

'He is coming,' they said; how familiar that phrase is to anyone who has spent any time in Greece!

But eventually there he was, urging us to the taxi rank.

'But what shall we do with the luggage?' we asked. 'Where is the left-luggage office?'

The concept of a left-luggage office turned out to be something impossible to convey in either French or Greek, but eventually we made ourselves understood.

'Why, you can leave it here,' he said, pointing to one of the pillars in the centre of the departure hall. We stared incredulously but in the end did just that, finding it safe and untouched twelve hours later when we returned to the airport.

It was starting to get very hot now and we were glad of the air from the open windows of the taxi in which we set off for central Athens, its driver determined to live up to the popular image of Greek taxi drivers. We were certainly wide awake by the time we found ourselves under the trees on the road leading to the Pnyx.

In my memory, the next few hours have become a montage of dazzling images.

The Parthenon, the ice-cold melon in a shaded café, walking on stage at the Herodes Atticus Theatre (unbelievable that!), lunch somewhere, followed by ice cream in Syntagma Square, where tables filled the central area and waiters risked life and limb as they dashed through the traffic. Happiness seemed everywhere that day, only the glimpses of gold braid through the curtained windows of the sinister black-limousines added a threatening note – that and the sudden gaps in conversation as we stumbled on something we should not have said in a *cafenion* full of uniformed soldiers.

We were hot and tired now and happy to follow Nikos up into Kolonaki and into his apartment for a shower and a sleep. As we left the square I looked back at the sea of tables now rapidly emptying and I wondered when I would be back. I little dreamed then that on that second visit I would be on a belated honeymoon and sipping my coffee, my husband at my side and I would fail, try as I would, to find a justifiable reason for phoning Nikos in the Athens flat. Sometimes you just have to let go, if only for a while! But all that comes later.

Meanwhile Nikos woke us as the shadows were lengthening and a soft evening breeze was stirring the net curtains – it was like a scene from a Bergman film. In the excitement that was Athens we had lost the dread of leaving, but now it came back, folding itself round us like a London fog. There was a ring at the doorbell and friends appeared with a car to take us to the airport. We said farewell to people whom we had barely met but who already seemed like old friends, and we waved as the car sped down the hill, careless of my tears.

We were six in the car squashed tight. All the way to the airport they tried to persuade me to stay. They said Nikos wanted it, that they would look after me, find me work in the theatre. Why didn't I? I'm not sure. True there was the *Junta* and there was Barney dog waiting in London. I think I just didn't believe that anyone was serious.

Anyway, I said no, that it was not possible. It was not to be the only time I was to make that mistake.

The road to the airport was lined with lamp-posts, each surmounted with a rising phoenix. I looked out of the windows at the view across the sea, but my eyes kept returning to the tops of the lamp-posts. Years later, driving along that same road I went very quiet.

'What is the matter?' said another Nikos. 'Are you unhappy?'

'I was just remembering another time I drove along this road,' I said.

'Ah, yes,' came the reply, intimating an awareness of that earlier trip which he should not have had. There were questions I should have asked then, and many more not long after, but by the time I realised the oddness of that reply there was no one left around to ask and the questions still hang heavy in my life, foremost among them the most tantalising of all time – 'What if…?'

The airport was busy now but our luggage was exactly where we had left it, untouched. Even my two Cretan gourds were peeping happily from an open carrier bag. We turned for the last goodbyes, and as J. headed for the check-in desk, I watched Nikos and the others pass through the doors and out into the forecourt where they became vague shadows which finally dissolved into the evening sunlight. I think J. was relieved when they had gone and I followed her like a robot until I found myself sitting on the plane, whose doors were still open because of some delay. Halfway down the plane a young girl burst into tears and ran to the exit. The air hostesses held her but she was adamant in her insistence that she had to stay in Greece. Reluctantly they eventually let her go as the plane was still close to the airport buildings.

I turned to J. 'She wants to go back to her boyfriend,' she said. I said nothing, but J. continued, 'She's crazy. By the time she finds him he will be with someone else. They see one holiday maker off in Departures and then go straight round to Arrivals.' Well, she may have been right about some of the boys but this romantic hoped that she'd got it wrong this time. I must admit that I had been tempted to leave the plane too but just couldn't believe in the reality of it all.

As the plane reached the end of the runway and surged into the sky I felt as though I had lost something out of my life, something that I would never find again. Crete, the Cretan people, Nikos, Athens, impossible to describe the feelings I had then, but I can remember them clearly even today. Later other Greek friends were to say, 'Greece is in your blood now, you will always come back.' That, of course, was it exactly.

I don't remember the flight. I know J. was seriously annoyed with me and we barely spoke. Then, as we approached Luton Airport, it became obvious that there was something wrong with the plane. Finally they told us that the under-carriage had jammed and the wheels wouldn't come down. The plane started climbing and then dropping to try to dislodge them, but to no avail. People began to get hysterical and I felt so sorry for the cabin staff. We flew round and round, emptying the petrol tanks and giving the airport time to arrange emergency services at the edge of the runway. I remembered an envelope that I had left in the chest of drawers in the hall in my flat. It wasn't the first time that I had been abroad, it wasn't the first time I had flown in an aeroplane, but the night before we had left for Greece I had written my will and left it where it would be easily found. That was when I started to be very afraid. Next to me J. started screaming and I think I slapped her. They told us to take up the crash position as we were going down at the end of the next circuit. Somehow I stayed calm. I started thinking of the days in Crete and the last few hours in Athens. It came to me that my life in Greece had been so perfect that there could be no future, that there was simply nowhere for it to go. But that romantic illusion didn't last long and was soon swamped by the will to live.

'Don't let me die,' I prayed silently to anyone who was listening. The screams in my head were so loud that I didn't hear the captain's voice at first. Then, incredibly, the words started to penetrate.

'The wheels are down, the wheels are down!'

We went on to make a perfect landing, taxiing past the waiting fire engines and ambulances right up to the Arrivals hall. Almost as we stopped the mobile staircases were put in place and the doors opened. I walked off the aeroplane in a daze and found the luggage already beginning to appear. The first suitcase was mine so I took it and walked out of the as yet deserted Customs Hall.

One man stood by the door looking towards the runway. As

I approached him our pilot appeared and the man patted him on the back. 'Well done,' he said, 'I thought you'd had it that time.'

'So did I,' said the pilot and walked on.

I don't remember saying goodbye to J. or getting back to my flat. I only know that for several days after that the world was a very precious place and I repeatedly thanked whichever gods had been listening that night.

Nikos and I kept in touch for a while, by phone and by letter. He sent me a Cretan scarf and an ancient votive tablet and I sent him, naively and probably stupidly, a record of the theme music from *Z* (the film by director Costas Gavras), I just hope the package arrived unopened. He sent me his photograph, too, standing in a denim shirt looking like Oliver Reed. Today it is blue-tacked on to the wall of my Poros kitchen above the poster for his Spetses exhibition. But the *Junta* remained firmly in power and the letters and the phone calls came at longer and longer intervals until they finally stopped.

I was still working in television and life was exciting. My circle of friends grew and grew but I never completely lost my interest in Greece. I came across a book entitled *Inside the Colonels' Greece* by, unsurprisingly, an anonymous author, and armed with this I tried to interest my new and sometimes influential friends in the deteriorating situation over there. But Greece was not a cause célèbre that year and it proved impossible. Then I took myself and everyone else by surprise when I got married!

I awoke one Saturday morning to a call from someone I had not known for long. First, I was told, I must go and buy a new dress and meet him at our local pub wearing it. Suitably intrigued, I complied and found him already there in a new pair of jeans that were at least six inches too long. This slight complication was solved when I remembered I had a stapler in the car that I had parked outside. My suspicions only began to be aroused when three friends arrived in suits clutching bottles of champagne, but before I had time to ask any questions or protest in any way I was whisked into my car and driven to Hampstead Town Hall, which was then a registry office. Fifteen minutes later we were back in the pub – and I was a married lady!

The celebrations went on all day. Back at the pub then down to the ICA and on to the infamous Buxton Club. All great fun until we fell asleep in the early hours of the morning. The next night we stayed with friends, so bewildered by the news and the stress of meeting my new husband that they put us to sleep in bunk beds. The following morning my new husband leaned down from his top bunk and enquired,

'Hello, what's your name?' Well, I suppose it set the tone for the next few years!

The honeymoon was difficult to arrange. My husband was heavily involved with the infant National Theatre so I went to Spain on an already planned trip with one of the 'suits' who had been at our wedding. We stayed, I hasten to add, with Carl's brother, his wife and her heavily protective Spanish family. Eventually, however, Phil's ever generous parents paid for us to have a fortnight's holiday together. We went to Greece.

I was so excited to be back and for the first few days all was well, but we had not chosen our island carefully enough. We were very close to the coast of Turkey, indeed on a clear day we could actually see it, and we were in Greece at a rather sensitive time not long after the Turkish invasion of Cyprus. The British were not very popular and the islanders began to make it very clear that that included us. I explained to the travel agent that I felt unwelcome there and we were quickly transferred to Glyfada on the outskirts of Athens.

And so it was that that one hot September day we sat in the middle of a café in Syntagma Square at the very table, I think, where I had sat not so very long before, and I watched the same black-curtained cars slip round the square and caught the same glimpses of gold braid while, as I said before, I slowly became reconciled to the fact that it really wouldn't be very proper to sneak off and make that phone call to the flat in Kolonaki!

Our one dream that summer was to visit Epidaurus, and it would have come true had we not got ourselves totally muddled over the departure dates on our airline tickets. We planned to go on the last day of our holiday, a super climax, so to speak, but the day we chose to go turned out to be the day after our scheduled flight to England – something we only found out a very short time before the flight. We packed in minutes and left for London swearing we would be back very soon. But it was not to be. And when we did return it was not together and the marriage was heading for divorce.

Back in London life went on quite swimmingly for a while. There were lots of visits to Greek restaurants, lots of bottles of retsina, and I began to cook a mean moussaka. We had Greek friends and 'next year' we were always going back but somehow we never did. Then the marriage broke up and for a time life hit one of its black-spots. Barney dog died and was buried in the garden. Life drifted on.

One summer it rained and rained and rained. A group of us were supposed to be going down to the South of France to stay in a cottage near Avignon, owned by someone's friendly aunt. But the departure date kept being put off and then put off again and every day it poured. I went across to Swiss Cottage to John Barnes and then popped into a nearby travel agent, suddenly determined to have a week in Portugal, one of the few bits of the continent I hadn't yet visited. Nearly three hours later we still hadn't managed to find a vacant seat on a flight that weekend to anywhere reasonably sunny. I left, buying an evening paper on the way home. Back in the flat, I picked up the phone, all thoughts of Portugal now banished from my mind.

Santorini – fully booked; Zante – fully booked; Poros (where?) – one week still left, but say yes now. I said yes and reached for Lawrence Durrell's book on the islands. After checking several times that it was Poros and not Paros I decided it might be OK. Durrell had been very happy there. Forty-eight hours later I set off to find out for myself.

Since that first trip to Crete, I had not been on a package tour, so I was unaware of the procedure. As soon as I had retrieved my luggage at Athens Airport, I ripped off the labels and headed into the airport foyer to try and work out how I was to get to Poros. It was the middle of the night and the Arrivals area was packed. I think I expected to see ferryboat times and the times of buses to Piraeus, but there was nothing like that, only hordes of people all following young men and women dressed in brightly coloured blazers and holding clipboards in the air. I was rather fascinated by all this and watched for some time until the airport emptied and I reconsidered my problem.

By now, I had found out that most of the ferries left at eight in the morning, so it was really only a question of getting to the port. Then I heard my name called over the loudspeaker and I stopped, incredulous that anyone should know that I was there! I went to the Olympic Airways desk and met an exhausted and somewhat exasperated Greek gentleman who was standing there with a young English couple already in his care. Considering the irritation I had caused, our Greek rep was surprisingly civil. He drove us down to Piraeus, gave us our ferry boat tickets, bought us coffee and then, deciding that I really did know my way around Greece, he left me in charge of the young couple and went home to bed. The three of us waited for about two hours in a tiny café surrounded by backpackers until finally we clambered aboard the right ferry. Then the sun rose, lighting up the long remembered Pappastratos sign, and I sat in awe on the top deck, vowing that I was going to stay in Greece for longer than one week.

The boat was the old *Eftikia* (Happiness) which plied daily around the Saronic islands and was filled with a thousand memories. It was a Sunday in early September and the boat was packed with Greek families all determined to enjoy a day away from the city. The noise was incredible, there was music and dogs barking and everyone talking at once. A group of gypsies sat on a bench behind me, the exotic colours of their clothing adding just the right note to a scene that was already beginning to resemble that of a carnival. The young couple went off to sleep but I could not bear to miss even one second of my return to Greece. I walked around the boat with an insane grin on my face that spread almost from ear to ear.

I love sailing through the Saronic Gulf for you are never completely out of sight of land. I was desperately sleepy now but had made some acquaintances and they alerted me on our approach to Poros. I went in search of the young couple but they were not where I had left them and there was no sign of them on the boat. In the end I got off without them and found out later that they had fallen asleep and had got off in a panic when the boat docked at Aegina, the first island. Well, it wasn't a disaster. Someone retrieved them, fed them and later stuck them on the afternoon boat to Poros.

I stumbled off the boat on to the quay of my temporary island home. An expert in package tours by now, I stood and waited for a rep to claim me, but there was no one in sight. The other passengers drifted away and I stood, a solitary figure, with my suitcase at my feet. Eventually I saw two figures run into view round a corner at the edge of the harbour. My rep (and her small daughter) had come to find me. The taxi took me quickly to my accommodation. I still have a memory of geraniums and bougainvillaea, a riot of colour in the gardens, orange and lemon trees and glimpses of a blue, blue sea stretching into the distance. Even at that first glance it seemed a magical island but its proper acquaintance had to wait a little while yet, for now I only wanted to sleep.

I awoke about four hours later, surprisingly refreshed, and took stock of what was to be my home for the next few days. I rehung the curtains where they had come off the curtain rail, decided that I would not be cooking dinner there that evening or ever, and then took a long cold curtain-less shower. As I had forgotten to move it out of the bathroom before turning on the water, my towel got soaked, so I had to hop around until I was more or less dry; I then put on some fresh clothes and hung my sopping towel to dry over the balcony rail. Obviously my Hampstead persona was going to have to make one or two fundamental adjustments, and with this thought in mind, I set off to see if something that had looked like a small shop from the window of my racing taxi was indeed just that. Of course it wasn't, it was more like an off licence, but it sold coffee and sugar and milk and biscuits and wine, literally by the barrel, so, armed with the basics to get me through to the next day, I returned to my apartment and faced the fact that I was going to stay in Greece for longer than my one-week holiday. Only I wasn't going island hopping or anywhere else for that matter, I was going to stay right here!

At what I vaguely remembered to be the appointed hour, I headed for Poros town, the tour office, and something described as a 'welcome' meeting. Poros town was delightful in the evening sunshine. Warm, welcoming and very foreign, exactly what I had been dreaming of those light years away in England. I got pleasantly lost and when I finally found the tour office it was well past the time I should have been there. There was only one person in the office, obviously Greek. When I explained I was looking for the rep, I received the reply,

'Ah, you are late.'

'How can I be?' I countered, '"This is Greece, time is nothing.'

'But we keep English time here,' He replied.

'Then I must leave at once for I came to be in Greece!'

I was eventually sent on my way to a nearby restaurant (*taverna*, I snapped!) where the rep was waiting, but I left the office determined not to return and if at all possible to avoid any further contact with this extremely rude Greek who, I fervently hoped, was not typical of the other inhabitants of the island. Later, I was to revise my opinion and we became, and still are, very good friends.

I think Poros had everything I was looking for that summer,

I was certainly in the right place at the right time. Mass tourism was still in its infancy and the local Greeks had a far from sophisticated approach to it all. But it was such fun! Like a long-running Greek pantomime it just went on and on. Days full of laughter, nights full of music and dancing, and what the Greeks call *kamaki*.

Kamaki is a fishing term but it has been borrowed to apply to all the romance that a Greek puts into 'chatting up' a female friend. You are paid the most extravagant compliments, gazed at with such lovelorn intensity and made to feel like Aphrodite herself. Age has nothing to do with it and I still revel in it today, especially when alone in Athens or in some relatively remote mainland village.

Believe it and you are lost. Many young girls did, and were. And many made disastrous marriages. Play the game and it is a delightful way to pass an idle hour in some idyllic café while the business of the Plaka hustles and bustles around you. But you must be resilient. Leave the café table after an hour of happy chat and you leave a devastated heartbroken lover. Return to the table ten minutes later, ready to devote the rest of your life to your Romeo, and you find him busily at work on the next foreigner who has stopped for a coffee.

Well, *kamaki* was alive and well and busy on Poros that September. And it made for an easy way to meet people and make friends. Go to a *taverna* two evenings running and you are practically part of the family. And the island was small. At that time there was only one *taverna* and bar and one supermarket in Askeli, so every evening most of the holidaymakers staying in the little tourist village set out for the main town, often on foot. I too, used to walk in most evenings as it got dark, for there was Greek music everywhere and the scent of the jasmine and the pine. The other tourists were friendly and it was rare for me to eat alone. We sat in *taverna*s and swapped information about buses and bars and newspaper shops.

My first week was filled with laughter and could have stretched into eternity as far as I was concerned. On the

Wednesday I finally went to Epidaurus! I went to Mycenae and Naplion too, for it was a guided tour. The guide was excellent and for once I was glad to be part of the crowd, for I learned far more in the group that I would have done on my own. There seemed to be hundreds of tourists at the Epidaurus theatre, many queuing for that magical centre spot where the slightest whisper can be heard in the farthest seat. Fourteen thousand people it held in the past and in the very near future I was to experience it filled to capacity many times. But for the moment I managed to find a quiet spot away from the crowds and touch with my finger tips that peace so brilliantly described by Henry Miller – the peace which 'passeth all understanding.'

But almost as soon as I touched it, it was gone, and I climbed down the ancient marble to the ringing tones of 'to be or not to be' and the guitar strains of 'Bye- Bye, Miss American Pie'. It seemed such a brief moment, but later I was to return time and time again, bringing tourists to the summer festival and sitting bewitched by the tragedies and comedies of the ancients, so brilliantly performed by the National Theatre and the other great companies of Greece – the actors, actresses and directors being household names there, Minos among them.

We always arrived early and those first summers before security became necessary I found myself free to wander at will and often alone around the amphitheatre. It was easy then to hear the voices echoing down the centuries together with the rustle of the gowns as they brushed against the marble seats. Now the magic is of a different kind, for this epitome of ancient Greece, this monument that people travel thousands of miles to see, has become part of my everyday life and that is something that even I never dreamed would be possible. I wander contentedly to 'my' piece of marble, chosen for its properties as a back rest, and watch the familiar contours of the amphitheatre fill out with Athenians, Corinthians, Spartans, Peloponessians and even, on occasion, the odd Persian. But the wars nowadays are only fought by actors, though Aristophanes still speaks loud and clear against war, an honorary member of the Peace Movement and a champion of the so-called 'common' man.

After my trip to Epidaurus my first week started to come rapidly to a close. I was determined to stay so it was time to beard the tourist agent in his office and inform him of my decision.

'There are no empty rooms,' he started categorically.

But he was, of course, quite wrong and I soon found something a little nearer the town. I watched the last ferry leave the island on the Saturday night and then, feeling like some intrepid adventuress of the ninteenth century, I turned my back on Europe and set off, metaphorically speaking, to discover the Balkans.

I stayed until November and watched the island slowly regress into the 1950s. The *taverna*s closed one by one, and then the bars. Donkeys re-appeared in the main square and the *cafenion* filled with men. No women were around after darkness fell, and that was early now.

Eventually it became too difficult to stay and I was due to start work in England anyhow. I packed up my few possessions and left, the dark glasses hiding my tears as the Flying Dolphin (hydrofoil) sped towards Marina Zea on the first stage of the journey to the airport. Something special had happened but I was not sure that I would ever come back.

In London the answerphone was jammed with messages, bewildered friends demanding explanations. But I couldn't tell them what had kept me there or why it had all become so important. Eventually life settled back to the way it had been and I pushed the memories away from the present.

I was working for the satirical television programme *Spitting Image* over the winter, and at the end of the long series the company paid all the airfares for us to have a week's holiday in Barcelona. It all went really well and we had a great time, going our own ways in the day and then meeting up to eat in the evening in a variety of assorted groups. On the Sunday before we flew back I took the local bus out to the beach and there looked across the Med to where I imagined Poros to be and suddenly found that I wanted to be back there more than anywhere else in the world.

Back in London I booked a six month, open return to Athens, turned down another long-running series and headed for London Airport.

This time when I stepped off the boat I did not expect to find a rep waiting to greet me but I had a room waiting and I knew where to go. The little square was busy and there were familiar faces in the harbour cafés. I even heard someone call 'Welcome back, Anna.' And I sighed with relief. I had not known whether or not I was wise to come for I had always made it a rule never to go back, and that first summer had all been so extraordinary. But almost from those first minutes I knew that there had been a sort of inevitability about this return and I was not going to need the other half of my air ticket for quite some time yet.

There was an air of innocence about those first two summers and Poros was still enchanted with the tourists. They spilled off the boats and the motor coaches, bringing with them a glimpse of the West, which conveyed an image of sophistication and a taste of the exotic.

Look at the history of Greece and you will find centuries of foreign occupation and tyranny; now, although access was still strictly regulated, there was a sense of change in the air. The arrival of commercial television had opened the airwaves and the newspapers were enjoying an unprecedented freedom and popularity. Greece had its President and Democracy was learning to stand firmly on its own two feet in the country that had been its cradle. Tourism was bringing undreamed of wealth and opportunity to some of the poorest islands and it was welcomed with open arms.

Not so welcome but as yet barely visible were the radical changes that were to occur far too rapidly in a way of life that had hardly changed for centuries.

But that summer we laughed and danced the nights away. Dreams and hearts were broken and promises were made which were to fade with the sunlight. The days sped by. My friends of the previous summer were delighted I was back. A group of musicians in one of the *taverna*s broke into 'my' song every time I walked past and we sat up into the early hours of each morning arguing and chatting and pondering the possibilities of this or that liaison.

As the end of that particular summer approached I did not know how I was going to make myself leave the island, it all seemed too idyllic to be true – and of course it was. Still, when I left this time the going was a little easier and I believed the Greeks when they said to me, 'Poros is in your blood now, you will always come back.' So I boarded the plane with a thousand memories to last me until my return, and went back to London to get on with my 'other' life.

Unexpectedly, I had a chance to buy the flat I had been living in for many years. Friends persuaded me that I would be stupid not to and for once I listened to them.

Everything went ahead very quickly. Other friends had bought the rest of the house and were bent on radical restoration. At first everything was fine and I planned to do my repairs rather more slowly and pay for them with money I earned; but the day the builders fell through part of the kitchen wall I had to think again. To cut a very long story short, I decided to go for broke and called in builders of my own. Within two weeks the plaster was off the walls, the floorboards were up and the electrical wires looped down over doors. I existed, for I can't say lived, with a bed, a gas cooker, a loo, a cold-water tap and an ancient black and white television lent by a neighbour.

Mrs Thatcher and her Government, who had been waiting with infinite patience for this very moment, smashed the unions and plunged the country into recession. I had always worked freelance in films and television, so for me any chance of work disappeared almost overnight. People I had known for years and often helped out on low-budget projects no longer returned my calls, or if they did, simply couldn't help.

At first I hung on, expecting the phone to ring as it always had before, but slowly it became clear that the work had simply evaporated. Non-union people, desperate to get a toe into television, were willing to work for virtually nothing. Expertise was no longer an asset. Union practices had certainly become too restrictive but they also ensured that their members were trained and professional; this no longer seemed to matter.

My money ran out and I laid off the workmen and went on the dole. For nearly two years I tiptoed over broken floorboards and went to friends for a bath. There were many people worse off than I was but I was unprepared for the depression that set in and left me sitting day after day incapable of making any sort of positive move at all. Eventually, friends kickstarted me and I did what I should have done many months before, I borrowed far more money than was sensible, finished the flat, let it, and went back to Poros for six months to sort myself out.

Actually I was running away.

I left England the day after Boxing Day and arrived on Poros with exactly £63 to my name. It was the morning of 27 December and I think I must have gone a little mad, for I simply took a taxi down to the apartments where I had stayed before and arrived completely unexpectedly. It had never entered my head to contact anyone on the island and no one knew I was coming. To their credit the family there barely seemed surprised and quickly opened up one of their summer apartments and provided extra blankets and rugs and plates of hot food.

They must have guessed that something was wrong, or maybe I just looked odd, for I stayed the whole of that winter and they would not take any rent.

'I get no rent from the apartment in the winter,' said my landlord, 'why should I take any from you?'

We have since all become great friends but I don't think that they have ever realised quite how much I am indebted to them. If they didn't exactly save my life they certainly saved my sanity! As the rent started to come in from my flat in England I slowly managed to pay off some of my personal debts and come to terms with the fact that I simply could not afford to live in my own country. Without Greece I would have been on the streets, for even if I had sold the flat in London, the situation there was so complex that I would have ended up with nothing.

The winter passed; I walked backwards and forwards across the island until I was able to look clearly at my situation and contact one or two long-suffering friends in London. Each day the family continued to cook too much food 'by mistake' and two little girls continued to bring huge plates of it to my door, and I continued 'to do them the honour of eating it'! It was delicious. Other friends on the island found out I was back and bags of fruit and vegetables appeared on my balcony. If I stopped for a coffee in town, it had been mysteriously paid for.

When the tourists arrived there was work, and life continued to get better and better. Without the Greeks, I hardly like to think what I would have done. In England door after door had closed in my face. Here, somehow they understood and simply helped. Back in London I had had faith that if I got to Poros everything would be all right, so I came. My friends here, all Greek, will probably never know how much I owe them. I came to Greece because I had nowhere else to go. I stay because there is nowhere else I want to be.

In the early days of the blitz on the flat, I left the workers to it and came to Poros for a quick holiday. All things seemed possible still in those days and I was planning to work in England for six months and come here for the rest of the year.

'Why do you not come for all time?' I was asked and I explained that a Greek friend had told me that Greece was not for everyone and I was to be sure that I could really live there.

'Come slowly.' he said. So I did.

During the summer after my sudden flight from England we

were sitting in a group in one of the bars and the same question was asked of me again. I gave the same reply and then heard the ironic comment from behind my head, in the same voice as before.

'Anna,' it said, 'I think you've come!'

I love Greece and the Greeks but here is not paradise. I have had to learn a very different lifestyle and sometimes it has not been easy. The Greeks think I am a little mad and I think the same of them and that, to my mind, is a pretty good basis for a friendship. And like all close friends, we sometimes fall out badly, but there is always a way back. I have been happy here and desperately sad. I have laughed and cried and shouted and sulked, but that is life. It seems to me that I owe the people of Greece, and especially those of Poros, an enormous debt of gratitude for all they have done and they will reply that I am welcome. My days in this staggeringly beautiful country have been some of the best of my life and what follows is an attempt to share them with you.

•

When I awoke today I knew it was winter at last. The mountains pressed close to the little island and the colours had seeped out of the landscape, only the brilliant shades of the bougainvillaea still held the vibrancy of summer.

I walked down the old coast road to the supermarket. Once the main road to Neorion, it is now little more than a donkey track, and weaves reassuringly between some of the old stone houses of Poros, now more and more frequently interspersed with the new breeze-block apartment buildings. Still, it was easy to lose myself in the past as the first wood fires of winter threw their smoke into the sky and the new crop of oranges and lemons bobbed in the breeze. The fig trees, much loved in the summer for their leafy shade, now stand awkward and redundant, soon to drop their leaves and become stark statues in the winter landscape; but the day will come when new green shoots will magically appear on the branches, bringing messages of spring and the promise of summer to come.

There are few people about today; no sign of Eleni on the balcony of the hotel, though the door is open so she can't be far away. One shout and she would materialise, eyes sparkling with laughter and curiosity. But I am in a hurry and don't call out, for we have the whole winter for the chats and the gossip which make up such a large part of the island life.

The supermarket is busy and hums with bits and pieces of conversation half heard coming from behind the fruit juices. I slip easily into Greek, forgetting the earlier agonies of trying to remember the word for cheese and then not daring to ask for some because I had no idea how many grams I wanted. Now, though, there is even time for a joke before I slip out and head for home. Gina meets me by the little church and insists on escorting me back. She is a tiny blob of a dog belonging to my Albanian neighbours and she has a personality way in excess of her size. I call her the 'levitating ball of fluff', for she leaps very high from virtually a standing position and with her coat brushed she is almost as wide as she is long. On her daily visits she sends the rugs and furniture flying, for she has limitless energy and closely resembles a whirling dervish. Today she is in one of her more responsible moods as she escorts me safely to the bottom of my mountain.

And then, suddenly I have the answer to the problem I have been considering all morning, the problem that precipitated the walk to the supermarket. Where shall I start my Homeric account of island life, my very own *Iliad*? Of course, I must begin at the end, well with an ending anyhow. I must start with a leaving!

You can depart from Poros in many ways but most of our visitors prefer to do it by boat, leaving the faster Flying Dolphins to the people who live here and are anxious to reach their destination, knowing that they will soon be back. But some people do not know if they will ever be back and so it is best to leave slowly, savouring the last sight of this magical little island. You stand there watching the cubic houses of the old town slowly merge into a picture from a child's colouring book. The blue dome on top of the clocktower is a vivid landmark but it gets smaller and smaller and it seems as though there is a cord tying you to the place, a cord which stretches as the boat moves away, faster and faster now, tearing you from friends and memories and dreams – and something else, but what, a sense of belonging perhaps? Familiar places pass, the pretty bay of Neorion, with the bus trundling down the hill to the local *taverna*s where newly made friends still sit drinking coffee or beer for they are not leaving yet. Love Bay, so aptly named (!), and Russian Bay, with the little island of Daskalion sitting low in the water, its tiny church a brilliant white against the blue of the sea. Next comes the point light, off duty and sleeping soundly in the hot sun, while a friendly herd of goats cluster round its base for company.

And now... but something is happening for the boat is turning and within seconds Poros has gone and the cord has snapped. You stand looking back in disbelief. Was it ever really there, this fantasy island in the Saronic Gulf? Well, if you never come back you will never be completely sure!

Almost without thinking, you find yourself moving away from the back of the boat, into the bar maybe with its noisy computer games and that throb of Greek conversation which never seems to stop. Or perhaps you just move to the side of the boat and watch the dotted villages of the mainland slide away. Certainly by the time you reach Methana your mood will have changed and you will have started to think about the rest of your journey home.

'Home' – that is such an emotive word. Is it really just the place where your heart is? I think not. Home is also the place where you understand the culture, the traditions, the history and, of course, at least something of the language. I have lived in Greece for quite a number of years now and somewhere during those years it has begun to feel like home. The first 'leaving' was terrible but the first 'return' – well, that was something else.

The excitement really starts to build once you are safely aboard the boat in Piraeus. I suppose the Flying Dolphins are better for your return, for you have been suffering a form of impatience to be there that they are most able to satisfy, but we left on the boat so let us return that way.

As the clock ticks on to the hour you hear the rumble of the engines and the slight vibration as they settle into a rhythm and almost imperceptibly you slip away from the quay leaving the other ferries behind teasing you with their images of Crete and Santorini and Mykonos. The Pappastratos sign provides a familiar landmark until that too slowly fades and you are leaving the hustle, bustle and noise of the big city behind. Ahead, beyond the huge tankers in the foreground, framed by the hills of Salamis, lies the open sea. Then they too disappear and you find yourself looking towards the outline of Aegina, already visible on the horizon. Aegina, the island famous for the Temple of Aphaia, and Aghios Nectarios and pistachio nuts. Well, we'll visit Aegina later. Now there is just the image of the tiny white church on the harbour front and the remains of the Temple to Apollo, no time to see any more, for the Greek boats only stay in harbour long enough to set down and pick up passengers and cars amid a cacophony of shouting and engine revs. What seems at first glance to be chaos quickly resolves itself into a highly efficient operation and we are soon on our way to Methana.

It is not unusual to find entertainers or raffle-ticket sellers on a Greek ferryboat, together of course, with the ubiquitous seller of lottery tickets who offers the possibility of instant success. So sit back now and enjoy the music or the patter of the raffle-ticket seller – the Greeks will. And before long, the faint smell of sulphur tells you that you are nearing the spa town of Methana with its healing waters and what is confidently believed to be its dead volcano. And the excitement is really mounting now; next stop Poros, and you will be back, back on the little island whose images have haunted you the whole time you've been away. The Poriotes say that once you have been there you will always come back and here you are! First you come to the headland light, the ever-present goats grazing peacefully at its feet. Then the tension builds unbearably for the boat starts to turn and for a split second there is the thought that the island will not be there, waiting, as you have imagined a thousand times. Perhaps after all it was just a dream. But no, slowly but surely, the pyramid of the old town rises before your eyes while the blue dome of the clocktower stands out against the backdrop of the mountains. Time seems to hang suspended for a moment and then picks up speed. Russian Bay, Love Bay, Neorion, all flash by until the loudspeaker warns you that you must be ready to disembark. You plunge into the shadowy depths of the hold, claim your luggage and stand with the other returning pilgrims as the door drops down to reveal a close-up of the harbour front before it crashes down on to the quay and you are there. 'kalos oriste' (literally, 'Good here you are'). Welcome to Poros!

What follows is a highly personal, totally biased glimpse of a small Greek island, its people and its way of life – with occasional forays into the highways and byways of Greece itself.

Chapter Two

THE CAST LIST

•

When you visit any country, the memories you bring away are not only of mountains and beaches and architecture; far more important than any of these are the people you meet, sometimes for only a moment, sometimes for long enough for you to return from your holiday convinced that you have bonded with them for life. Convinced, too, that you will return again and again, taking 'Manuel' his English cheese and 'Maria' her Marks and Spencer underwear. Mostly, of course, you never do.

Poros, as in so many things, seems to be an exception to the rule. The first time I left I hardly dared to think I might return, and the people who had become so real during those first three months I quickly and cruelly relegated to memory; a part of a one-off magical experience. But over that first winter their images remained, clear and sharp, and after that first return my new friends became an enduring part of my life and most are still there today. As you are about to meet them for yourselves I think it only polite to introduce you properly, roughly in the order I met them myself.

It was my passion for antiques that caused me to enter one of the little converted houses in the old town. A long thin room hung with traditional rugs and old Epirus copper pots led into a shadowy cave from which a disembodied voice said, 'Welcome.' I squinted into the depths of the back room, my eyes slowly becoming accustomed to the lack of light. There was a slight movement and Takis appeared smiling, his eyes full of curiosity.

I'm not sure if I bought anything that first time, but I returned again and again to sit on the small upturned barrel, enjoy the coolness of the thick-walled room and to listen to Takis as he told tales of village history and of the gypsies who regularly visited the shop. They came to collect the old, empty shell cases and took them away to engrave them with assorted patterns and scenes from the past. His stories were full of characters who sounded larger than life, but it didn't take long for Takis to emerge as a veritable character himself. The family came originally from Tripolis, but they had spent some considerable time in the Plaka in Athens where Takis's father had been a respected, if broke, member of the community. This was the time of the *Rebetika* (music that arrived with the Greek refugees from Smyrna) and the *Karaghozoi* (shadow puppet) theatre, itinerant musicians and poor children kidnapped by rich, childless Athenians. It all sounded much more romantic than it actually was, but Takis grew up with a love of music and later, with a friend, toured the *Panagyri* (Saint Day) markets selling 45rpm records and living a life that was perhaps 'no better than it should be'! Later he went to university in Italy and later still met and married Giorgia, eventually producing a daughter, Leda.

Leda spent many happy hours asleep in her carrycot in the shop at her mother's side and was frequently admired by a visiting, but incognito, Greta Garbo; until, that is, Giorgia, without thinking, addressed her politely as 'Miss Garbo' and saw her quickly leave the shop, never to return. I, on the other hand, returned often, regardless, and was to spend many happy hours listening to stories of village 'comeuppances', rumours of non-existent brothels, and tales of icon painters getting drunk and painting pictures of the Virgin Mary in the nude. Thanks to Takis and Giorgia the island characters began to emerge from their backgrounds and the island took on a life all its own.

Today Takis and Giorgia have their own olive-oil-soap business and Leda is at university. The little shop is shuttered and dark, its memories relegated to the past, like the flaking paint and the dusty cobbled floor, but for me they are as vivid as ever and every time I walk past I remember something new.

Nikos I met in most atypical circumstances. It was all quite out of character for him, but great fun for the rest of us .The day started quite normally with a morning walk into Poros town to collect my mail. On the way back I stopped for a coffee with some friends, one of whom owned a bar downtown. This bar had something of a reputation for the expertise of its tequila-drinking clientele. Phenomenal quantities of tequila were reputedly drunk every evening, helped along by the story of Costas's father. Not surprisingly, this story was pure fiction, but at frequent points in the narrative, tequila glasses had to be banged on the top of the bar and their contents downed in one go. Sitting in the warm morning sunshine we drifted into *mesi meri* and after a couple of lunchtime beers it became imperative that we should visit the bar and hear the epic story for ourselves. So, when evening came, by now rather wishing that we had not got ourselves involved in all this, we ate a substantial meal and sat drinking coffee waiting for the appropriate hour to descend on downtown Poros.

It was at this point that Nikos appeared in his little Mini, bought us a drink and enquired of our plans for the evening. We explained. 'Oh, I'll come too,' he said, rendering us open-mouthed for Nikos was known not to drink. Still, the more we thought about it, the more the idea appealed, so we all squeezed into the Mini and set off. And indeed it was all rather good fun, though mercifully we were excused most of the rounds of tequila. Then a group of Australians appeared and the evening took a turn for the better – or worse, depending on your point of view! The bar became increasingly lively and someone introduced the ritual of lying flat on your back and having a shot of tequila poured into your mouth. 'I think I'll have a go at that,' said Nikos, now fully entering into the spirit of things. In vain did we try to persuade him that it really wasn't a good idea and that it would all end in regret, but he insisted on going ahead, so he did. By this time, not exactly sober myself, my homing instinct locked in and I set off down the harbour front in search of my apartment.

Next morning I woke late but felt fine until I remembered Nikos, and then the guilt set in. I found him sitting in his office wearing dark glasses, a cup of Greek coffee on the desk in front of him. This was a bad sign, for Nikos was known never to drink coffee either, besides which, he was obviously concentrating very hard on not moving his head. It took most of that day for him to recover. He has never repeated the experience, but remains staunchly proud of the one evening he really let his hair down and became a tourist!

Later he was to marry, and over the years he and his wife have become my good friends and it is usually to Nikos that I go when in need of a photocopier or a fax machine or the use of a car for a couple of hours.

Petros is my good friend, my very good friend, and the islanders these days refer to him as my brother. He is very good looking and has one of the kindest hearts on the island. Until recently it was one of my greatest pleasures to go with him up the mainland mountain roads on a visit to his father at his farm there. Alas his father died a little while ago and there is a great gap where he once was. He was one of life's true gentlemen and I am so very grateful for the memories of him that I am able to share.

One of Petros's ambitions was to own his own *taverna*, something he finally succeeded in doing a year ago. It came a little too late for his father to see but I for one feel sure that he is quite aware of everything that is going on in Neorion Bay.

The *taverna* opened in a thunderstorm with just a few faithful friends sitting damp and shivering in the gloom, but since then it has gone from strength to strength and it is great fun sitting and watching Petros fly round the tables – but then watching other people's dreams come true is always a joy for their friends.

One of the first ways you meet people in Greece is by eating in the *taverna*s, as I know by experience, but it took a while to get to know Yiannis and Andreas. Their *taverna* is the oldest on the island and has some of the loveliest views from the tables that are set at the edge of the sea and look across to the old town of Poros. Whenever I walked past in those early days it always seemed full of sophisticated Athenians, all off the luxury yachts moored in the bay and hopelessly out of my league. Of course I should have known better for everyone is always welcome and at the height of summer there are some pretty lively evenings there. The Greeks have a wicked sense of humour and these two are no exception, so what pleasanter way to spend an evening than to sit by the sea eating good food, drinking a little wine and being made to feel like a very special guest. This latter talent is one the Greeks have in excess – English gentlemen, please note!

Meanwhile, down in Askeli there is Andonis and his family. Once to be found sailing the world as a captain on the large merchant ships, he woke up one day and realised he was missing the best years of his daughters' lives; so he took early retirement and came home. Now he owns a block of apartments and runs the swimming pool bar there where he plays mine host with something of a natural talent, if not exactly practising the skills of a Warren Beatty or Tom Cruise.

Andonis is generosity personified and it is fortunate that Christina is on hand to see that some of the guests occasionally pay for something! His two daughters, Yiota and Evi, are delightful and obviously adore their father, though there is enough of Christina in them to throw him a look from time to time which states quite clearly that 'enough is enough'! This was the first family to welcome me into their home and we have spent some good times together – again, a little food, a little wine and just a hint of the local gossip.

Captain Kiriakos and his family will pop up frequently in the pages of this book. Because of their boat, the *Anna II*, we have spent a lot of time together, but also I live very close to their house and usually meet at least one member of the clan on a daily basis. When I first knew them, Kiriakos's mother was still alive and I soon grew to love her. Sometimes she came with us on the boat and we used to walk slowly round the harbour at Spetses talking ten to the dozen. She spoke no English and my Greek then did not stretch to more than a few words, but somehow we understood one another and, like Petros's father, she impressed me with her quiet dignity and deep love of life. She told me once that she had had an exceptionally happy marriage. She said she never knew why her husband chose her for she was not beautiful (although people have since told me that she was, in fact, one of the local beauties and widely admired). Happily, he would have no other and they went on to have four children and a good life. It must have been a happy family always, for it still is to this day, and there never fails to be a warm welcome in that house and a love of laughter which draws you back again and again. In fact the whole of the area around me is populated with cousins and second cousins and aunts and uncles and if ever there is a family get-together, it really is a case of 'hang on to your hat'! They tell me now that I am part of the family, and I consider myself most privileged.

Matina is my swimming friend and many summer mornings we are to be found neck deep in the sea and local gossip. The ladies of Kanali beach are a formidable bunch and I am constantly in trouble for not wearing a hat and sitting in the sun longer than I should. I seem to have been accepted as a deserving member of the group, however, or at least as some sort of mascot. As it happens, Matina and her husband George have also run a local *taverna* for over twenty years. When I first came to the island it was well known for the dancing of their sons, often in traditional costume, but the boys grew up and went on to other jobs and those evenings became rare; still, even without the dancing it remained popular, and until the day it closed it was one of the most traditional *taverna*s on the island.

There are many good dancers on Poros, and there is perhaps no better way to complete an evening than in a *taverna* with good food, good wine, music and good company, for then the *kefi* will come and the dancing will start. By the end of the evening you are flying, your feet barely touching the ground, completely in accord with the other people dancing with you. It's quite simply one of the best feelings around. But if you want to meet one of the famous dancers of Poros, then take a load of washing to the launderette and ask for George. Giorgio was a dancer almost before the days of the foreign tourist. He worked on the big international cruise boats and danced in films. It is even said – well, I'll leave him to tell you some of those stories.

When I first came here, he and his brother ran a *taverna* down at the far end of the harbour and every night the place was packed and the dancing started early. People used to hover on the road just to watch and envy those fortunate enough to be part of the party. There were many places like that on Poros, and even now, with fewer visitors, one of the *taverna*s will suddenly erupt and you just have to hope you are there to be part of it. Down in Askeli there is dancing most summer evenings. This is now done professionally and in traditional costumes. Another Giorgio leads the field here and he has danced all over Greece and specialises in the regional variations of all the great dances. There is always a great atmosphere, but even these evenings can suddenly reach another level and 'take off' and then word spreads quickly; if you see people suddenly start arriving on motor bikes then hang on to that table and order another round of drinks!

Fanni is a friend of mine. Her mother and father are very special people, and their *taverna* is much loved by the tourists and Greeks alike. Fanni works in the family *taverna* and dances the Greek dances with enthusiasm. More and more women are learning and performing the characteristically showy male dances. They do it well but somehow the effect is never quite the same as when they are danced by a man in love with his girl, for the dances were, and still are, part of the courting ritual and the better the man danced, the better his chances of winning the lady. They are also an expression of lost love and are danced even on the death of a loved one or as a prelude to an act of dering-do. As a courting ritual they worked sensationally well, and still do!

Although it is easy to eat out alone here, I do have Magda to share some of my summer evenings. Magda, one of my truly cosmopolitan friends, spends most of the winter in Athens and most of the summer on Poros. She is one of the few people with whom I dare to discuss Greek politics and catch up on all the inter-party gossip. We are also avid music and theatre lovers and every winter look forward to the new season's events with great enthusiasm. Married to Vassilis and with one son, Orestes, she is nevertheless something of a free spirit and seems to have boundless energy. She is also a good friend, and always there when needed.

Kleopatra is my other Athenian friend. She is rooted almost completely in the city and it is difficult to persuade her to come to Poros, though it has been known. We met when we both worked for a new television station, Skai, she as the designer and I as the adviser and, later, director of the Greek version of *Spitting Image*. These were exciting times for we actually went on air without a licence, albeit to only a small part of Athens in the early days. But these really were the actual *Spitting Image* puppets and nothing like them had been seen in Greece before. We worked hard, all of us, but Kleopatra and I quickly found a rapport and, when the going got a little rough, we tended just to forge ahead and do our own thing. The friendship survived the end of our contracts and since then has gone from strength to strength. She studied at the School of Fine Arts here in Athens and now specialises in modern sculpture. With two exhibitions to her credit, she is beginning to make a name for herself, and I am told that she is very talented. She, too, is married but as Dionysus works long hours in his advertising business, Kleopatra is free sometimes to sneak off with me to the cinema or to an exhibition, often accompanied by her very youthful mother. We are close friends now and my life would be infinitely duller without her in it.

Catherine is one of my English friends here. She is married to Kostas and has two boys, Stash and Daniel. She has long been one of my experts on various aspects of Greek family life and is always ready when the strain of struggling in basic Greek becomes so overwhelming that English must be resorted to for a while. Between us we manage to keep a reasonable supply of books circulating and she is my connecting link in the Sunday Times chain, thus making sure that Jeremy Clarkson and A.A. Gill keep me up to scratch on all matters relating to current 'thinking' and culinary etiquette. Over the years we have experienced comedy and tragedy and somehow managed to survive both.

Sue and Andy come next. They visited the island originally as tourists but found something special for themselves and eventually moved out here lock, stock and mildly agoraphobic dog. They have settled well and love the life here and they can always be relied on as companions at any special event where going alone could be a decided disadvantage.

The other Sue lives in London and without her I would not have been able to stay here for such long periods, especially in the early days. Another friend who helped to save my sanity in the difficult days, she has now become an indispensable part of my life. I met her here on Poros where she was a regular visitor; now she comes less often, but is remembered with great affection and is often asked after. It was for her that I wrote so many of the letters and articles on which this book is based in an attempt to make her feel she was still here on Poros – and sometimes just to make her laugh, for laughter was one of the things which originally bound us together. Long may that laughter continue.

These, then, are just some of the people you are going to meet as you turn the pages of this book; they are the people who help to make my life in Greece so special. If you are reading this and you are someone who already comes to our island again and again then you will have your own special friends, and they may not be mentioned here, for Greece, and Poros especially, is full of warm, generous people who take a delight in welcoming their visitors from all over the world. Of course, you will have your own *taverna*s and bars and your own stories to tell. Well then, you will just have to write your own book ! If, however, you have never been to this crazy little spot in the Saronic Gulf, then buy that plane ticket now and come and see for yourself and make some friends of your own. For only then will you begin to understand what I am writing about.

Chapter Three

SNAPSHOTS

•

Poros

Wednesday morning, 4 a.m., and in the London flat the alarm goes off at the appointed hour; so far, so good. It is cold and pouring with rain but eventually there is a taxi, whose driver, after driving round and round Victoria Station swearing blind that there are no trains to Gatwick at such an early hour, drops me, panic-stricken, at the main entrance and simply drives off. Of course there are no trolleys, so I stagger along the concourse dripping spare coats and cameras and a hundred other items I had sworn to leave behind. And there is a train! The guard tells me not to bother to get a ticket; he loads my luggage into the guards van and then seats me in a first-class compartment. The train leaves immediately, revealing a notice saying that the next two have been cancelled – the omens seem good! Gatwick is humming; I queue for my ticket in one queue, then in another, then back to the first. Then I have to pay excess baggage (surprise, surprise) so I return to the second queue where, for no apparent reason, I am now informed that everything is OK, I no longer have to pay anything; my suitcase is taken from me and I appear to have checked in.

In the departure lounge I long for a coffee but have only a fifty-pound note and a few pennies. I sit down and two people arrive with a tray of fresh coffee. Their names are called and they rush off, leaving the coffee untouched. I drink it! The flight is uneventful and arrives in the early afternoon, exactly on time. The airport is empty and the sun is shining. I ask at the Tourist Information desk about Flying Dolphins to Poros and the girl tells me that the last one went at half past three.

'But it's only half past two,' I protest. 'Oh, I'm so sorry I am wrong,' she says. 'Go quickly.' The taxi driver is over seventy and doesn't speak English so we have to rely on my Greek. Somehow I explain the situation and we are off – through red traffic lights, the wrong way down one-way streets, through petrol station forecourts and over pavements. He must smoke, he shouts to me over the roar of the Athens traffic, his heart is beating so fast. We both start laughing and continue giggling until we arrive at Marina Zea at twenty minutes past three. I gratefully over-tip him and we stand thanking one another profusely. I stagger to the ticket office but it is closed and I must go to the other office on the main road; so I dump all the cases and packages next to a bewildered old lady and run. At the office I gasp out a request for one ticket to Poros. 'Of course,' says the girl 'The Dolphin leaves at five p.m. And indeed it does!

I stagger ashore at Poros to find only strange faces on the people waiting at the quay. The suitcases are dumped again and I set off across the ploughed field that was once the road. A voice yells, 'Anna', and I see Petros standing there, grinning from ear to ear. I am safely returned!

Now it is as though I have never been away and I know it was right to come back. Whatever it was that was here for me the first time is still here now, even though so many things have changed. The island is still full of flowers: mimosa and poppies, geraniums and the wild yellow daisies. The light is settling and changing and the sea, calm as a millpond, is slowly turning into myriad shades of blue. At night a full moon spreads a carpet of light across the bay and it is, oh, so beautiful that sometimes it still takes my breath away. But the weather is always good when I first arrive. The God Poseidon is my friend and I am sure that this is his way of telling me he is pleased to have me back. Evening is arriving and it is getting cold but behind me on the mountain a man is singing softly for himself, the sound carries clearly and I am loathe to go in until he has finished.

Poros

Another arrival.

What a nice surprise to find your letter tucked cosily amongst various left-behind bills forwarded from London. Yes, I am safely returned with reams of excess baggage and crumbling carrier bags, all of which fortunately passed unobserved at the check-in. The flight was delayed while they found a gap between the cruise missiles and then, when we got to Athens Airport, the carousels were not working and there was a near riot there that was coped with admirably by the airport officials. They simply faced firmly away from us all and drank their coffees with the rapt attention usually to be found in a highly paid wine taster. Eventually, however, someone cracked and invaded the downstairs area and the cases were brought up by hand. By this time, in that extraordinary way the Greeks have, lifelong friendships had been formed and most of the world's political crises had been taken out, discussed at length, solved amicably or otherwise and tidied away again.

All this worked in my favour, of course, for I was on a night flight and by the time all my bits of luggage had surfaced it was time to grab a taxi and head for Piraeus and the Flying Dolphin. I must say that it was the first time I had experienced any delay with the carousels but it did make me start to remember the good old days at the Airport – with great nostalgia I might add. Do you remember how you used to have to squeeze out through the trolley gap into the airport car park in order to collect a trolley, wheel it in past the customs officers who pretended not to see you, load up all your luggage and walk back past the same custom officers who then often questioned you in detail about the contents of your bags? I also vividly remember going to the airport to buy a ticket back to the UK. That involved turning up at the airport with the requisite amount of cash carefully concealed in a newspaper and under orders to ask for K. When he eventually appeared, usually around two in the morning, he collected the money and your passport and disappeared. (Nervous travellers usually panicked at this point.) A little while later he returned with your ticket and, if you had influential friends, with your boarding pass. At this point your suitcases magically disappeared and you all went for a coffee. I'm afraid computers have a lot to answer for!

But to continue with my arrival: the harbour at Piraeus was noisily awake so coffee and sesame-seed rolls were quickly to hand. I chatted happily with a priest and several ladies off to Sifnos and then it was time to heave myself and all my packages on to the Flying Dolphin for Poros. I arrived at nine o'clock to find the little town deserted except happily, for one taxi with a driver I didn't know. I thus achieved my return unspotted – much to the annoyance of the Poros grapevine, which to this day cannot understand how it could have happened! 'But WHEN did you come back exactly,' is the puzzled cry, for I have obviously shown up an unforgivable gap in the café surveillance system.

•

Poros

I know it is 30 April today because tomorrow is 1 May and I must make my wreath of flowers. I have made the base, rather successfully, though I say it myself, and tomorrow I must go and collect the flowers. We are just about recovered from Easter when, as usual, rather too much food was eaten and far too much wine drunk. This year I was invited up to a friend's house – well, farm actually – in a valley right on the top of Kalavria. The views are stunning up there! It's on the way to the temple, and on a clear day you can see as far as Athens and just about make out the Parthenon. The house is old, quite simple, with odd bits added on from time to time, and it is all smothered in vines and bougainvillaea and looks romantic, blending in with the background of pine trees and eucalyptus. It was a beautiful day and the food and the wine tasted amazingly good out in the warm sunshine. Greek music came pouring out of the television set and in the short breaks for adverts you could hear other music played loudly at various homes across the valley.

It's difficult to go far without hearing music on this island and after a while it seems to enter into your bloodstream and become part of you. When you reach somewhere it hasn't penetrated, the silence is awesome; that is until you become aware of other sounds, the sighing of the wind, the singing of a single bird or someone far away exchanging a piece of gossip with their neighbour. Sounds travel for miles here and often come at you from odd angles.

So lunch was noisy and full of chatter too, until finally even this slowed down and the food stopped coming and the wine glasses stood half full their contents unwanted, on the table. Someone was going back down the mountain with a car so I said my goodbyes and thank you's and begged a lift back. The sounds of other people's Easters drifted across to us and several times we caught a glimpse of people dancing, but the *kefi* was going out of the day and siestas were beckoning. I slid into one of those deep, dreamless sleeps which are an essential part of Mediterranean life and enable you to bounce up an hour and a half later ready for whatever the world has next on offer. Today was no exception and mid-evening found me down in Poros town sitting in a *cafenion* in the main square watching several friends, less restored than I, endeavouring to start on the night celebrations.

•

Poros

I've just spent four days in Nea Makri with friends who live there, and so I don't feel like moving again at the moment. We had a marvellous time eating too much (amazing fish), drinking too much and talking, talking, talking. One night (actually early morning), we sat on the roof terrace, with the full moon spilling its light across the sea and the dark shapes of the islands mysterious on the horizon, and played Maria Callas at full volume. It was something I will remember forever and there were tears spilling down my cheeks. The next day we went to Marathon and visited a country farm selling local wine, and we ate *barbouni* (Red Mullet) with a local cheese millionaire and walked by the sea. It was a lovely time, the first warm days. Now it has turned seriously hot and the heat drains all thought of action from your head; The 'Lazy Hazy Crazy Days of Summer'!

•

Poros

It's been another beautiful day today, really hot. The island is still full of Greeks, (of course it is, but I mean mainland – mostly Athenian – Greeks) and all the cars have been going around covered in spring flowers, ditto the bikes – and in some cases the people riding them. I dutifully went out early this morning (surreptitiously), in order to acquire, i.e., steal, a few geraniums, etc. and found rather a large number of Greek ladies doing exactly the same! But it was worth the effort and the wreath now looks great and has been proudly photographed. It is hanging from my balcony for all to see and there are others, too, hanging from the balconies of the neighbouring houses, on this May Day holiday.

After lunch I set off for Neorion and sat by the sea, twiddling my toes in the water. I was just about to doze off when a party of Greeks arrived, complete with picnic table and two transistor radios. (I find radios in Greece to have been infected with the national hatred of being alone, and it is not unusual to find them in large groups all tuned to different music stations.)

Next to me, on my other side, two rather large ladies of a certain age decided to sunbathe topless and hold an intense conversation on some topic or other. In order to be heard above the noise of the radios they screamed rather a lot, a fact which resulted in the radios being turned up even higher. At this point I gave up and set off back home. Democracy, I decided, not for the first time, has its disadvantages and is definitely not for the faint hearted.

A few minutes later I was sitting outside my apartment, glass of wine in my hand, watching Vangelis water-ski across an indescribably blue sea, thinking how amazingly lucky I am sometimes.

Tonight I was really determined to go into Poros Town for a *volta* (early evening stroll), so I cleaned my shoes, sewed on two vital buttons and thought out a superb outfit to wear – and here I am with no intention of moving at all. One day I'll get bored, and THEN I'll go!

•

Poros

Last weekend I was 'baby sitting'– the four-legged type of baby. Takis and Giorgia had to go to Athens and Rokko had to be left behind. We brought this apology for a dog from Athens a month ago and he quickly settled in here and is now extremely full of himself. He lives with five half-grown cats in a huge garden in Phousa and operates a reign of terror up there, though they all seem to love him really and spend hours in his company. His favourite cat is *Arapitsa* (the little Arab), who is all black and a glutton for punishment; they are inseparable. At feeding time Rokko is chained up to give the cats a chance and they all group round their dish confident they are safe. Ha Ha. But one cat always make the big mistake of ending up too near to Rokko, its tail stretched out towards him; so Rokko grabs the tail, the cat usually clutches the dish of food, and they both arrive within Rokko's grasp. He is one smart little puppy.

Anyhow he arrived at my apartment to stay, with his blanket, his feeding dish and his food, but they forgot his toys, so one of my slippers was quickly sacrificed (without my noticing) and an old duster seemed a source of comfort too. He obviously regarded the whole thing as a great adventure and settled in really well. Night came and I tucked him up on his blanket and we both went quickly to sleep. Around half-past four in the morning I was awakened by something cold in my ear, careful examination of the situation revealed that it was his nose; Rocco was on the bed. 'Er, no,' I explained, 'this is not on.' And I resettled him on his blanket where he went quickly back to sleep, all four feet in the air. I then awoke at half-past seven to find Rokko IN the bed, his little head cuddled into my armpit. 'Oh really!' I exclaimed, as I was covered in good-morning licks and enthusiastic tail-wags. Then, giving up for the moment, I escaped to make some coffee. He was still happily in the bed when I returned, but as I put down the cup of coffee he ran to his feeding bowl and cried, so I returned to the kitchen to get his breakfast. As he tucked into his food I slipped gratefully back into bed and reached for that longed-for coffee – only to find that he had drunk it! I stomped back into the kitchen to start all over again and while I was waiting for the kettle to boil I looked into the little salon. Everything that had been on the coffee table was on the floor, the books had been pulled out of the bookshelves and the cushions from the sofa were under the dining-table. By this time Rokko was chasing round the flat, presumably doing his early-morning exercises. In sheer desperation, I yelled 'Sit down,' in Greek, whereupon he slithered to a halt and sat like the perfectly trained dog he isn't. He then looked at me as much as to say, 'If that's what you wanted, why didn't you tell me?' I just burst out laughing.

We spent the rest of the weekend doing an audition for *Turner & Hooch II* and by Sunday lunchtime he was bilingual in such words as 'don't' and 'no'. But I fell for his enormous charm and I missed him dreadfully when he finally disappeared back to Phousa.

•

Athens

It's been very windy here the last few days and other people's washing keeps arriving in the garden. I keep retrieving it and folding it carefully but I've no idea where it came from. I've got two T-shirts and a pair of shorts so far. I can't say that I would ever contemplate wearing them but they're probably all deeply loved by someone.

Escaped washing seems to be one of the delights of the area as, in the trees beyond the garden, there is a sheet, a towel and a pair of green knickers. Do you have these problems in North London?

Supper break: prawns and mushrooms in a cream and wine sauce with rice and Gosh this Cretan wine is very strong!

•

Poros
(The week of *Kreatini* or Meat Week)

The final week of *apoxrias* (carnival) here in Greece is called Meat Week because its Sunday is the last day on which meat can be eaten before the start of the Easter fast. But we decided not to wait for the very last minute and set out to enjoy ourselves on the Saturday. Giorgios, our dance teacher, had asked Sue, Andy and me if we wanted to go out after the class with him and his girlfriend. Of course, we took little persuading and ten o'clock at night found us climbing the old streets of Poros to what used to be Drougha's and is now run by Theo, but in much the same traditional way. Inside there is the same huge log fire and the food seems still to consist of what was freshest in the market that day. We had fava, and beetroot salad with a pungent garlic sauce. To follow there was the ever-present Greek salad, and gigantes, and finally a huge platter of lamb chops cooked on the open fire and suitably singed. It was all delicious, the wine too, fresh from the barrel and lightly chilled in the cold night air. It all slipped down easily and, together with the excellent company, quickly produced the *kefi* that is an essential part of all Greek celebrations. So it wasn't long before the dancing started and George was shouted to his feet. He danced beautifully and people were still calling 'Bravo' when the music for the *Hasapiko* started and Giorgios pulled Sue and me to our feet. With George's guiding hand on our shoulders and a few whispered instructions to help, we danced well, and people's faces were a picture as we walked back to our table. I loved it all!

By this time we were chatting to the people at the next table. They were not from Poros but lived in the mountain village of Arachova near Delphi and were here for the weekend only. But it was one of those evenings when people instantly become bosom friends, so we all went off to one of the harbour bars to continue the evening there. A bottle of champagne was bought to celebrate the dancing and we were invited to Arachova any time. Of course we all vowed we would go and Giorgios and I said we would dance to seal the promise but the music was never right and the disco took over. Heaven knows what time it was when I finally walked along the icy harbour front, a half moon throwing sharper shadows than the street lamps, but just as I was beginning to think longingly of a warm bed a friend drove past in his car and delivered me safely to my door. It had been another of those memorable Poros evenings and I was only glad that I had been there to enjoy it.

•

Poros

Yesterday I finally made it up the mountain to visit Petros's father. We worked out that the last time I had been there was in 1985 and we weren't quite sure why it had taken so long for us to repeat the experience. The night before, Petros had telephoned to say that he would be along 'not before eleven', so I sat reading in the hot sunshine until he appeared at five minutes to twelve. We just made the noon ferry and started up the mountain into a different world. It was like entering a secret valley between the two mountain ranges where time had stood still; and here was rural Greece, the women in headscarves with the goats and the men on donkeys or pruning the olive trees. There were little fires burning brightly at the edges of the road every few yards or so, the smoke making hazy the way ahead.

As we turned the corner before the house the dogs came running, Petros's father could be seen sitting at the table in front of the open door, the radio playing. He had his cap in his hand and for a split second I had the impression he had not moved once in ten years, but of course that was nonsense. He had aged a lot and shrunk as old men do, but the wicked twinkle was still in his eyes and he seemed delighted to see us.

We sat drinking coffee, looking across the Saronic Gulf to Poros where the whole waterfront of the little island fitted neatly into a gap in the hills; the land dropped away so steeply from where we sat, that it was almost as if we were suspended in mid-air. The two dogs now regarded us with interest whilst the curiosity of three cats finally got the better of them and they came to inspect us. We must have passed muster for they quickly disappeared into the branches of various olive trees and went to sleep. Petros, too, quickly disappeared up a ladder into an enormous olive tree, from which large branches and odd comments descended from time to time. His father and I caught up on a few of the intervening years and he told me of his trips to Naplion and the mess the E.U. was making of everything and how he believed Greece should get out. He also complained loudly that he enjoyed living up his mountain and wished people would leave him alone and not keep dragging him off to places he had no wish to visit. Half an hour in Galatas was all right, but no more than that! This last was obviously directed at Petros up his tree, but he did not rise to the bait.

Lunch was artichokes and potatoes in a rich tomato sauce and *retsina* from a village high up on the mountains. We ate at the table outside while the sun danced through the leaves of the chestnut tree, dappling the plates and glasses as we ate, and bathing the whole gulf in light. The three cats now sat in a neat row and looked hopeful and in the gaps between them sat the two dogs, all so beautifully spaced they made me laugh out loud. After lunch Petros took me on a tour of the 'estate', which was pretty big. It is divided up now between the siblings but the whole farm must have been huge when Petros's mother brought it to the marriage as her dowry. This practice is illegal today but was once very important when daughters had to be found suitable husbands. Petros has two hundred olive trees and once there were peach, lemon, pear and cherry trees growing on the terraces – it must have been breathtaking when they were all in blossom. Now just a few remain together with almonds, figs and the occasional walnut. Petros was like a different person, walking across his land and describing how he must care for it.

'I think you are a lucky man to have all this.' I said.

'Well it is hard work,' he replied, 'but yes, I am lucky; it is a gift from the gods.'

As we climbed back up the terraces we found anemones, wild crocus, wild orchids and a delicate wild asparagus, the latter being delicious to eat and quite unlike the cultivated variety. We fetched water from the mountain stream that ran into a huge concrete tank and Petros said, 'Do you want any fish?' and when I looked closer I saw eight or nine huge goldfish swimming contentedly around.

'Why goldfish?' I asked.

'Why not goldfish?' came the reply, and I couldn't think of any answer to that, so I went with Petros to the edge of the yard and we lit an enormous bonfire with the cut-off branches and watched the smoke drifting towards Poros, where we imagined all our friends sitting in the *cafenion* and arguing about politics and money and football! As we raked the ashes later to make sure the fire was safe I asked Petros how his father came to be in Poros when he was born in Tripolis and he answered that he thought he must have come with the sheep for the winter grazing; but when we asked the man himself he came out with a very different story, Yes, he told us he had been born in Tripolis, but his mother had died when he was six years old and he had been brought up by an uncle. When he was old enough to work he couldn't find any in the area near his home so he and his brother had made their way to Athens where they had become mixed up with the *Mangas* for a time; then someone had suggested they go to Poros and so they did, eventually finding work with one of the important families on the island. A short time later he met, fell in love with and married Petros's mother and enjoyed a long and happy marriage. Petros was obviously surprised by all this, especially the part about the *Mangas*, for they were streetwise, spiv-type gentlemen of the 1920s and the 1930s and were often part of the *Rebetika* singers and musicians and were famous for a less than reputable existence in the many bars around Piraeus and some of the poorer areas in Athens. I was fascinated and longed to hear more but, much to my annoyance Petros said we had to be going, so we left the rest of the story for another time and sadly never returned to hear it before his father's death not long after.

As we drove down the mountain road we came across two hunters standing rigid and silent in the scrub at the side of the road. They were dressed like two extras out of a French art film and looked somehow surreal. Farther on we stopped and picked up a straying Poriote and gave him a lift back to the ferry, driving on to it just as it cast off and arriving back in Poros as the daylight faded into night. It had been, said Petros, a good day.

•

Athens

I'm pretty expert on Greek buses now, even when they are packed. Getting on is relatively easy, you just stand in the middle of the crowd waiting on the pavement and let them do the pushing, and suddenly you're on! You then must establish a position near the door even if you are not getting off for some time. And when new people get on you must never, never move to let them pass by as they simply don't, they just take over your two square inches, and you are left contorting horribly with no centre of gravity and liable to collapse of top of everyone when the bus moves off. Anyhow, yesterday I had sort of achieved a niche and the bus was full to all intents and purposes, though you knew full well that another twenty people would get on somehow at the next stop. And then we passed a very famous little church. Now, everyone standing on the bus was clutching a strap or rail with their right hands and holding on to loads of shopping with their left. As we drew level with the church everyone freed their right hand to make the sign of the cross, and at that very moment the bus lurched and we all went down like a pack of cards. It was some time before we got ourselves sorted and by then I had the giggles – the sort you try to stifle until the effect makes your stomach ache and inevitably they break out again. And what made it all worse was that I kept catching the eye of a young man across the bus and we kept setting one another off again. I was much relieved to struggle my way out through the doors, nearly flattening a potted plant that was waiting to get on.

Did you know you buy lace curtains by weight?

•

Poros

It is still unbelievably hot, twenty-eight degrees centigrade, but the last of the tourists has disappeared and 'Life', with a capital 'L' of course, is slowly returning to normal. After a 'weally, weally' hot summer we are all desperate for winter, and grow wildly excited at the first cloud or drop of rain. It did look quite promising two weeks ago and I got out all the winter sweaters, polished the copper and dug out the rugs from their mothballs, but yesterday I capitulated, fetched the step ladder and retrieved a large part of my summer wardrobe from the suitcases, only thankful that I had not dispatched it to the rubbish bin where it sorely belongs. Still at least the birds have returned and the air is full of birdsong. The sounds of the pneumatic drill and the ever perambulating dustcart have, if only temporarily, disappeared.

I saw a robin yesterday, a sight that took me completely by surprise, for he looked so ridiculously English sitting on his spray of bougainvillaea and looking at me quizzically. The other birds who visit the garden are so much more exotic, at least in part, with flashes of brilliant blue or yellow. I have no idea what they are and ought to buy a book. On a less romantic note I exiled an enormously long and flat multimillipede from the garden earlier; he was slurping up a snail and was quite revolting, about nine inches long and an inch thick. What's more Eleni, or rather Yiannis, killed a four-foot snake yesterday, and they live just around the corner from me! I firmly locked all the shutters last night and shook my shoes this morning.

Another rather annoying fact of nature is that we are now into the olive-picking period. I am taking this personally as my hairdresser extraordinaire has disappeared in order to pick his olives and I am left desperate for a haircut. Fortunately this is the bad year for olives so he will only be away for two weeks instead of his more usual month. The note on the Malibu Bar's door says 'Gone Fishing.'

•

Poros

I have just been forced out of bed by the arrival of a white, fluffy cannon-ball seeking her daily treat of half a rasher of bacon. This is the lump of fluff that lives next door and is called Gina. [I introduced you to her earlier.] She is a tiny, white version of the Barney dog, with much the same kind of personality, for she is a right little bossy boots and very sweet and full of life.

But she is quite a heartless little minx, because once she has had her bacon she zooms off to sort out the rest of her day, and that rarely includes me. So I am left to do the same with my day, one that is lived at a much slower pace than hers.

It has become very hot and humid, not at all like our regular summers that are known for their dry heat. Consequently we are not very happy bunnies and we all drip and droop around complaining of the weather and being generally bad tempered with one another. My apartment is deliciously cool, so I am better off than most, but even so the desire to go into Poros town for a social life has to be really worked on and doesn't come easy. I have, however, been down the last two evenings because we have groups of foreign dancers here giving special performances with live music and national costumes – something Spiros, the mayor, organises for us most summers. Last night it was the group from what was Yugoslavia dancing beautifully and, in the light of the events of the last few months, with a great deal of poignancy.

Tonight we have the Russians and tomorrow the Bulgarians.

Later. Last night the dancing was very good indeed. There was a lot of Georgian leaping into the air and the women had truly perfected the art of gliding. All the performances take place in the main square with the good old *Two Brothers* boat providing the backdrop. The moon was slightly on the wane, but the summer sky was jam packed with stars, and the lights from Poros and Galatas were beautifully reflected in the sea, distorting dramatically whenever a boat passed through the strait. A romantic idyll had been achieved but was rather shattered when the woman sitting next to our table started a continuous battle with the people who repeatedly moved in front of us and then stood blocking the view. This got very heated on several occasions, for no Greek will put up with being told what to do, especially if he or she is in the wrong. These eruptions were further complicated by the fact that the couple had with them an elderly spaniel that barked loudly and lengthily every time anyone applauded. These complications aside, however, it was a most enjoyable evening and we all left the square looking forward to the two nights of dance still to come.

Later still. The Bulgarians and Moldavians were good but not quite like the stars of the previous evening. The elderly couple were there again, but had taken the precaution of securing a front-row table and had left the dog at home. Peace reigned and the evening passed calmly, though I couldn't help feeling that it had lost a little of its character.

I spent the last evening sitting with Takis and Georgia – the first time I had seen them since I had persuaded them to take Little Piece of Fly S-, their cat, to the visiting vet to be 'seen to'. Generally the Greeks are very much against interfering with nature, but I thought I had persuaded the family at Phousa that it really was for the best and would make for a greatly less complicated life. But when I arrived at the house on the day the vet was on Poros I found only Takis still committed to the project. Little was said, but an air of deep gloom hung over the house and finally Giorgia and Leda joined forces and announced that the cat would not be going after all.

'Oh, yes, she will,' declared Takis.

'Well, I am not driving the car,' said Giorgia, and an uneasy silence reigned, until the assurance or insurance man arrived unexpectedly and talked for hours. By the time he left the lunch was ruined and the day had taken another downward turn. Still, somehow we got to the improvised clinic with Giorgia clutching the cat protectively but not actually daring to defy Takis on one of the rare occasions he had put his foot down and further underlined his decision by forgoing his siesta and driving us all down to Poros town. Happily all went well, and now of course everyone is pleased it was done, but few things come easy here and so it was nice to spend an uncomplicated evening together and catch up on the gossip which is such an essential part of small-island life.

Leda, their teenage daughter, was the first topic to hit the headlines, and I was sorry to hear that her problems with Communism were continuing! She had hoped to form a Young

Communists' group but discovered that you needed a minimum of four before you could do so. After considerable effort four teenagers had been recruited and the inaugural meeting scheduled for last Saturday. Alas, only the two female members turned up as the two boys had gone out to the bars on the previous evening and simply overslept. I pointed out that this was hardly within the bounds of Party discipline but she seemed to think that there was little she could do for the time being. So now we are not too hopeful of a Communist resurgence here on Poros but are nevertheless prepared for anything.

I must say I am rather glad to be writing to you today as Nostradamus had prophesied the end of the world would be yesterday. So far so good, but we are not out of the wood yet as he also mentioned another two dates in July. Takis has advised walking around with a packet of sandwiches and a bottle of water as he thinks that it is all bound to be a bit chaotic at first and we'll need sustenance while we find the places where we want to be and the people we want to be with. He is not sure, he says, whether or not God has arranged for *taverna*s.

So, think on.

•

Poros

Sue and Andy drove me up to the top of the mountains opposite Poros this morning. The view from up there is stunning, down to Spetses one way and Athens the other, whilst Poros looks tiny, like something sketched on a map. The colours, too, are stunning – greys, silver and streaks of gold one way, deep blues, white and greens the other. Indescribable really and one of those moments you'll never forget but can't actually share with anyone.

Yesterday Giorgia brought me flowers from the garden in Phousa. The seasons have gone crazy for the spring poppies are out and the yellow clover flowers and even the anemones.

Are we in for a horrible shock or is it just going to be a very mild winter?

Maybe we have the answer today, for I awoke to hear the rain pouring down and bouncing off the palm tree on to the balcony. It's the sort of day when you think the world has turned upside down and the sea has become the sky with the water desperate to get back to where it belongs. The colour has drained out of everything and it makes me think of England.

One of the tourist reps told me of another rep who was waiting on the harbour front with a group of homeward-bound clients for the soon-to-arrive Flying Dolphin. By chance it was one of the new luxury ones, known as the Flying Cat.

'Look out everyone,' he cried, 'here comes the Flying Cat.' And everyone looked up at the sky and moved their heads as though at a tennis match. And if that story isn't true, it should be, for it makes me giggle every time I think about it.

•

Poros

The trip to Ermioni was a great success. I love driving along the little coast road with its irregular hazards of mountain goats and gypsy children and lazy tractors blocking the way. You follow the sea almost all the way there, through the carnation fields where the plants always seem to be in flower, and then back into the more traditional olive groves surrounding some rather beautiful old farmhouses. The carnations are grown for the *Bouzouki* Halls in Athens where the flower heads are now thrown in place of the more traditional plates. More romantic I suppose but nowhere near as exciting. Plate throwing was actually banned during the time of the military dictatorship and is still illegal I think, though you do find it happening in some of the more traditional bars and clubs. As always in this delightful country, the fact that something is against the law does not necessarily stop it being done. Of course, 'sensible' laws are strictly observed, well, most of the time anyway, it's just that it's rather difficult sometimes to know which is which. Living in a democracy as opposed to a bureaucracy can be difficult and a large sense of humour is required at all times. But to return to the trip to Ermioni. We went for the market there, which happens every Thursday and sells most things from local produce to household goods. This trip was aptly timed for the new wine was just on the market and very good.

We came back on a detour through the mountains and found people already picking the olives, surrounded by vast herds of goats. This was the old Greece of the 1950s and before, the women wearing the coloured skirts and the white headscarves, the men in well-patched suits and the flat, black caps. In the distance the sea poked through a gap in the mountains and briefly framed the daily car ferry as it ploughed back from Spetses. Here, suddenly was every foreigner's idea of Greece and a scene that can hardly have changed over the last hundred years. Happily though, every town and village has all the so-called blessings of modern life and it is rare to find a home without a television set among other twenty-first century essentials, even including the ubiquitous mobile phone. But for the moment we were back in the pages of Lawrence Durrell and daring to dream. It is so nice when the tourists have gone, you can almost hear the countryside sigh with relief.

•

Athens

Athens at least is still its usual crazy self. I have spent all day being screamed at by taxi drivers for walking in the road. I only do it because it is impossible to walk on the pavements for the cars and bikes parked on them, the chairs and tables from the cafés arranged there, the produce from the shops spilling out sometimes as far as the road, and the old furniture and the rubbish which has been dumped there.

The local market this morning presented a hazard too, going on for streets, with fresh fruit and vegetables smelling sweet enough to make any British supermarket mogul weep. The butchers were selling game, and the herb stalls nearly knocked you over with the smell. Round every corner now, you find a little group of lit-up snowmen or Santa Clauses and every car has a Christmas tree sticking out of the boot.

Going into the centre of Athens yesterday I was lucky enough to find a seat on the trolley bus before it was packed. At one stop, just when it seemed impossible that another body could squeeze on, four Albanian musicians burst up the steps and struck up with their violins and hand-organs, playing that well-known Greek number, Rudolph the Red-Nosed Reindeer with enthusiasm. Hats were knocked flying, old ladies fell to the floor, feet were trampled and one elderly gentleman had a nosebleed, but no one seemed to mind and we were soon struggling to reach into our purses for the obligatory small change.

In Ermou Street, which is now closed to traffic, the Christmas trees all have their red bows and the barrel organs play away with their operators dressed up as *Mangas*, in their 1920s' jackets and painted-on moustaches. Even the dogs have got into the spirit of things and are charging around happily, some wearing tinsel collars. All in all there's quite a buzz in central Athens at this time of year.

•

Poros

We spent yesterday in the little market *taverna* next to Aphrodite's shop. The rain bucketed down and the owner, who is something of a natural clown, was wishing '*Kalo taxidi*' (good journey) to anyone who was stupid enough to leave. Alas, the famous roast pork was all gone by the time we got there, but the octopus and macaroni dish was excellent and our table seemed to have one of those never-emptying wine carafes which are so common in Greece. We were advised to drink no more than three litres of wine each and certainly, given the inclement weather, not to drink less than three litres of wine each. The friend who was advising us on this vital issue went on to confide that he himself had drunk exactly three litres of wine and was feeling great, although he was a little apprehensive about the mood of his wife for he was already two hours late for his dinner. When he got home, however, he planned to ask her if she really wanted him to get soaked on the journey home and run the risk of some terrible illness? Was she not glad, he would go on, that he had stayed in the warm *taverna* with some good company and a little wine?

After about another half-hour, it seemed he had convinced himself of the certainty of his wife's understanding nature and he finally got up to leave. As he passed our table we asked him where he lived. 'Ah,' he said; 'at the little house on the corner.'

We gazed rather carefully at our glasses, still half full of wine and then we reluctantly pushed them away. It was time to leave the talk and the laughter and the companionship and head for home. The light was fading as I walked along the harbour front and the rain had almost stopped. One taxi was waiting and we clambered in and were soon returned to our various homes. I walked into my flat, the noise of the *taverna* still ringing in my ears and the taste of the wine on my lips. It was nearly nine o'clock in the evening when I woke up. It had been a good day I thought, and I only went into Poros town to post a letter.

•

Poros

On Monday I went to see Eleni and ended up staying for supper – of course! Kiriakos was on the telephone from the *cafenion* where he was watching the football and he was most insistent that we should eat meat rather than the freshly cooked *pastichio* (macaroni and mince meat) or the freshly caught fish. This presented a small problem as the meat in question, a large lump of pork, was sitting frozen solid in the freezer. Despite my protestations that pastichio was what I most craved, Eleni seemed to think that she had no choice in this particular matter and so the pork was put into a large pan and placed in the oven. A little while later we had a minor crisis when the olive oil from the tray of pastichio cooked in the oven earlier caught alight and caused black smoke to billow into the kitchen. Well, the moment soon passed and tranquillity returned but when, shortly after, Kiriakos arrived home, clutching the wine and obviously very hungry, the meat had barely thawed and it looked as though we were in for a long evening.

By midnight the meat had started to cook well but we were pretty desperate by then and had drunk most of the wine so we gave in and ate the *pastichio*, which was delicious.

•

Athens

Have just been to an exhibition of theatre and costume design and was enthralled. Many of the designs were by Ghikas and I realised how close the Greek theatre and the French theatre must have been until quite recently. British design seems to have been more influenced by America than Europe. Pity!

Later I went for a long walk round the Acropolis which I now know almost as well as Epidaurus. Coming down I found a group of Peruvian musicians playing the music of the Andes, so I sat and listened, the Parthenon in front of me. The music sounded perfect for the setting, as though it belonged there and not thousands of miles away in South America. I treated myself to one of their tapes, and am listening to it now.

Later still, I found three members of the Bulgarian State Orchestra, playing superb classical music. It seems unbelievable that such talent has to earn a living playing in the streets of Athens, but it was a rare treat for us.

I spent a lovely day with Magda last week. She lives in a magical neo-classical house by the edge of the sea near Piraeus. Once the whole road was composed of similar houses but now they have mostly been replaced by apartment blocks. But her house looks like something out of an Angelopoulos film and makes you dream of times past.

My favourite television moment of recent times remains the news story recorded in Omonia Square. The reporter was interviewing a *periptero* (kiosk) owner about the inconveniences caused by the work being done there on the new Metro line. All was going well and the reporter was just winding up his piece when an enormous hole appeared beneath his feet and he, the *periptero* and all disappeared into it. As no one was hurt it was all very, very funny and has greatly amused the whole of Greece.

•

Poros

Christmas and New Year here are not the big holidays that they are in the UK for they really only happen on the actual day, but they are none the less enjoyable for that and in fact I prefer them that way now.

So, Christmas morning I trotted out for Buck's Fizz at the house of a friend and then went on to Captain Kiriakos' house for what I firmly believed was the appointed hour of one o'clock. Alas there had been a slight mix-up, as quite often occurs between us, and the captain had been up and dressed since twelve. This would not normally have been a problem but he, his brother and no.1 son had been out partying until six that morning so a great effort had been made on my behalf, whilst there I wasn't. Poor Andonis had had to start on the turkey and everyone else was clutching cans of soda water; except that is Eleni and Mitsos, who had stayed at home and found it all exceedingly funny.

The meal was excellent, with the turkey cooked as a rich, game-type stew, pork chops from the barbecue and lots of other goodies, and after some food everyone livened up a bit;

but by three-thirty I could see that sleep was the necessary next step for most people and I left to take a siesta myself. Not one person said, 'Stay,' so they really must have been pretty desperate for their beds!

For New Year's Eve, the mayor had organised live music, and free brandy and cakes, all available in the Post Office Square. By this time in Greece the last thing you want to eat is more cake but these evenings are fun so I trotted up to Poros town in good time for the magic hour. With only minutes to spare I tried to phone Sue in London so that she would hear all the Greek music and get very jealous, but she didn't get back from work in time. The next time I tried the phone gave up the ghost and all I could hear was a scrabble of Russian, French, German, Albanian, et al. But with the new year duly celebrated and yet more cakes loyally eaten, I had one last try and got through straightaway, only to be accused of being drunk when I tried to tell her about the two tiny ponies I had just seen walk by and climb into the back of a little van driven by Father Christmas, or *Aghios Vassilis* as he is known here. As it was all true, and as I had only had two small drinks anyhow, I was quite miffed and felt the New Year had got off to a less than perfect start.

•

Poros

We have been wading through a series of cultural events that have been presented and received with great pleasure. First was the Archaeological week that was actually ten days and would have been very interesting had my Greek been good enough for me to realise that it was happening. I caught up with it on the last night when (rather ambitiously, I thought) Homer's Iliad was presented in its entirety as a dance drama. This took place in Russian Bay, and when I arrived there I found the old ruined trading post made a magnificent backdrop and had been beautifully lit. With a full moon trailing light across the sea and the occasional shooting star exploding in the heavens, it got off to a sensational start.

Alas I had not eaten for some reason or other and so the hour and ten minutes of speeches found me longing for action, and I really was not alone in this as the audience, too, were becoming increasingly restless and it was imperative to find somewhere to sit. But finally the music started, the dancers appeared and the ancient galleon (actually the trusty *Two Brothers* again) sailed round the headland bathed in pink flares and with exceedingly handsome young men in very short leather skirts hanging from the rigging. This produced a well-deserved round of applause and it was generally felt that the epic poem had got off to a most impressive start. But, as so often on these occasions, enthusiasm eclipsed common-sense and the boat came closer and closer to the shore and finally stuck in the shallows.

There then followed something of a hiatus, although alas not one that was shared by the music or the dancers on the shore. After a lot of engine revving and some timely help from two contemporary policemen, the boat was finally freed and successfully moored to the specially built jetty at the far end of the bay.

After that I'm not sure what happened for hunger overcame my artistic needs and I was lured away by the temptations of a *taverna* in Neorion. Walking into the unlit unknown with two friends, I gratefully accepted a telling off and the offer of a lift from a handsome stranger who seemed to know me quite well. As he dropped us safely at our chosen restaurant I was amused to learn he was not someone who's name I had most unfortunately forgotten, but instead he was a member of the local police force! He wished us a pleasant evening, warned us again against walking along unlit roads and complimented us on our choice of restaurant. We thanked him warmly and headed into the buzzing and brightly lit *taverna*, still a little guilty about our abandonment of the Iliad, but too hungry by now for our regrets to last long.

Following on from all this came the Navy Week, relying on word of mouth, usually so devastating here but this time completely useless, the whole week managed to pass again without my knowing anything about it. Certainly a large stage appeared in the middle of the main square, and I caught glimpses of schoolchildren in National costume, but on the occasions I sat hopefully in one of the harbour cafés nothing happened. Only on the final Saturday night did I stumble across the remains of the free food and wine, which had appeared briefly on long tables, and find a *bouzouki* group from Athens playing to an empty square; while across the road, the cafés were packed with people, everyone glued to a selection of televisions that were all tuned to the World Cup.

•

Poros

I am off to the cinema tonight with Takis and Giorgia. It is a very special event, for they are showing selections from all the old films which were shot on Poros and some of the actors and actresses taking part are expected to be there too, so it should be an interesting evening.

Later.

The trip to the cinema was really great and someone had done a very good job of compiling the videotape. It is going to be on sale to raise money for the construction of apartments for elderly, impoverished thespians. Last week one much loved actress committed suicide because she couldn't pay the rent. There were about fifteen or so of the stars there, all famous in the 1950s and the 1960s and it was all very moving. The mayor presented each of them with a commemorative statuette and they were all taken out to dinner, while we lesser mortals trotted home treasuring memories of a very nice evening and a series of images of 'the way we were'.

•

Poros

It was Magda's idea to go to Sirocco for the *bouzouki*. We had been out to dinner and were sitting having a late night-drink when a friend of hers passed by and told her it was the last night of the summer up there. So we finished our drinks and set off along the harbour front, round the headland and finally up the steep white steps into the open-air nightclub.

A hundred memories of other summer evenings briefly flooded my mind but then the music reached down to take us high into the night sky and hint at the evening ahead. It was only one o'clock in the morning and early by *bouzouki* standards but there was already enough atmosphere around to hold us and make us glad we had come. I think, between us, we knew everyone there.

The *kefi* was good, but only just beginning to move up to that level which is necessary for a really great evening, so we settled at the bar with our drinks and sat exchanging greetings with new arrivals and generally doing our best to help the atmosphere along. It really wasn't long before one of the girls got up to dance the *sheftalia* (belly dance). She was from one of the villages high up the mountain and was with an older man who obviously adored her. She danced beautifully, every movement controlled by the music, and she was loudly applauded when she sat down; her companion escorted her to her seat watching, warily, for covetous glances from the younger men in the room.

After that the pace of the evening quickened. Some of our best dancers were there that night and the energy seemed to spin from one to another; Tassos, Yiannis, Takis, Vangelis, and finally Theo, who almost ran into the other dancers as the *kefi* soared; all held us in thrall. Theo is a self-taught musician who writes his own songs and almost lives for music. He danced divinely, taking over the room, applauded and encouraged by the other dancers. We sat on our bar stools, forgetting the discomfort of the metal frames, and as Theo flew, we flew too. Then I became aware of Magda pulling at my arm. 'Anna,' she said, 'come, its time to go.' I looked across the rapidly emptying bar and then peered at my watch. It was five-thirty and the glow of dawn was creeping across the night sky over Askeli Bay. Someone, if not us, had danced all night!

•

Poros

Another big event has been that of the 'Chair Buying'. My problem dated from when I moved, for the dining-chairs belonged to my old apartment. The need to acquire some more was originally low down on my list of priorities but slowly it worked its way to the top until finally it could be ignored no longer. I then could not find any I liked.

I had searched Poros and Spetses and Hydra, now really only Aegina remained, but this time somehow I felt more confident of success, so, as the *Anna* pulled into Aegina harbour, I fluttered my eyelashes at the captain with my usual success and set off down the backstreets of the old town where I soon found exactly what I wanted – well, all seven of them to be precise. Then, huffing and puffing and soaked in sweat, one very small boy and I arrived back at the *Anna* only to be met with incredulous laughter. Why on earth did I, living on my own, require seven chairs? In vain did I explain that four were for the table, the green one for the bedroom and the two canvas ones for the balcony. Comments were made all the way back to Poros and it was impressed upon me that I should sit on each one in turn so as to allow none of them to get lonely.

Now, however, I dare not tell them that only a few days later I peered down from my lofty heights and saw what looked like two very nice period chairs lurking by the rubbish bins. Binoculars confirmed first impressions and I scuttled off to retrieve them – and very nice they are too. So I have now somewhat OD'd on chairs and am running out of space for the useful chest of drawers I was planning to buy. A few extra friends would not come amiss either!

Poros

The French have returned to Paris, ecstatic about their holiday but leaving me exhausted. As I collapsed thankfully on my sofa, the family 'heirlooms' arrived from England, followed closely by Marina who informed me graciously that I should wash my rugs upstairs on the larger balcony as it would be easier for me. Rug-washing not actually being foremost in my mind, I nevertheless hastily put it there and set about rolling them up and buying a large bottle of carpet shampoo. They are now safely dried, moth-balled and stored ready for winter, the curtains have been washed and the cupboards emptied and reorganised. Things have been thrown away, pictures have been hung, Victorian tablecloths washed, bleached and ironed. Only my floor remains a nightmare, covered with the annual black blobs that throw reproachful glances at you when you arrive with a mop and scuttle off to dark corners to await the end of the mopping process. Once the floor is dry, twenty-eight spiders and fifty-three small beetles of assorted species return to their original positions and glare smugly at you for days.

Outside, my path resembles the M1 – cats march past delivering kittens for me to admire and tortoises stomp, their shells shining in the sun and their little heads rotating slowly.

Somewhere in the middle of all this, the *Anna* started working and I finished Part 2 of my coffee-table book of photographs for my father-in-law's birthday. You think you have stress in London? Think on!

Outside in the garden it is a time of plenty. The lemons are ripe, the loquat fruit is falling off the tree outside my door and the cherries are freshly arrived from Tripoli. Also freshly arrived are the tourists. The summer is nearly upon us.

•

Poros

Magda and I went to see a feminist version of one of the *Karaghozoi* plays at the school on Galatas. Her niece and nephew (twins) were appearing in it and it really was very good. There is a professional group in Piraeus that goes round the schools working with the children and putting on productions. The children were playing the parts of the traditional shadow puppets and the women's parts were taken by the boys and vice versa. It was all very funny and there was a great atmosphere there. Afterwards we met Vassilis and Orestes (I do worry about Magda calling her son Orestes!) who had arrived from Piraeus on the late boat and we all went to eat enormous beef chops and drink lots of the local wine.

Crossing back to the island in one of the little water taxis we found Takis and Giorgia. All is well up at Phousa and Leda has passed her English proficiency exam and finally seems to be making some progress with the Communist Party, the *KKE*. Alas, it still seems to have a rather small membership here on Poros. They are staging a protest march against the NATO bombing and the group will consist of Leda, a lady and her husband from one of the shops, Leda's best friend (male), someone's grandfather and a twelve-year-old child. Realists, they are hoping to have a greater impact later when they join forces with the larger group on the mainland.

Meanwhile the photo of Tom Cruise has been removed and now Che rules alone. Takis was under the misguided impression that Che Guevara was there for his political importance but I was able to pour some light on this misconception and after some thought he said he had to agree for the more he thought about it the more unlikely it seemed that anyone would have a picture of a politician displayed on their bedroom wall and Che was everywhere.

I then had to confess that he had appeared on my bedroom wall when I was fourteen and I didn't even know what a Communist was at that time! At this point the little water taxi pulled into the quay and so, laughing, we all went home to our respective beds.

•

Poros

Up to Poros town for the traditional blessing of the waters when the priest throws the cross into the sea and all the young bloods of the island dive in after it. This year 6 January is warm and sunny so you don't have to grit your teeth in sympathy as the participants hit the sea. All over Greece people are doing the same and it is one of the big, annual religious festivals. Our priests and dignitaries board the trusty *Two Brothers* boat which makes for the middle of the strait between Poros and Galatas; afterwards everyone heads for coffee or *ouzo mezere* (aniseed drink accompanied with small plates of food) and a long chat in the harbour *cafenion*s.

Shortly after this, the weather turned bitterly cold. 'Ah ha!' we thought. 'Winter is upon us,' and out came the boots, the sweaters and the hot-water bottles; but two days later it thought to put off the evil day and reverted to hot sunshine.

And so, with 6 January safely behind us, life returned to normal. Kleopatra phoned to see when I was going to Athens and Takis suddenly appeared on my doorstep to see if I would help him with his stand at the Trade Exhibition in Piraeus.

'Of course,' I said.

'Good,' said Takis. 'We leave tomorrow on the 7.15 a.m. ferry to Galatas!'

So, a bag was packed, Kleopatra was phoned in a torrential rainstorm and the alarm was set. Wednesday dawned bright and sunny and off we went. It was a beautiful morning and the previous night's rain had taken all the dust out of the atmosphere. The climb through the mountains revealed spectacular views and you could see for miles. As we reached the highest point we stopped to admire it all – and smoke poured out of the engine, obscuring our view and sending our spirits into a sharp decline. Hoping that it was merely a Takis oversight in not checking the water before we left, we located a mountain stream and filled up. Eternally optimistic we set off down towards Epidaurus and five minutes later stopped to check the radiator. It was empty! We filled up again and carried on, stopping every five minutes or so to fill up with water, collecting it from whatever source was available, and eventually we covered the hundred and thirty kilometres into the centre of Piraeus. I was astounded at the way in which Takis stayed cheerful and controlled throughout. It later transpired that we had blown a gasket and were extremely fortunate to have been able to move at all, but to have got to Piraeus without destroying the engine was little short of miraculous.

Once safely in the exhibition hall – and after a large and very necessary coffee – we set about creating a little gem of an exhibition stand and were suitably gratified when people began telling us how unusual it was and how much they liked it.

We finished around nine o'clock that evening, whereupon I headed for Kato Patissia and Kleopatra's studio. There I dug out the lion blanket from its hiding place, poured myself a large vodka and tonic from K's vast supply and passed out in a happy, exhausted, semi-stupor after a deep, hot and vastly satisfying bath!

Two days later I returned to the exhibition to find that all was going well. Giorgia and Leda had arrived and everyone was happy, so I arranged to meet them on the Sunday for the journey back to Poros and set off into Athens to carry on with my social life.

I left just as it was starting to get dark and strolled back along the busy harbour front, lost in my thoughts, imagining the music from the long-gone *Rebetika* cafés drifting in an almost tangible form across the shadowy streets and into the night- life of the city. A gipsy and her child walked quickly away down a side street, adding a vivid dash of colour to the greys and greens of early evening. A ship hooted and pulled me back into reality and I became aware of someone calling to me from the waterfront. I stopped to enquire, politely, what he wanted and, when he explained, equally politely I found myself definitely unable to help and walked rather more quickly to the station, giggling to myself. Once there I spied a letterbox, purchased an envelope from the *periptero* and sat down on a nearby bench to address it. When I had finished I looked up and found the bench no longer empty – five hopefuls sat watching me closely. At this point I sealed the envelope, posted the letter and fled towards the train. Although I didn't feel in the least threatened it was all getting a bit much!

The next day found me luggage-laden and back in Piraeus to meet Giorgia before we caught the Flying Dolphin at three-thirty. I tottered into the exhibition hall to be told by Giorgia that an immediate and violent storm was forecast and no Dolphins or ferries would be running for the rest of the day.

I decided to have a coffee and return to the studio but within half an hour the stupendous storm was raging and no one was going anywhere. We were slightly on the edge of it, but even so the streets of Piraeus quickly found themselves under three feet of water and the radio was reporting floods all along the Corinth highway. The exhibition closed at 10 p.m. and only about then did the rain begin to ease. When we finally set off through still flooded streets towards the centre of Athens, the Metro was closed and the streets empty. I did eventually get a train at Thisseon but the carriage floor and the seats were soaked and only about ten people were travelling. Kato Patissia seemed a haven and I was happy just to remake the bed and collapse into it.

The next day Giorgia phoned to say the mountain roads were still blocked and people were being advised not to travel. There were no boats or Flying Dolphins because by now everyone was back on strike again, so I gave up worrying about getting back to Poros and went to see the film of Evita, which I thought was stunning. On Wednesday we borrowed Takis's brother's car, loaded up five people and one very small puppy and set off for Poros along the Corinthian Highway. The journey was excellent and showed no sign of the recent flooding; we made it to Poros in around three hours. Only when I switched on the T.V. here and saw the pictures from Corinth town did I begin to understand how terrible it had all been. Bridges had disappeared, and vast lengths of the local roads had just crumbled away; houses had collapsed and cars and lorries were tipped upside down and buried in the mud. It was like the film footage you keep seeing from the Philippines and people had lost everything. Miraculously only two people had died, though that was tragic enough. The storm was on Sunday afternoon but by Wednesday the sun was scorching and on Poros everything looked normal. Ten days later, however, Corinth was shown on the news still trying to clear the mud from the streets and the houses.

•

Poros
28th Oct.

It was *Oxi* Day today – the day the Greeks said 'No' to the Italians and sided with the Allies in World War 11.

At the first Italian invasion a relatively small group of Greeks, badly armed, single-handedly forced the Italians back over the Albanian border, only to face another, more determined invasion by the Germans in the depths of a terrible winter. Many died fighting bravely before the defending force was left with no choice but to flee to the mountains and continue fighting as partisans. Today is set aside to honour these men and all the others who have died fighting for Greece. In a way it is like the British Remembrance Day, though there are no red poppies. There are events all over Greece, ranging from impressive military parades to simpler but equally moving ceremonies – like the one on Poros. I always try very hard to attend for the men who died, died for my future too, and that of my family and friends. So this morning the bare feet of summer were forced into shoes and the T-shirt and jeans replaced with something more respectable as I joined family groups and excited children, all heading for our main square and the war memorial there. This year I sat with Andreas and Maria in one of the harbour cafés surrounded by friends and familiar faces. Then, as the ceremony started, I remembered another year. It had been hot then, too, and I had stood with Takis and Giorgia watching Leda as she marched past carrying the Greek flag. It was a solemn and moving moment but, as we kept the two minutes' silence, the mid-morning ferryboat pulled into the harbour immediately behind the line of dignitaries and I knew it was going to hoot. With something approaching horror, I felt the laughter rise up inside me until my stomach was in knots and my suitably respectful face threatened to split into a wide grin. Then I looked up on to the prow of the ship, and there, standing proudly to attention, was a little old man, a small Greek flag in his hand. The laughter turned to tears and they streamed down my face. As so often in this country, tragedy and comedy walked side by side.

•

Poros

October here is our rainy season, and this year was no exception. I woke up this morning to the sound of torrential rain beating down on to the balcony, shivered slightly and disappeared back under the duvet. Today was not a day for outside but later, when I had adjusted to the fact that winter was coming, I donned my trusty wellingtons and set off for the supermarket, remembering with nostalgia the first time I was here for the autumn rains.

That time, like so many of the foreigners, I was taken completely by surprise. With only summer clothes and tennis shoes I was ill prepared for the first downpour, and something had to be done. So down to Poros town I went and, dripping and soaked, I entered the only shop I thought was likely to stock a mac and wellingtons. And I was not disappointed. The mac was quickly produced and accepted but the wellingtons created major problems, not the least because of the deficiencies in my command of Greek. Still, after much head scratching and graphic hand-waving, a rather dusty pair arrived from the back of the shop. Alas, I take size 38 and these were 43. The hand gestures grew more frenetic as I was urged to try them on. Not wishing to offend I did, sliding them across the floor in a desperate effort to keep them somewhere near my feet. Then an interpreter arrived. 'Perfect,' he said. I tried hard to explain tactfully that, on the whole I felt they were less than perfect, in fact I felt they were hopeless. At this point the unfailing Greek optimism broke through. Two pairs of thick workman's socks were produced as the ultimate solution. I burst out laughing, paid for the mac and fled. The next day the sun returned and the mac lay, unused at the bottom of the wardrobe.

•

Poros

Today was the day of our big Greek wedding – and christening! These two events had been talked about for weeks; talked about, and rejected, and planned, but now it seemed that it really was going to happen! Petros had been up to the farm on the mainland and then sat for hours in a *cafenion* on Poros complaining about all the work that had still to be done. Things seemed to be on course. I left for Athens to attend the opening of Kleopatra's latest sculpture exhibition and returned on the Saturday afternoon. The *combaros* (best man) had arrived from England and the weather looked hot and sunny for the wedding tomorrow. There was only one slight problem – I had no idea when, or indeed where, it was all to take place. The reception would be at the farm halfway up a mountain, of course, but at which Church? At half-past eight my nerve gave out and I seny a text-message to the *combaros*, 'How, when and where tomorrow?' The reply was immediate. 'How should I know?' it said! I waited some more. At ten-thirty came another text-message: 'Be at the ferry at 10 a.m.,' so I went to bed happy.

I arrived at the ferry point early, so as not to be late, and at five minutes to ten there was another text-message: 'Now coming 10.30,' it said. So I sat on a wall and watched the sun playing on the sea and decided that the world was really rather a good place sometimes.

They finally arrived without the bridegroom and we chatted as the ferry pulled in. Then Petros screeched on to the boat on his bike and we all made it safely to Galatas. Next, there was a stop for coffee and a long discussion about how to solve the problem of not having a cassette for the video camera. Happily Petros knew the man with the shop and he was prevailed upon to open it. Panic was now running through the proceedings until the bridegroom casually revealed that we were not due at the church until noon. Then, we climbed up the winding road to the farm, where we found tables and chairs and the porch of the little house decorated with tulle and raki waiting to be drunk. We also found that no one else had yet arrived!

It was so beautiful up there, the sky a deep, deep, cloudless blue, the sea almost the same colour, and the old town of Poros still framed in that dip in the hills. Hydra lay basking in the sun and just visible through a morning mist was Cape Sounion and the old prison island of Makronissi. So we sat, happy with our glasses of raki, until the bridegroom and the combaros appeared in suits, with the bridesmaid in her white dress, over a T-shirt in case it turned a bit chilly; and Petros's sister from Naplion took the curlers out of her hair. It was time to go to the church.

But before the wedding, there was to be the christening of Petros and Sophia's small daughter, Maria. The marriage was to follow on from that! True, there had been a civil ceremony some months before, but the busy summer schedules had left no time for a full Greek Orthodox service, so today really was the big day.

The church was a tiny one, about two hundred metres away, and when we arrived we found it full of people and the preparations well underway. And so we eventually christened Maria. She hated the font, wouldn't wear her hat, and the *bou bounieres* (sweet meats) were blue – but never mind! We relaxed outside in the shade for a few minutes, and then moved back in to the church for the nuptials. Sophia looked stunning, like some classical statue, her hair, in a bun at the nape of her neck, was decked with stephanotis, and she wore a simple white linen dress embroidered with white flowers. And Petros had on his new suit. It all went surprisingly calmly, and even Tassos, not always the most organised of people, knew exactly what to do with the wedding crowns. True, Sophia almost forgot to stamp on Petros's foot, but the women shouted and she remembered just in time. Then we pelted them with rose petals and rice and that bit of the ritual was over, bar the photographs. We went back to the farm and there Petros's sisters tied a shawl around Petros, Sophia and Maria before they walked under the wedding arch and into the little house.

By now the tables under the olive trees were all spread with the best white tablecloths and the food began to arrive – and with it the wine. It wasn't long before people started dancing and my feet soon took me into the circle of dancers, it was impossible to stay seated.

Then, inevitably, the shadows of the olive trees began to lengthen and the *kefi* slipped out of the day. We looked at Maria fast asleep in her pram, said a regretful goodbye and drove back down the mountain. And there you have it – 'Our Big Greek Wedding'! It was the happiest wedding I'd ever been to, and such a great day!

Chapter Four

MILESTONES

•

On Getting My Hair Cut

For many days of the year life on a small Greek island has little to do with reality. It took me several years to accept this fact, and by the time I did I was so immersed in the daily routine of the island that it all seemed completely unimportant anyhow. The Greeks are the most delightful of people and events on many occasions can and do give one the feeling of living in the middle of a pantomime.

A Greek once asked me who I considered to be the best actor in the world. I thought hard, choosing carefully between the great knights of the English theatre, American superstars and the superb classical actors of Greece. He saw my hesitation and laughed. 'The ordinary Greek,' he said, 'he is the greatest!' Over the years I have come to agree with him totally. The English may have a reputation for a dry sense of humour, or for tongue-in-cheek repartee, but the average Greek can outsmart him any time. Everyday in the highways and byways of Greece there are hundreds of performances going on, each one worthy of an actor from the cast of a play by Aristophanes, Euripides, Socrates or Aeschylus. Watch a Greek child cry real tears and hurl itself into a histrionic tantrum when denied a second packet of crisps and marvel. Many a trained thespian would turn green with envy at the ease with which the violent emotions, and indeed the tears, can be switched on and off to order.

It was not by chance that Maria Callas became and remains one of the greatest divas of all time, though of course a superb singing voice was no handicap. But you don't need to go to the theatre or the opera to witness these great performances; sit in a *cafenion* or a *taverna* or, as I happen to have done last week, simply go to the hairdresser's. You don't have to wait long for something to happen.

I went in the evening, rather late in the evening, and found my favourite hairdresser sitting outside the shop reading a story to his young son. I waited a little hesitantly, not wishing to disturb what was obviously a close moment between father and son, but when finally the eyes were raised and the familiar smile appeared, I took a step forward to say hello.

'Are you working?' I asked.

'Of course,' came the reply.

'And will you cut my hair?'

'Of course, he said again. 'but sit inside, I will come. First I must finish the story.'

Now it was my turn to say, 'Of course,' for I learned long ago that everything in Greece has a time of its own, and to push things is to court disaster.

So I went inside and sat on one of George's antique chairs and it really couldn't have been more than half an hour before father and son appeared in the doorway holding hands, the little boy eating an enormous icecream.

By this time several more customers had appeared and some were already becoming impatient, but I was the first, so as I was already dreaming away in the barber's chair I was unfortunate enough to miss the opening move in the ensuing drama; something I was greatly to regret, for the reason behind it never really became clear. All I remember is that the scissors were suddenly flung down and I was abandoned in mid-snip. Voices were raised, speech patterns rapidly accelerated and across the room a middle-aged client, halfway through some sort of colouring process, stood up and made for the door, still wearing the rubber cap with odd bits of her hair poking through. For one glorious moment, I thought she was going to leave, but something must have drawn her back for she finally returned to her chair. There was a long and ominous silence, and I feared for the success of my haircut, for all hairdressers are creative artists of the first degree and George is no exception. The atmosphere in the salon was terrible and time hung suspended, not even the clock dared to tick.

Then, as the woman sat down, I saw a pair of hands reappear with the scissors and it seemed safe to breathe again. Now the atmosphere quickly returned to one of calm and serenity and all seemed well. My hair-cut was superb as ever and the clock ticked loud and clear.

As I left, no longer the scruffy orphan who had sat so patiently waiting for the end of the story, I looked back over my shoulder and saw the lady in the rubber cap glowering at her image in a small-hand mirror.

A familiar voice followed me down the street. 'Come back soon,' it said.

And I will Giorgios. For sure I will!

•

On Understanding Greece

I have always said that Greece is like an artichoke – you pull off one leaf and there is another, and so you go on, round and round, until you reach the heart. Or do you?

Well, sitting this morning in one of the harbour cafenia I saw no reason to change my opinion. It was the first warm day of what may well turn out to be the summer, and the first tourists, totally unsurprised by the heat, were striding around, their little white legs and bare arms already showing signs of early sunburn. The islanders of course were still wrapped in their layers of winter clothing or hiding in the shade, already complaining of the sun.

I listened to the market traders chattering on around my ears, their conversations providing a fascinating background of sound to the comings and goings of the shoppers and the tourists. Occasionally a half-sentence raised itself above the general cacophony, hinting at dark political intrigues or the rumour of someone's downfall on the *Chrimatisteria* (the Greek stock market).

Given Greece's history, and especially that of the last hundred years, it is hardly surprising that there is a sub-text to many an ordinary conversation; even when the mouths remain closed, a slight movement of the head or an arm can communicate a wealth of information to the perceptive eye. Look at the recent history of Greece from the time of the Turkish occupation, through the Second World War and the ensuing civil war, and you begin to realise how survival itself often rested on these talents. And alongside all that went the need to slip into the shadows, under no circumstances could you afford to draw attention to yourself, for to stand out from the crowd could sometimes result in torture or death, or both. Even now many of the older generation run from a confrontation and seem threatened by the slightest argument.

Not so the majority, however, for whom argument is the stuff of daily life. I suppose not all arguments are about politics, though it often seems that way, and I certainly think the one I witnessed one particular warm summer afternoon had more to do with politics than anything else, but my Greek was not good enough to be sure.

I think it was around six in the evening and I was up in Poros town, but about to set off for Askeli to shower and change. As I entered the little main square I saw the one bus just leaving and I decided to take the water taxi instead. I leapt into the half-full boat that I thought was about to leave, but once seated I became aware that its owner was some way down the line of boats and involved in an argument which was becoming noisier by the minute. There were signs of impatience amongst the waiting Greeks and one or two shouted down the line for our owner to hurry up. Reluctantly he left his adversary and moved back towards the boat, only to turn round and continue the argument yet again. There were more complaints from our boat and its owner returned, but just as he bent to start the engine, some insult from the harbour front sent him running back. One by one the Greeks started to leave and soon only I and a couple of tourists remained, loyally sitting there. Eventually, I too gave up in despair and set off to walk.

Later that evening, showered and changed. I returned to Poros town to eat. It must have been around eleven-thirty when I reentered the main square, intent on returning to my bed, and heard an all-too-familiar sound. The same boat from early evening sat at the quay, half full of weary tourists, while its owner stalked back and forth angrily still exchanging insults with the same adversary down the line. I shrugged and walked to the waiting bus, there are some arguments you simply cannot win.

Only twice have I ever attempted to enter into a political discussion here and I have promised myself I will never do it again – not because of fear for my own sanity but because of the quite awful furore it produced on both occasions between the people around me.

Not for nothing was alcohol banned until only a few years ago on the night of the final speeches before an election. Of course, like most things in Greece, this never presented a major problem; and if you sat in a *cafenion*, the white wine appeared in the water jugs, the beer in the coffee pots and the whisky in the teacups. I don't suppose any of the local police were fooled but, provided everyone behaved themselves, they were prepared to turn a blind eye. After all, livings had to be earned and on a night, often in winter, when almost all the local people were down in the main square the opportunity to earn a little extra cash was too good to miss.

Election speeches here rouse powerful passions, and heated debate rumbles round the packed tables of the cafenia. The candidates are mostly listened to with respect, but later the passions rise and to express one's sympathies at the wrong café table can cause problems and serious argument. Politics are a part of the lifeblood of island life, together of course with sex, football and the weather. You can hear the discussions echoing around and around the centre square, though it is often unclear which particular subject is arousing these passions, for the same vocabulary seems to work for all topics. It is easy to find, when sitting among a party of Greeks listening to a conversation about the previous evening's meal, that when you venture some comment on a particularly succulent steak the entire group explodes with laughter. In retrospect it is easy to guess why, but when your Greek is still somewhat hesitant then the potential exists for deep embarrassment. As you can see, the hazards of social conversation at a Greek dinner table are limitless – though you may discover after one such occasion that you have just pulled off another leaf from that artichoke.

•

Galini

It's quite amazing sometimes how you can live in one place for a long time and never see it properly. You can talk about it, even inform other people about, it and yet never see it for yourself.

I have lived close to *Villa Galini* for twelve years, seeing it almost every day and sometimes describing it to other people, and yet only today did I stand a few metres away and see it as if for the first time.

Villa Galini stands on this small Greek island of Poros, close to the edge of the sea. The house itself is reached by a curved flight of steps which makes you wish for an exotic evening gown so that you can float up and down it for a while. It is built of red brick and I suspect it is Italianate in style, at any rate it conjures up pictures of gentlemen in tight-bottomed trousers and ladies in plunging necklines, and ice cold wine and plates piled high with food, filling the air with the smell of exotic spices. But it is more than just a beautiful house and you will find quite a few references to it in contemporary literature and biography. I fell in love with it the first time I saw it and I have just fallen in love with it all over again.

Today I looked down the road to the villa and suddenly caught a glimpse of it as it must have been in the past. Lawrence Durrell and Henry Miller have both written about it, for George Seferis, the Greek Nobel Prize winning poet, brought them here just as the skies of Europe were darkening at the approach of the Second World War. Chagall stayed there too and many of the Athenian celebrities of the past fifty or sixty years. After the war Yiannis Ritsos was to walk along the road from Neorion and it is probably Ritsos I see most clearly as my eyes follow what must have been the old coast road along the edge of the sea to the villa gates. From here, the house is enclosed in an assortment of tall trees; some are the sweet-scented pine, others are more exotic. There is mimosa too on the sea edge of the road, a dark dry green in summer but always the first to signal the end of winter and the certainty of warmer days to come when I retrace Ritsos's footsteps down to Neorion and find the trees in bloom. Today the road curves quite dramatically, bending into the rough foliage of the rambling gardens. It must have been a donkey track for many years until the tourists and progress brought Tarmac and the lorries to spread it. But in the strong sunlight of *mesi meri* it is easy to half close your eyes and see the shadows of the villa's famous visitors moving behind its white damask curtains as they drift softly in the breeze. You can maybe see Ritsos too, striding towards you, while Chagall must surely have his easel perched at the water's edge as he roughs in the watercolour sketch of Poros that he did from the villa.

Then stand in the same place on a soft summer night, the sound of the *trizoni* (cicadas) chuckling from the pine trees and the shooting stars cutting vivid arcs through the black sky, and if you strain your ears, you can just hear the notes of the last waltz played on an old accordion, the music of the 1920s and 1930s wafting wisps of cigarette smoke and the faint clink of the newly fashionable Martini glasses in your direction.

There is no doubt that this house is full of memories, but like those of most buildings with a romantic past some are best left to the imagination; and of course there is no shortage of that on a small Greek island. So engage your imagination and walk with me back down the road to the nearby *taverna*. This *taverna* merits a mention in the story of Galini for it has been standing there for nearly a hundred years and it, too is still owned by the original family. You only have to enter the old part of the building to smell that heady blend of resinated wine, olive oil and lemons and perhaps, too, a hint of wet winter jackets fresh from the little fishing boats as their owners swap stories of the day's exploits; stories which get more exotic as the level of the wine in the jug drops and drops.

Surely Durrell and Seferis, Henry Miller, Chagall, Ritsos, Pathenis, Tsarouchis and all the others must have sat here at one time or another? If not I shall certainly claim a writer's privilege and place them here for there is nothing to suggest they haven't. And you can somehow see them fitting in easily here – just a simple island *taverna* as it then was, with none of the exuberance of Galini, not even a log fire to fan the flames of your imagination, only the heat from the kitchen to warm in winter and stifle in summer, though by then the customers would be sitting outside round the little metal tables, the sea practically lapping their feet.

Until the 1960s this was the only *taverna* outside Poros town, a twenty-minute walk away, or more likely a twenty-minute row in one of the small fishing boats. There would be some regular weekend visitors from Athens too, for local memories place the ferryboat in the little bay opposite this *taverna*. As the boat was unable to dock in the shallow water, the passengers were taken off by the same small fishing craft and ferried to the hotels on the town seafront. Some say that this daily ferry from Piraeus had a small orchestra on board to help pass the hours as the boat steamed through the Saronic Gulf, and of course there would have been the dolphins to watch, or the flying fish skimming away from the hull; maybe even a swordfish, leaping through the surface of the sea, turning in circles as the water droplets caught the sun like crystal before they fell back into the blue.

But I am hungry and so for now I turn my back on Villa Galini and the past and concentrate my thoughts on the more immediate pleasures of freshly grilled fish and cold white wine.

•

On Needing a Tin Opener

There are days for doing things here in Greece and days for not doing things. So, when both gods and men decide they are against you, and that certainly seems to be the case sometimes, then patience is of the essence; this is a lesson I learned only too well the first time I tried to buy a tin-opener here.

I'm not quite sure why we get these problem days, though I think perhaps it might be something to do with the elasticity of time. Once you get past Lyons in France and move into the real Mediterranean area, time begins to stretch, and the farther east you go, the longer the distance between the seconds and the slower the pace of life. I suppose there must be a place where it all speeds up again, but it certainly isn't Greece.

But to return to that most riveting of subjects, the tin-opener.

When I awoke that particular morning there had been no indication of the difficulties that lay ahead. It was winter I recall, but the sun was shining and it wasn't one of those bitterly cold days that take your breath away and come as such a surprise to any newly arrived expat. Indeed, so golden is my memory of that trip down to Poros town that it could almost have been one of those *halcyon days* which arrive late in January to give us a taste of the summer still so far away. Anyhow, I walked slowly along the harbour front, savouring the moment and contemplating the pleasures I would derive from owning an efficient tin-opener, and also wondering vaguely whether or not to indulge in the luxury of a new kitchen knife as well.

I think I had almost decided in favour of the knife when I walked round the corner and found, for no apparently obvious reason, that the shop was closed.

I must have been fairly new to Greece at that time for I remember looking for a sign telling me why the shop was closed and when it would reopen, and then peering hopefully through the shutters to see – I know not what. Eventually it must have dawned on me that I had inadvertently stumbled across a bad day for buying tin-openers and so I set off back home empty handed.

Nothing daunted, I set out again the next day and found the shop open, and a man inside. My excitement grew – until I reached into my pocket that is, and discovered I had left my wallet at home. Still predominately British at this stage, and as yet unacquainted with the finer points of Greek-island shopping, I had yet to understand that money is probably the last thing you need when making a purchase here. 'Pay me tomorrow' is the familiar phrase which so astonishes tourists and expats alike. So I returned home empty handed yet again.

On the third day, still operating on the principle of nothing venture nothing gain, I found myself back on the harbour road, my wallet clutched firmly in my hand and hope in my heart. And yes, the shop was open, and yes, there was a man inside, but alas it was the wrong man! Alas, the right man, the one who knew where the tin-openers would be, had gone to Athens and would not be back until late. Despairing of ever opening whatever it was that had necessitated the purchase of the tin-opener in the first place, I walked around the harbour until I came to a favourite *taverna* and there I sank thankfully into a chair. Once I was thus settled, time changed down another gear and the day moved into evening without my noticing. Finally, full of good food, good wine and good companionship, I made my way home, the tin-opener no longer the thing of urgency it once was.

And so it came to pass that on the fourth day, which was again bright and sunny, I once more walked into Poros, bought a tin opener and a new kitchen knife, and all was well.

•

A Trip to Galatas

Friday, 18 May, and today I went to collect a pair of shoes I had ordered and found the shopowner taking delivery of a pan of roast meat and potatoes, courtesy of his small daughter. I was immediately asked to join him for lunch and soon found myself enjoying some of the best roast lamb I had eaten for years. These things don't come as a surprise any more in Greece but they do delight, and maybe the English shoeshops should take note.

Most Greek-island shops are an extension of their owner's home, indeed they are often its centre during the long hours and days of summer tourism. With only five months to earn a living for the whole year, every sale counts and no opportunity must be missed. So you can see people sitting playing *tavli*, the local backgammon, in an open supermarket well into the early hours of the morning, or whole families eating and drinking together during the scorching hours of *mesi meri*.

Well, you could! Nowadays bureaucracy invades almost every part of Greek life, though in a healthy traditional style, ways can usually be found to circumvent it. The Greek motorcyclist for instance can be seen driving around with his helmet on his arm. Visitors from England are appalled by this and usually remonstrate with him loud and long, but the helmets are hot in summer and very unpopular.

'Look, there is a law insisting they be worn,' cry our visitors.

Well yes, there is, but alas, although the law does state quite clearly that they must be worn, it doesn't specify where, so for the moment the police can do nothing. A similar wave of creative thinking operates on the side of bureaucracy too. With the arrival of Common Market subsidies, many land-and-stock owning Greeks found themselves substantially better off. Very soon, perhaps not surprisingly, an element of human greed crept in. In the case of the shepherds of Galatas, there quite suddenly appeared to be a considerable rise in the number of sheep they had grazing on our local mountains. Or was there? The local government minister in charge of subsidies was inclined to suspect a midnight migration of large flocks into the area he was due to visit the next day. As he said to a friend of mine, he was somewhat prepared for this, and as long as the numbers stayed in single figures he was willing to turn a blind eye; but when a man he knew had never owned a sheep in his life, suddenly acquired a flock of eighty, then he decided it really must be time to take action. After a few days he hit upon a plan and was later seen crossing to the mainland, a Super-Eight camera in his hand. The next day he told my friend what had happened.

When he reached that day's waiting shepherd and his surprisingly large flock, he produced his camera and proceeded to explain that it was the latest piece of technology, so sophisticated that it could distinguish one sheep from another and so could tell whether or not it had passed in front of the camera before. Nothing was said, not an eyelid was battered, but after a slight pause a cup of coffee was offered to the government minister. This he gratefully accepted and stepped into the warmth of the shepherd's house to drink it. Later, when he came to do the census, the flock appeared to have shrunk and from then on there was a dramatic drop in claimants for the government subsidy, and a return to undisturbed sleep for the people of the mountain villages. But the traditional way of life is fast being stamped out by the romantically challenged European bureaucrats, and while we once laughed at the idea of a straight cucumber and smothered it in slightly risqué jokes, it is now rare to see a cucumber in the local markets which has even the remotest kink in it. And thus the fruit boats on Aegina are almost a thing of the past. It is difficult to imagine how a few locally grown vegetables, sitting on a small fishing boat could cause such waves of consternation and create such a passion to exterminate, but somehow they did. Of course, the local people fought back and solicited signatures from the foreign visitors, but it was all to no avail. Some overpromoted jobsworth managed to steel his heart against all pleas and now the little boats are fast disappearing from the waterfront, to be replaced by yet another flotilla of yachts.

Here on Poros we were hit by the 'Thou shalt not serve food which has to cross a road whilst travelling from kitchen to table' regulation. A restriction, this, that hit just about every harbour-front *taverna* in Poros town. So, vast amounts of Common Market money were spent moving the road so that the tables were no longer on the harbour front and most of the atmosphere disappeared, along with the brightly checked tablecloths. Most of the *kefi* disappeared too, *kefi* generated by the waiters as they dodged the traffic and balanced large trays of food on one hand, or danced the *hasapiko* (fast dance, performed by men) between the motorbikes and the local buses.

One or two of the *taverna*s survived away from the town centre, but I am loathe to mention these by name for fear that yet another piece of paper will arrive from Europe and something more will be lost from the quality of our island life.

But to return briefly to my shoe-buying excursion to Galatas. On this particular day there was no one to stop me, no piece of paper to threaten me. I wandered backwards and forwards across the road, knuckle of lamb in my hand. '*Kali orixi*,' shouted the local people. 'Good eating.' Indeed it was, and I made a mental note to keep buying shoes.

•

Death of a Hero

Minos Volanakis died today. It was on the television news. They said some nice things about him and showed a brief clip from a recent interview and some slightly older photographs and the face was still the same.

I remember him so clearly on that first day at the Oxford Playhouse, standing there dressed in black and seeming so stern, so forceful – but the eyes always laughing.

We met for the production of *The Mad Woman of Chaillot* by Jean Giraudoux, years ago when I was a young, naïve and terrifyingly over-enthusiastic stage manager and he was an exotic species of director from Greece. The leading lady was a star of the international cinema and intended to be treated as such. Minos wanted ensemble playing, a group, an entity, a whole – and they clashed almost from the first day. There were furious arguments, loud explosions and long silences, and for days they only communicated through Mike, the ASM (assistant stage manager). One day we reached some sort of a climax and Minos stormed out of rehearsals and disappeared, leaving me in charge. As he left I noticed the eyes were twinkling and he winked once when he knew his leading lady couldn't see him. I thought he was wonderful. Eventually, of course, some sort of ceasefire was drafted and accepted – mostly on Minos's terms, I seem to remember – and rehearsals moved on, leaving us all considerably more experienced in international negotiations. Peace returned, and with it the awareness that we were working on something rather special. By now we were charmed by this man, who was like no other director we had known. By opening night we were all part of something that was already responsible for a buzz of excitement in theatrical circles. Yolanda Sonnabend had designed the costumes and the set, a glorious riot of fabric and colour that matched the production. For me it was the stuff of dreams and I remember it vividly to this day. I was one of the red ladies. Clad in a tight red satin shift, I had stiletto-heeled shoes, a long table-tennis-ball necklace, a cigarette holder and a mask through which I could see little and which made my eyes water if I looked anywhere but straight ahead. Our first entrance was down a particularly steep and narrow staircase.

It was all, to put it mildly, something of a nightmare – but we never complained, not even the third red lady, who was Mike the ASM in identical costume.

Anyhow, things were going well till we got to Guildford and personal disaster struck! I had made my entrance, said my lines and turned to exit when I realised that one of my stiletto heels was firmly jammed down a hole in the stage. I couldn't move and tugged but to no avail. Then, aware that an unsuspecting and severely sight-limited Mike was rapidly approaching from stage left, I decided to abandon the shoe and limp off. But this was easier said than done, for the shoe was half a size too big and had been attached to my stockinged foot with a tenacious heel-grip. I struggled and struggled until there was a loud ripping noise and my foot came free. Most people in the audience by this time had latched on to what was happening and they were beginning to enjoy themselves thoroughly. I limped off to a round of applause and then watched in suspense as the still unaware Mike missed the resplendent red shoe by a hair's breadth and completed his part of the scene successfully.

I turned away in relief just as Chris Gable signalled to me that he was going on stage to retrieve my shoe. 'Don't,' I hissed, trying to warn him that it was very firmly stuck indeed – but he was gone.

Chris, known internationally as one of Britain's great ballet dancers, had recently sustained a seriously torn ligament and had turned his considerable talent towards acting. But it was as a ballet dancer that he flew on to the stage, stooped elegantly down to the offending shoe and tugged. And tugged and tugged! The audience was now laughing long and loud as Chris found himself stranded there, not knowing quite what to do. But the shoe must have grown tired of being capricious for it suddenly came free, taking its rescuer by surprise and throwing him on to his back, legs in the air. Somewhat chastened he picked up both himself and the shoe and left the stage to a thunderous round of applause.

Minos was not in the theatre that afternoon, but when told what had happened seemed delighted with both the event and his actors' reactions to it. So much so that for a moment we were afraid he might say, 'Keep it in.'

You see, we were beginning to understand the workings of our new director's mind and, what is more beginning to enjoy it all.

Later that season Minos was to direct *The Good Woman of Setzuan* by Bertolt Brecht, and I was to learn more about the art of directing in a few short weeks than in all the rest of my career in the theatre.

The play and Minos were well suited and this time his leading lady was a much liked and respected theatre actress. Rehearsals were happy and exciting times. Of course, there were still the explosions and long silences – and still the twinkling eyes and the winks when he thought no one was looking. One or two of the older actors said they found him 'difficult' but he wasn't really, he was just an impatient perfectionist who had little time for over-inflated egos.

And then, just as before, this new cast began to understand and relish the freedom they were being given to try out different interpretations. And they became aware too that Minos was always totally in control and knew exactly where to take them. What had seemed like chaos turned slowly but surely into something with many depths and of many layers and finally became a piece of pure theatre. He had scored us like an orchestra.

There were new things to be learnt too from the designer – how the set and costumes must grow out of the original concept and find their own level in the production as a whole. Nikos Stefanou had come over from Athens and worked daily alongside Minos. As Nikos spoke French and Greek but no English and I spoke some French, I was attached to him as helper and translator for when Minos wasn't there. How I enjoyed that. My enthusiasm grew alarmingly with each passing day but somehow, in spite of this diversion, rehearsals continued and the play developed in content and stature. Then one day it grew up completely and we had to let it leave home and share it with an audience. It should have been a beginning but it felt like an end.

Minos worked in England for quite a while after that and we kept in touch until that glorious day when the BBC broadcast the news that the Colonels in Greece had been deposed. Many people's dreams came true that day. I phoned the London flat but Minos had already left for home, and after that I lost track of him for a while.

Unsurprisingly, I found him again in Greece. I came to Poros on holiday and saw a poster for the Epidaurus Festival in one of the tourist offices. It was in Greek, but I knew enough to make out three very important words: 'Minos', 'Volanakis' and 'Medea'. That night at Epidaurus, even if I had not seen the poster, I would have known the name of the director of that play. Everything he had taught us all those years ago was still there working brilliantly. Maybe he had matured or maybe he was more at home working in Greek with Greek actors – whatever, it didn't matter. I sat on my little piece of marble transfixed by a production that was outstanding by any standards.

I looked for Minos that night but was not surprised when I couldn't find him. I imagined him prowling along the upper limits of the ancient site or merging into the shadowy darkness of a convenient tree.

Soon after that I came to live in Greece and saw other productions of his in other theatres. I was never disappointed. Eventually I found someone who knew Minos and I sent a message to say I was living here in Greece.

'Tell her to phone,' he said. So I did, but somehow it all never quite worked out and I never met him again. Now it is too late. When I heard he had died I phoned Mike in London.

'Ah,' he said, "A part of the past gone for ever."

But here and for me he is a part of the present and I am still angry that he will now not be part of the future. I am so proud to have known and worked with him all those years ago and I know there are so many people who feel the same. I will never forget – and I can still see that face with the twinkling eyes and then the long slow wink.

He was a theatre director of international stature and a true innovator and he was a delightfully charming human being. He was special and we will miss him dreadfully.

Monday, 15 November 1999. Minos Volanakis has died and the world is a colder place.

•

A Walk to Neorion

The sun was so hot today it was impossible to stay in the house. Like the sirens of yore it lured you outside with promises of sparkling seas and haze-wrapped mountains straight out of a Japanese painting.

So I allowed myself to be tempted and walked down to Neorion following the sea and almost dazzled by its brilliance. Neorion is one of my favourite places on the island. Its little bays and friendly *tavernas* make for one of the loveliest places to spend a summer evening. Now, of course, it is deserted. The chairs and tables stacked away, the shutters closed. The little boats are pulled clear of the sea and tied firmly against a sudden storm. But in the shade of the fir trees, tables, and mismatched chairs still stand, neatly arranged and awaiting the first game of *tavli* or chess that will herald the season.

But there are people about. Some are parents here for the weekend to see their sons during the three hours they are allowed free from the Naval Base. Anxious mothers these, with the car filled with cakes and favourite foods lovingly cooked by *yiayia* (Grandmother) and other family members, convinced their favourite child is starving on an alien isle. Mothers are the same the world over.

Here it is so nice to see middleaged couples walking hand in hand enjoying each other's company. A lone water-skier curves an arc across the bay, leaving a trail of spray and memories of the summer past. The beach too is full of summer ghosts – friends who were here, sometimes only for a few hours, but who are now part of my island life.

Stelios is sweeping out the forecourt of his hotel and waves in greeting. Other friends toot as they pass on their motorbikes, going heaven knows where – to a relative maybe along the headland or simply out for a *volta* (stroll) to see what is happening and who is where.

It is impossible to disappear on an island. I remember one day walking miles to a distant and deserted bay where I sat totally at peace with the silence and the sound of the sea until I slowly became aware of a familiar buzzing sound that quickly turned itself into an approaching *mykhanaxi* (motorbike). This ground to a dramatic halt and a complete stranger shouted down to me, 'Anna you are to go to the office immediately, there is an urgent message for you.' His speech delivered, the messenger turned his bike around and disappeared, leaving me to walk the not inconsiderable distance back to Poros town. But how had they known where I was?

Today there was no messenger and no summons back into town. So I walked on to the end of the bay, had a daydream and then turned round for home. On walks like these I really miss smoking; my daydream would once be accompanied by a cigarette, and the dreams could drift off with the spirals of smoke until they too disappeared into the air.

But cigaretteless I was, so I wandered back picking some greenery for the Christmas decorations. On the whole I don't do Christmas, but this year, it being the Millennium, I decided to make five new 'somethings' to add to my minimalist one which is hung each year with great ceremony.

Back home I made myself a cup of tea and sat back feeling very content indeed.

•

A Christening

On Friday the phone rang. It was Eleni inviting me to a christening. Mitsos our very own 'juvenile delinquent' was to be the *noonos* or godfather. Eleni had told me that this was to happen while we were still working on the boat together. But it all seemed a long way from the Mitsos I had first known as a young boy who refused quite categorically to go to school. Since then he had worked long hours on the *Anna*, pushed by his father in the hope that he would see school as the easy option. But he never did. He just took whatever was thrown at him and got on with it. I nicknamed him 'the juvenile delinquent', though that hardly seems a fair name to describe him, for he bears no similarity to the real thing, now to be found in large cities throughout the Western world. Ours rebelled early, but his 'crimes' consisted only of a stubborn determination to go his own way, and a nightly habit of escaping through his bedroom window to spend hours at the local disco! There had been many angry arguments on the *Anna II* and Mitsos must have felt the whole world was against him, but nothing would make him go back to school and we never really found out why.

Over the years I have got to know him well and I have a great respect for him. He also has a wicked sense of humour, one that more than matches mine. But Mitsos as a godfather? Well, why not? Anyhow I have been invited to the christening to see for myself how it will all turn out.

'But I don't have a present,' I said.

'Anna, you must not bring a present, it is a privilege for us that you will be there. There is no need for a present.'

Such is Greek hospitality but I still feel a little British – uncomfortable. Even so, on Saturday, still presentless, I crossed to Galatas and made my way to *Aghios Nikolaos* (Saint Nicholas), the big church in the main square. The whole family seemed to be there and Mitsos looked amazing in his first ever suit. Is that really the person who never wears anything but jeans and refuses new boots even when his current ones are falling off his feet? It seems so.

I watch him carrying his godson to be, holding him so firmly yet gently, and I think what a lucky baby young Nikos is for he will have a really terrific godfather. Mitsos is all heart.

Of course the baby does not yet have a name, so 'baby' it is for a little while longer as everyone tries to catch his attention, making him wave excitedly. His father, who is carrying him again, doesn't realise what is happening behind him and he slaps the baby's hand and tells him to be still – It hardly seems fair but maybe it's an early lesson on the injustices of life!

The priest has been bustling round the church checking that all is ready. The big christening candle with its ribbons and flowers stands by the font and one of the ladies of the church appears with the hot water. The nave is full of people now, all pushing forward for the best view. Mitsos's grandma insists I sit by her and refuses to let me stand at the back. As we came into the church we all bought and lit a candle dedicating it to the baby – or maybe another Nikos from another time…

It is the tradition here for the first boy or girl to be named after its father's parents, the second one after the mother's, then you are free to choose, but they tell me that Angelica's father died only a few short weeks before his grandson was born, so this baby is to be named after him.

The service has begun now and the baby sits in Mitsos's arms quite composed, fascinated by the flickering of the candles and thoroughly enjoying being the centre of attention. His mother hovers nervously, just out of his sight. Greek christenings are not for young mothers. Until recently they were not allowed into the church. Today they are, but they do not hold the baby during the service.

Finally the moment of dedication arrives and the baby is undressed. He does not like this, nor does he like being dipped into the water three times and then smothered in oil. He screams loudly and healthily (a sign of a good purification) and the congregation are delighted. Only the mother stands close to tears, unable to take him in her arms until the service is finished.

But it is soon over and the baby is wrapped in a thick towel and brought to the table to be dressed in his new outfit. The women press round, anxious to be a part of it all and consequently making the process longer and more complicated than it need be. He is still screaming loudly but quickly stops when he is back safely in his father's arms.

Young Nikos, the little boy, is among us at last. We leave the church telling one another that it was a great christening. We file past the family wishing the traditional greetings to the father and his son and we collect our cake and *bou bounieres* and leave the church.

In our lapels are the ribbons that mark this special event and one which will remind us of it in years to come. And it works. I have a growing collection on a shelf in my bedroom and I can remember clearly which christening or wedding each came from.

As we go out into the early evening twilight, the women are clearing away the large copper font and all the trappings of the christening. Our candles, which have burned steadily for over an hour are put out now and dropped into a bin to be recycled.

I set off with friends towards the little taxi boat that will take us back to Poros but when I reach the corner of the square something makes me look back towards the church. My last image of this special day is of young Nikos clasped firmly in his mother's arms. Both are laughing, while just behind them stands Mitsos, no longer the 'enfant terrible', but standing proud, basking in the limelight. His father reaches out and pats him on the shoulder and Mitsos beams. Perhaps it was only a starting point but I walked on towards the waterfront feeling that something momentous had happened that day; and maybe it had.

•

A Funeral

Kiria (Mrs) Dimitra died during the night. Katherine telephoned to tell me this morning. I didn't know her terribly well but I lived next door to her for two years and once she realised I could understand a little Greek she always spoke and asked how I was. The funeral will be later today, just a simple affair but very moving none the less. This isn't like Minos's death, no announcement on the television, no state funeral, no eulogies by famous actors and actresses but here in this little corner of the island she was well known and loved. Two summers ago we used to swim together on Kanali beach. I think the doctor had told her she should. She was afraid of the sea for quite a long time but then I think she began to enjoy it, savouring the cooling effect of the water and the companionship of the other ladies, some from Athens and bearing rich gossip. She seemed to find the whole adventure rather risqué – wearing a swimsuit in public, I suppose. But her new-found friends reassured her, and I am afraid of the water too and that helped.

As my Greek improved we chatted for longer, nothing important, just this and that but she always smiled and seemed genuinely to enjoy our casual meetings. In the summer I used to come across her on my way to the *Anna*, she coming back from church, both of us the only people around in the cool early morning before the full force of the sun came over the mountain. We used to meet in almost the same place, just before the Naval Base accommodation buildings, and she quickly became part of those summer memories.

Last year she was already ill and rarely left the balcony. The television was moved outside and I would see her sitting there, a silent silhouette. But she would always smile and wave. Today the balcony is empty and the church bells toll her passing. The marching music came across the water from the parade ground, a sound she must have heard so many times, but today she does not hear and suddenly there is silence – someone must have told them.

In England death is such a private thing shut behind closed doors and curtained windows. Here you do not die alone and you are remembered with joy. '*Kalo Taxidi*' they say – have a good journey, a good passing over – and sometimes a coin is dropped into the coffin, the payment for Charon in his little boat.

The funeral was at three o'clock, the middle of the day, and a beautiful day too. I went with Katherine and we stood outside the house with the family and friends and the people of the neighbourhood. They brought her down just before the Naval Base clock chimed the hour, her coffin open and filled with flowers freshly picked from the garden she loved. There is something about intense grief that changes the very air around the people involved. It seemed as though even the birds had stopped singing and the sound of the coffin being placed in the hearse was muffled somehow and slowed down.

We walked with her to the little church in the cemetery and filed slowly into the cool interior. The singing was beautiful but the pain on the faces of the people around us made it almost unbearable. We lit our candles and filed past the coffin, stooping to kiss her goodbye, and then we moved on to the living. Her husband, children and grandchildren stood by the door, lost and helpless, and there was nothing we could say to comfort them. Here in Greece you do not die alone but the final parting is just as terrible. Dear Kyria Dimitra, your death did not make newspaper headlines but you were deeply loved and we will miss you.

•

For Another Dimitra

You were born in Greece and you spent your first summer on Poros, a little island in the Saronic Gulf where the mountains stand guard over the community here and the little fishing boats chug out at night, their sodium lights flaring brightly against the dark shapes of the land.

At the full moon a swathe of silver light cuts a path across the sea and in the height of summer it is so hot that the sun distorts the image of the old town and the little clocktower that stands proudly at its peak. Here the summer days are long and filled with music and talk and the sound of the sea. The winters smell of wood smoke and the spices from the cooking and everywhere the chink of glasses can be heard as the new wine is tasted and found good.

Now you are going to a place very different from all this, but if you look you will find beauty there too. Go into the Peak District of Derbyshire (I know it well) and there you will see the rough edges of the granite rocks, the purple of the heather and the ling and the gold of the bracken in autumn. In summer everywhere is a rich shade of green you never see here and the air is full of the smell of roses and freshly mown grass. In winter you will have to keep warm, as the wind roars down from the hills bringing with it snow and icicles and early-morning frost. It seems to go on for ever until one day, just when you begin to despair of the cold ever coming to an end, spring arrives bringing with it the catkins and the bluebells and the song of the birds.

Yes, you were born in Greece, in Athens. I sort of knew you before then and many people from many countries awaited the news of your arrival. You must have known, for you kept us waiting for quite a while! Once you got here, of course, you just grew and grew and the summer rolled along until one day it was 16 October and the day of your baptism.

The day dawned grey and cloudy, a fact that came as something of a shock, for the long hot summer days had stretched on into the winter and only the day before we had been complaining of the heat. The cooler weather was actually welcome, apart that is, from the problem of what to wear to the church; there was a chill in the air and our summer clothes looked decidedly thin, while the winter ones still lay crushed in some forgotten suitcase. In the event, the people at the church reflected both seasons, the young girls looking especially beautiful in their long dresses and high-heeled shoes, the rest of us erring on the side of caution in our quickly pressed winter jackets. But it turned out that the girls were right!

I arrived far too early, having allowed myself too much time for the walk up the mountain to one of the prettiest churches on the island. It is one of my favourites, and I have spent many happy hours in the shade of the huge trees, listening to the sound of the running water as it comes bubbling out of the mountainside. The water is clear and sweet and quite famous. People come from Athens and all over the Peloponnese to take it for its beneficial properties.

The priest arrived early too and he and his family began to bring the icon from the church and fill up the font with water. Then people began to arrive, mixing in with the kittens and geese and guinea fowl that had come running down from the nearby farm to see what all the fuss was about and to wish you well.

We put our presents on one of the wooden picnic tables and waited impatiently for you to arrive. Aunt Jenny came next, bringing the *bou bounieres*, the special candle and the new clothes for the little girl who would come out of the church also wearing her new name.

And then finally, we saw the car with you in it. 'Baby' we called you for the last time. Your mum was trying to smile but she looked nervous and complained that her hair was still wet. Your dad looked handsome but he seemed nervous too and quickly got involved in checking that all the arrangements were in order. He had brought the hot water to add to that already in the font and he went to find the priest. You were not in the least nervous and you smiled happily as your mum took you into the church. At that moment the sun came out and stayed out for the rest of the day. You were a sunshine baby.

The service began but the church is tiny so I stayed outside and watched from there. I caught glimpses of you still smiling as you were carried round by your godmother, and I heard the priest declare that you were to be called Dimitra. People came and went and the sun poured down through the trees, causing intricate patterns on the tables and the faces of the people standing there. There was a great silence outside, just the voice of the priest and the smell of the incense associated with the centuries old ritual of the Byzantine Church. There was a great sense of continuity and tradition and I began to wonder how many other Dimitras had come here to receive their names and the blessing from the priest.

Of course, christenings are about fairy godmothers too and there was a moment when I caught a glimpse of yours as she flitted away up the mountain. She was very beautiful and she was laughing as she disappeared into the trees. I'm sure she brought you many wonderful gifts.

You screamed as you were put into the font – most babies do – and it was very loud and very long. Your mum said later that you didn't like being dressed and undressed so you had a good excuse to scream for quite a while. This you proceeded to do while mum looked very unhappy and asked your Dad when it would be all right for her to hold you again. Your priest is a family man so it wasn't long before you were back in mum's arms and both of you started to look happier.

As you both came out of the church a lone turkey wobbled up and squawked his greeting, making us all laugh; he turned and then walked away with great dignity, past Aunty Jenny who was waiting by the stream with the *bou bounieres*. We crowded round you, admiring your pretty dress and welcoming you to Poros and the world as Dimitra.

We ate our sugared almonds and chatted whilst dad and the priest emptied the font and took everything back inside the church. Then we set off down the mountain back to your house to celebrate with some food and wine. Meanwhile, you fell asleep in the car and missed it all! You really should not make a habit of this for there was music and dancing and laughter and many more good wishes before we finally all went home and left you to embark on the rest of your life.

Such was your Greek Christening and maybe there will be

an English one, for you belong to two countries. What an interesting life you are going to have – though perhaps not always easy. But you should know that you have a mum and dad who love you very much and will, I'm sure, be always there for you. You were born into the sunshine of Greece, with music and dancing in your blood. Carry those with you wherever you go and enjoy.

I wish you good health and love and laughter (beauty you have already) and I give you the little icon to keep you safe and the little donkey to keep you company in England.

•

The Bolshoi Ballet Comes to Poros

Rumours had been running round the island for days, long before the first posters appeared. The older people nodded their heads and talked in a casual way of some dancers coming to Poros, but those of us who had travelled a little gasped, and thought it couldn't possibly be true. Maybe it was something on film, maybe a lecture of some kind. But when the posters did appear in Greek and English and with pictures, it seemed there was no longer any room for doubt.

By some mysterious, unbelievable, miraculous chance the Bolshoi Ballet was coming to dance on Poros.

The best in the world; first time in their history; for one night only, shouted the posters, and they were right. The island buzzed now and slowly it emerged that this was a personal success for Spiros the mayor. For a whole year he had begged, pleaded and badgered the Russian company, asking that, for the one night that they were not dancing in Athens, they would come and dance on Poros. And, finally, the best contemporary soloists of the Bolshoi had agreed. On 10 August they were coming.

Even after learning all this it somehow seemed too much to hope for, so we watched the carpenters building a stage in front of the new school, watched the electricians wiring up some mega speakers, watched the rows of chairs being put out in the school yard – and still we crossed our fingers and held our breath.

But miracles really do happen sometimes and so, that night of 10 August 1997, I found myself sitting on a hard wooden bench wriggling like a child in anticipation of what was to come. The last rays of light melted away across the sea. The sky turned to its habitual black velvet and the stars came out in their hundreds. All around me people chattered away, calling to friends and relations on the other side of the audience and then squeezing together even more tightly to fit in new arrivals.

I held my ground and resisted being pushed off the end of the bench while excited children ran past treading on my toes and grabbing me with ice-cream sticky fingers. There were even two or three stray dogs attracted by the commotion and the possibility of a fallen ice-cream or a half-empty packet of crisps. One in particular sat in front of the stage, gazing in anticipation, while Russian-speaking stage staff made last-minute adjustments to the lights and called to one another across the back-drop of the school buildings, thus adding another dash of excitement to an atmosphere which was already pretty electric by now.

Then, with no warning the floodlights came on, the music belted from the megawatt speakers and the first dancer appeared on stage. It was a programme of mainly solo roles at first, later they performed the duets and some ensemble dancing. The music was loud and not of a great quality and I'm sure the newly built stage left much to be desired, but the dancing was superb. Sitting near the edge of the sea on this perfect summer's evening with the best of the world's dancers performing there in front of us was something I shall never forget, and I wanted it to go on for ever. Looking round at the faces of those sitting beside me, I sensed they felt the same too. It was lovely to watch them – grandads, grandmas, young people and babies in arms – all there because they loved to dance and to watch other people dance. For some, I'm sure, the name of the Bolshoi meant nothing, but no matter – this was Art and it was available for everyone, just as it should be.

Bravo, Mr Mayor.

As the dancers took their bows, we cheered our thanks and the bouquets were handed across. Then the music started again, one of the traditional Greek dances, and they danced that for us. The cheers then must have awakened the gods. It was a generous end to a perfect evening.

Later, as I walked home, I eased one of the posters off its lamp-post. Today it adorns one of the walls of my apartment. I can see it as I write this: 10 August 1997, the day the Bolshoi came to town!

•

Two Weddings

I went to two weddings while the sun was still shining. Kleopatra got married in Athens and had her reception in the Plaka, while my landlady's son got married in Galatas and had his reception nearby.

There is always a problem when a close friend gets married for you are convinced that they are marrying the wrong person and that your relationship with them will change for ever. There is an element of jealousy I suppose. In this case, I'm delighted to say, I was wrong on both counts, but I wasn't to know that at the wedding. So it was with rather mixed feelings that I arrived at the church on a mild autumn evening.

Kleopatra, my friend from *Skai*, was married in the old Byzantine church in Syngrou Avenue very late one Sunday evening. It seemed strange to be arriving for a wedding at eight o'clock but we soon got into the swing of things.

She arrived looking very beautiful, but not a bit like the Kleopatra of the filming days at *Skai* where we spent most days working long, long hours, covered in paint and dust. This was the sophisticated woman, wife to be, and I felt a lump rise in my throat.

I love Greek weddings, the Byzantine music, the changing of the wedding wreaths over the heads of the bride and the groom, the stamping on the foot and the throwing of the rose petals. It all seems so very romantic, and I love romance. That evening the air was full of it.

After the ceremony there was a scramble for taxis into the Plaka. My driver was one of the uncooperative ones and dropped me quite a way from the nightclub after driving round half of Athens. As I wasn't really sure where I was going I was unable to indulge in a really good argument over the fare, which was annoying to say the least. I soon forgot all this, however, for there was a *bouzouki* band of ten musicians and it wasn't long before the hall was throbbing with the music. Once the wine was opened we were up and running.

Bouzouki is like the South American samba in that it starts almost lethargically, sometimes off key even, and then, as the atmosphere builds and the musicians pick up some *kefi* from the audience, the music gets more energetic and the rhythm more pronounced until it seems to flow through your veins at a quickening pace, along with your blood. Hands and feet start tapping out the beat and sometimes it is impossible to stop yourself from dancing. Once this happens, you can just go on all night and time flies.

I was sitting at a table with the elderly aunts who kept telling me that they didn't actually drink but would I mind topping up their wine glasses while their husbands weren't looking. Always happy to oblige, I poured away recklessly until I realised that they were all getting rather tipsy. When they started dancing round the tables I thought I had better slow down. The husbands, of course, knew exactly what was going on and gave me a conspiratorial wink from time to time.

I found out later that I was supposed to have sat with some of the younger couples but I was glad to have sat where I did.

The older Greek people have that enormous capacity for enjoying themselves that the younger ones seem to be losing. Too concerned with their image, I suppose, just like the Western Europeans.

I left in the early hours of Monday morning, the music still throbbing in my head as I walked through the silent, ghost-ridden Plaka to get a taxi. Kleopatra had looked beautiful at the reception in a dress made from a peacock-blue and silver sari. She is an exotic creature and the dress suited her to perfection. In it she looked exactly like the Kleopatra I had always known and I felt reassured for the future. I was soon to find that my new confidence was not misplaced.

The other wedding started off at a church in the same way as Kleopatra's, but this time we were in the church in a small village on the mainland, opposite Poros. Still, the service was the same except for the fact that I did not know the bride and so had no complicated feelings to battle with. The groom was my landlady's son and I was just delighted to have been invited; it was a kindness and consideration so typical of the family in whose apartments I live.

So we emerged from the church, clutching yet again, our *bou bounieres*, taking photographs and very much on our best behaviour. This continued until we reached the reception, but I am happy to relate that, once there, no one could keep up the formality for long and when they couldn't get grandad to take off his (new) tweed cap, well, things rapidly changed for the better. Very soon people were dancing and the music was getting louder and louder. The wine and the food just kept coming all night and the men were dancing the traditional dances with a passion and flamboyance you don't very often see these days. We have some very good dancers on and around Poros and it seemed as though they were all at that reception. Even the waiters were dancing in between serving the different courses.

This reception started at four in the afternoon and went on until dawn, and the bride and bridegroom stayed to the end. I left sometime during the night and as I was crossing back to Poros in one of the little taxi boats the full moon was cutting a path across the sea and the sky was full of stars. The other people in the boat were clutching flowers and singing, all of us a little drunk and full of love for all humanity!

'Nice,' as Kleopatra would say.

•

Recovered Faces and Keys Found

There's been a miracle. When Phil and I were here in Greece we went to the Plaka in Athens and I bought an old icon there. For me it was a 'dream come true' because I had always wanted to own one. This one is from Macedonia. It is not particularly valuable because you aren't allowed to take the good ones out of the country. But for me, that didn't matter. We were told that it was probably painted by a local artist and came from someone's home. It is of the Madonna and Child, quite simple, and the Madonna's face had been virtually rubbed away where it had been touched so often.

Anyhow, I loved this icon and it has always been one of my favourite things, so last year when I was in England I kidnapped it from my flat in London and brought it back to Poros – and the Madonna's face has come back. Do you think it's the change of climate or is she just glad to be back in Greece? Well, I think it's the latter.

We have a newly restored local church. This one is dedicated to Aghios Fanourios. He is an interesting saint and very useful to have locally. For a start he was rather unusual in that his mother was well known as something of a sinner. But he is also the saint who finds lost things and lost people. Well, he must be a hard worker because, since his church was restored, for me alone he has found several families, a Greek friend I knew in England twenty-five years ago, a pair of scissors and two nail files. When I met Margarita in a tizz because she had locked the door and then lost her keys, I sent her to light a candle in the church and learned later that within ten minutes the keys had turned up in a highly illogical place. Not bad eh?

I suppose he must be quite grateful to us all for his church was falling down and last winter we had a series of teas and ouzo evenings to raise the money for the restoration. The local people did the work free. Still, thanks are in order, though it's rather more complicated than lighting a candle. You have to bake a special pie that will help his mother to be forgiven for her sins. I'm not sure of the recipe but I expect Giorgia will know it or else Eleni from the boat.

Yesterday it rained all day, the sort of rain that makes you think back to the days of Noah and consider whether or not to start building a boat. Several times I looked across the straits to Galatas and saw nothing moving at all; the roads were empty, the harbour deserted. Only the big ferries from Piraeus broke the stillness, moving like the *Marie Celeste* across a millpond of a sea.

The mountains of the mainland seemed dark and oppressive, their tops disappearing into clouds that hung low, layer upon layer, almost down to the harbour. Time suspended itself; even the clock chiming the hours away in the Naval Base sounded muffled and remote. With relief I closed the shutters and switched on the central heating. It was winter indeed, and only some opera on the stereo could fit this mood.

Today I woke late and felt rather than saw the sun on the shutters. Once opened, they revealed a summer-like brilliance, and the heat had caused puffy little clouds to dance across the sea, disappearing almost as quickly as they formed. After the rain, the smell of verbena hung over everything and the lilac buds looked ready to burst open many weeks before they should.

Dimitrios in the supermarket was full of good humour and people were laughing as they helped themselves to the piles of broccoli, spinach, leeks, beetroot, *hortas* (wild greens) and spring onions, newly arrived from the mainland and still smelling of the rich red earth from which they had so recently been dragged.

It was another good day to be alive.

•

A Trip to Athens

As I descended my mountain, suitcase in hand, I thought I had every reason to assume (never assume) that I was off on my pre-Christmas trip to Athens. I had seen the early-morning boat head off towards Hydra and Spetses and it really didn't seem all that windy. But, as I turned the corner by the office of Saronic Gulf Travel, the full force of this same wind hit me, bowling me sideways for several paces. I began to have second thoughts.

An orange narrowly missed my head and danced its way through the air, finally bouncing into the sea. I crossed away from the fruit trees but then changed my mind and crossed back. The sea was pounding up and over the quay, as the seagulls screamed above it.

'No,' said Nikos a few minutes later 'there have been no Flying Dolphins – but go and ask. The boat will leave at three-twenty this afternoon.'

It was ten-fifty and I had come to catch the eleven-twenty Flying Dolphin to Piraeus. What to do?

Well, first I thought I'd try the Flying Dolphin office.

'Maybe later,' they said.

I tried to assess whether this remark was based on reports or, as was more likely, just the eternal Greek optimism that everything will work out the way you want it to in the end. I decided to wait and see, at least until eleven-thirty. Two hopeful Pakistanis waited on the seats by the place where the Flying Dolphins always moored; it really wasn't cold but the wind made staying out in the open unbearable. I admired their fortitude.

Taking refuge in Nikos's office I was entertained by the comings and goings of the other would-be travellers. I was also hoping to keep up to date on any information coming from the Flying Dolphin office but nothing seemed to be happening.

At eleven-thirty my nerve snapped and I walked through the cafés to see for myself if anything had changed. My appearance produced only that eloquent Greek shrug which can imply anything from, 'Maybe' through 'What can we do about it?' (i.e. nothing), to 'Don't bother me'. I retreated back through the cafés.

'Go home.' said Nikos 'Wait there and go on the three-thirty boat.'

But I was reluctant to go away. Winds can suddenly drop and boats can appear unannounced and many are the times hopeless situations have been saved by the arrival of the unexpected.

'I'm hungry,' I said, and stomped off to the market *taverna* delighted to have thought of such a sensible way to pass some time.

It is not really the 'done thing' for a woman alone to eat here, indeed only a few years ago I would never have dared to enter alone, but I was very hungry and I made sure that everyone knew I was stuck waiting for the boat and I just about got away with it.

The roast pork was superb as usual and I gained extra good-behaviour points by ordering only a glass of wine. Appearances are all, for the glass that arrived contained almost as much as the small carafe that usually appears automatically.

Linda was there with her husband and daughter, newly returned from a visit half way across the world to her own country, and it was nice to have a friendly eye to catch from time to time as I sat happily gorging away on a portion of the pork that would have been enough for two.

Time passed quickly now and when I finally emerged from the *taverna* there was only about an hour left before the boat was due. I walked slowly back to N's office passing the two

Pakistanis on the way – so there had been no Flying Dolphin then.

I phoned Kleopatra to say I was still coming – I hoped – and then settled back to wait out the rest of the time. The boat was late and had difficulty docking – I should have been warned, I suppose, but I didn't really think. I just walked on board and sat with some friendly looking Greek ladies, ignoring the ashen faces of the people already aboard.

Methana was difficult, but then Methana often is. They managed to get in long enough for the people to run up the ramp but the cars and vans stood forlornly on the quay as we pulled away and out to sea again.

Aegina was next, the people waiting eagerly for the first boat of the day but we simply could not get in at all, and after three attempts we left.

I have never known a boat not stop at Aegina and for the first time ever I began to feel afraid. Certainly the journey was the worst I've ever had. Twice, I really thought we were going over and even in Piraeus harbour the conditions were little better. They docked us at the far side, the Port Police running us off in groups while the boat tried desperately to break free.

The captain had done well; somehow or other we all got off, though the boat did not sail again that evening as it was scheduled to do. I gained the calm of the Metro and headed for Kato Patissia. There the phone was ringing, a worried Kleopatra concerned for my safety.

Well it had been quite a day and all plans for a trip to the cinema disappeared to be replaced by a longing for some food, a glass of wine and bed. I was soon asleep – and awoke to a sunny windless day where all things were possible again. Yes, I should have waited.

I love being in Athens. It is a vibrant, exciting city when you get to know it. After several months on a small island it can easily go to your head. Now, only a few days before Christmas, it was at its most chaotic. The preparations for the Millennium celebrations had suddenly got under way, the tree in Syntagma was up and lit and Father Christmas, or Aghios Vassilis as he is known here, was everywhere at once, often smoking happily or chewing on a souvlaki (kebab), his rather too modern jeans tucked into his boots and peeping out from under an assortment of red jackets. 'Jingle Bells' was playing loudly almost everywhere, and slightly embarrassed parents were attempting to explain away the glut of Aghios Vassilises by talking of Santa's little helpers – although the fact that several of them spoke fluent Albanian was not really helping.

But on a sunny morning only four days before Christmas it all seemed good fun, and I ploughed off in the direction of the shops like a child heading for a pâtisserie. Today was really just a preliminary skirmish for I had arranged to see Kleopatra back at the studio; we had not really talked together since the middle of the summer and there was a lot of catching up to do. I did manage to spend some money, however, before it was time to squeeze myself into the Metro and head back home. Kleopatra arrived soon after and with a mug of tea each we embarked on some serious talking; by the time she left four hours later we were pretty much up to date and ready to enjoy each other's company for a few days.

'What will you do this evening?' she asked, suddenly stricken with the thought that I would be on my own.

This, of course, is just about the worst thing that can happen to a Greek. I remember once being told once that I was extraordinarily unlucky, for the three worst possible things had happened to me: one, I had not been born Greek; two, I had been born a woman; and three, I had no family! With these misfortunes hanging around my neck I had learned to provide myself with some ready answers.

'I shall go to the cinema,' I said.

'Ah, yes,' said K, the smile returning to her face.

And so, not wishing to tell fibs, off to the cinema I went – though not quite to the cinema I wanted to go to, for that remained lost and unknown to anyone I asked, including the ticket girl in one of the cinemas I did find. Here I was met with

Poros Town at sunset, framed by the Peloponnese

The ruins of Theseus's birthplace at Trizinias on the mainland

Poros: The larger island of Kalavria with Aegina and Angistri behind

The Monastry of Zoodochus Pigi on Poros

The Clock Tower, Poros

War memorial, decorated on Oxi Day, Poros

Octopi drying in the sun with Poros in the background

Petros's father at the farm

Russian Bay, Poros

The ancient theatre at Epidaurus, where a pin dropping onto the stage can be heard throughout

Villa Galini, Poros

Captain Kiriakos at the wheel of the *Anna II*

Mistos serving lunch on the *Anna II*

One smart puppy and friends at Phousa

Athens: The Parthenon and Acropolis seen from the Pnyx

Sue (wearing headband)

Petro's wedding

The Mani: The old town of Monemvasia (top left); The lady owner of the hostelry in Kardamyli (top right); Maniote tower house and our hotel (middle); the little town of Gerolimanos (bottom)

The icon of love, peace and hope in the church
of the old town of Monemvasia

The monasteries of the Meteora

The bay of Vygonia, site of the ancient city of Poros

The little island of Daskalio in Russian Bay

Bourtzi (known as Snake) Island and the Venetian Fort

The crew of the *Anna II* hard at work

The monastery on Hydra built with stones from the ancient temple on Poros. Now the town hall.

The pink Turkish tower on Aegina. Home of the first free Greek government after the Turks were expelled from Greece.

The *Anna II* leaving the Corinth Canal

Corinth Canal, looking toward the Gulf of Corinth

another Greek shrug and so, having learnt a long time ago that no amount of further questioning will get me anywhere, I accepted the search was hopeless and settled for *The Runaway Bride*. It turned out to be far better than I expected and thoroughly enjoyable to boot.

I emerged from the cinema in a very good mood indeed, chuckling to myself at various remembered bits from the film, and walked out into a torrential downpour that looked as if it was going to last all night. I really wasn't far from home and so I decided to make a run for it and just get wet. This I successfully did, arriving dripping at the studio just as the rain stopped and the skies cleared. I went quickly to bed, hoping that my judgement would improve for the rest of what remained of the twentieth century.

Next morning, still feeling decidedly soggy from the previous night's adventures, I set off back into central Athens for some serious memory making.

This was the end of the twentieth century. Great moments had to be stored up so that they could be reproduced *ad nauseum* when I entered my dotage. Other people take video pictures, I talk!

Back in Syntagma they were putting the finishing touches to the Millennium stage. Quite a large *bouzouki* band was playing away, the *kefi* was rising and I stopped to listen. The music was good, piercing the cold winter air and making you forget your icy fingers. There was a man on stage, walking around and then talking into the microphone from time to time. There were not many people in the square and the TV vans were nowhere in sight. The music was so good it almost seemed like a special present just for me. Then the man spoke again into the microphone. '*Ti na karnoume. Eimaste stin Ellada, ola einai kala. Etsi then einai?*' 'What can we do about it? We are in Greece, all is good. That's enough isn't it?' And he smiled at me. The people in the square were all looking at me, and I suddenly felt incredibly happy. I laughed back at the man and moved away, the music following me like a party balloon on a long string. Memory number one safely locked away. Thank you.

I walked along past the Amalia Hotel, now surrounded by a thousand memories of the time I worked at Skaï and headed for the bus for Palero Falero. They had dug up the road and they had also changed all the bus numbers, so I walked through to the back road and stood at the bus stop in Filenenenon Street, only to find even more memories sitting there waiting to be patted like some stray dog. After what seemed like an age, I pushed them away and, forcing myself back into the present, leapt on to a bus that said Palero Falero but bore a strange number. By now it was the beginning of *mesi meri* and the buses were packed. Not daring to risk my sanity by requesting information from the driver, I elbowed my way across to stamp my ticket and stood, convinced I was on the wrong bus.

I was.

I made a wild guess as to the best moment to choose and pummelled my way off after about ten minutes. I really was nowhere near where I wanted to be, but telling myself that things could be a lot worse (they could) I set off to walk the rest of the way to my destination. It was bitterly cold, the wind tearing in from the sea, and I regretted not having thought of gloves. At least my dark glasses helped to protect my eyes and my wool and cashmere coat was surprisingly warm. I focused my mind firmly on other things and tramped away, ending up on the duel carriageway that ran alongside the sea and led ultimately to the airport.

At last I saw what I had come to find, to photograph in fact.

Every year since that first Christmas spent at the Poseidon Hotel I had seen the Christmas trees. Huge piles of them at the side of the road, looking strange I had thought at first, but every time looking more familiar. Why they should have appeared so strange I don't know. Maybe it was the brilliant sunshine or the sea with the huge tankers moored on the horizon. But anyhow, I had long wanted a photograph and now here I was.

But as I got closer I was disappointed. The characters selling them were not the wild, romantic looking creatures of other years and there was a wooden shed with plastic Father Christmases dangling from it. Also most of the trees had gone – well, only three days before Christmas I suppose it was not surprising – but somehow I had counted on the Greeks' love of last-minute action to guarantee me the photo I wanted. But it was not to be; so I clicked off a few quick shots, got shouted at for some reason and plodded back along the duel carriageway, finally risking all and darting across the busy lanes to a bus stop. I was now so cold that I resolved to take the first bus irrespective of where it was going. Fortunately it was for Piraeus, so I squeezed in amongst my fellow travellers, glad for once of the close physical contact and the warmth it brought with it. I descended at Neo Falero (more memories) and was soon on the Metro, heading home; where, rather surprisingly, I found Kleopatra waiting to take me to Kallithea.

After a vital, life-restoring hot drink, we set off through the Christmas traffic and soon got stuck. As we were planning to go together to the El Greco exhibition later that evening I was not sure why we were making this desperate lunge across Athens. But once we arrived at K's flat, all became clear. A small and ecstatic French pug met us, desperate for her evening walk that was obviously long overdue. She and K disappeared into the wilds of Kallithea while I sat looking at K's art that hung from every wall and provided a superb setting for some of the elegant furniture. When the daring pair returned they had exciting tales to tell of rescued kittens and thankful mother cats. One small dog was remarkably pleased with herself, and thrived on all the attention she was getting. Alas we had to leave her again almost immediately and head for the National Gallery, but as we walked along to the bus stop the memory of those two sad eyes reproached and threatened to ruin the start of the evening. We steeled our hearts and marched on.

The bus came quickly and there were even seats. We were due to meet K's mother at the gallery and were a little worried about the time but we needn't have been for a few stops later she struggled on to the same bus, rather surprised to find us there. The traffic was moving quickly into Athens and we soon passed the church in Syngrou Avenue where K was married, and then the Olympic Stadium as we pressed on towards Pangrati. The bus spat us out directly opposite the National Gallery and we went directly inside this gift to Athens from the philanthropic Lambrakis family. A few years ago it held a major exhibition of students' art, featuring K's work and that of her fellow artists from the prestigious School of Fine Arts here in Athens.

El Greco is not really my favourite artist but this was an impressive exhibition, almost overpoweringly so at times. The colours crashed into your consciousness leaving a vivid and lasting impression of an artist painting out of his time. His canvases were often large, his subjects austere with a hint of cruelty. His was the church of the inquisition, self- flagellation and pain – the Catholic Church; the mainly gentler influence of the Greek Orthodox Church was nowhere evident. Here the way to Heaven was paved with the transports of Hell. I shrank before them. In the end I had to go back to the softer images at the start of the exhibition, for reassurance, before we left for Kolonaki and an Italian restaurant.

In Kolonaki the little lights in the trees and the window dressing in some of the boutiques reminded me of Paris and the area off the Champs-Elysees. K. and her mother are easy company and we chatted happily as we climbed around the hilly streets.

There had been a bazaar at the National Gallery where they had been selling some of the remaindered posters from other exhibitions. I bought myself *The Straw Hat* by Nikolaos Lystras, it was of a man in (unsurprisingly) a straw hat, and it was a sunny, hot painting that made me think of Spain rather than Greece. 'My toy boy,' I said and then immediately regretted it as the continual worry of my single status was brought to the front of the minds of the two people with me.

There have been several attempts to provide me with a suitable partner; most of them have taken place on Poros and all of them have been disastrous. I simply cannot impress on my friends that being alone is infinitely preferable to being with the wrong person. I have no intention of changing my life unless that special someone should arrive and do it for me. Alas, this is something incomprehensible to all Greeks. Fortunately we were all hungry and it was easy to divert the conversation to food and wine. Anyhow, K and her mother are not really serious in their match-making but it really is a topic best left buried at all times!

The little restaurant was still half empty when we arrived at ten o'clock and we had time to place our orders before the other tables filled up and we became surrounded by the noise and bustle of a busy eating house. The food was good and beautifully served and it was a lovely ending to an eventful day. Afterwards we wandered down on to Academias and found two taxis to take us home.

Next morning I awoke and pondered which Dolphin to take back to Poros. It was the day before Christmas Eve and although Athens still held temptations there were presents to deliver on my little island and the apartment to clean ready for the visitors. The Toulouse-Lautrec exhibition beckoned but at a pinch that could wait until I came back for the Souvenir Exhibition in January. Then I realised that the trees in the courtyard at the back of the apartment were bent almost double with the wind. 'Ah ha,' I thought and opened the bedroom shutters. Plastic bags, chocolate wrappers and orange peel danced happily in front of my eyes.

The wind was back.

I phoned Nikos in Poros.

'No problem,' he said; 'the boats are running OK. Come this afternoon.'

I phoned my friends in Phousa. We have been friends for many years and they never interfere in my life or question what I want to do. This time they did.

'Stay there Anna,' they said. 'The sea is wild, dangerous even. Come when the wind has gone.'

It is surprisingly easy to do as you are told when that is what you wanted to do all along. An hour later found me sitting in the Metro telling myself firmly that I was not to buy any more books – and I nearly didn't, for the Palmides Bookshop proved remarkably difficult to find. Just as I was about to give up, however, there it was on Amerikis Street where it always had been. I should have remembered – an elegant lady had even asked me where it was an hour earlier in that serendipitous way that Athens has, but I had placed it far higher into Kolonaki and had been hopelessly off the mark.

Now, swinging my bag of books, I set off up Sofias Avenue for the *Megeron Musiki* (Classical music venue) and Toulouse-Lautrec. This exhibition I loved. It brought back memories of student days spent in Paris, writing bad poetry and sleeping illegally on the floors of student rooms in the various national residences. Of course I was deeply and unhappily in love…

The exhibition included some of the things from Lautrec's studio and there were many photographs. Somewhere around the middle of the exhibition he came alive again and I went back to the posters and could almost hear the can-can music. The little video room was showing the film of his life with Jose Ferrer in the lead. It was cold and windy outside and I was happy to drift back through the streets of Montmartre and Pigalle, and also to the cinema in London where I had first seen the film, and conjure up the life that went with all that – memories again.

It was dark when I came out of the exhibition and the wind seemed to be dropping at last. I thought briefly of making a dash for the evening boat but there really wasn't time and the parallel lines of lights lured me down Sofias Avenue and into Syntagma.

The square is fully restored now after the excavations for the new Metro line, only the café tables and chairs are still missing and the lurid signs of the fast food counters blaze where they shouldn't be. But if you slightly close your eyes, stand with your back to the Christmas Tree and imagine the temperature several degrees higher, it is still possible to be there in another time when the pavements were full of elegant women and the centre of the square was packed with tables attended by waiters almost dancing through the traffic, trays held high. Now, alas, that all belongs to a time long gone.

Disappointingly there were no musicians this evening, only a few shy children far outnumbered by Santa Claus's little helpers and the television crews who were laying cables and pointing cameras at the empty stage. I stopped to take a photograph and miraculously all the lights sprang to life, including those proclaiming the year 2000 in blazing figures. Was some sort of rehearsal going on? Anyhow, I had my shots so I smiled a thank-you across the now empty square and allowed myself to be pulled through the deserted Plaka to the souvlaki shop.

I wandered along the now familiar streets, with the Parthenon floodlit above my head and glimpsed from time to time in gaps between the houses stepped up to the Acropolis. Nikos had once called her the 'whore of Athens' because she lured the people and satisfied them for money. It seemed a long time ago now, so many memories in between. If tonight was a time for making memories it was also a time for rediscovering them.

I reached Hadrian's Library and glanced up at the temple – and caught my breath. Above it was a full moon, the light overpowering that of the spotlights, and the Parthenon stood in all her glory, proud to be Greek and proud of the goddess to whom she was dedicated. No whore this. I had never seen her like this before, there was such beauty there. I looked round, thinking I wanted to share the moment with someone, but there was no one around. Like it or not this moment was mine alone and I felt deeply privileged. Later, on New Year's Eve, when I saw her dressed in her blues and pinks surrounded by thousands of doting disciples, I had to look away from the television screen. I did not want to remember her in that way on that magical night.

I wandered on through the deserted Plaka, revelling in the dearth of tourists for once. Two cats came mewling out of the shadows so I fed them the last of my souvlaki but they weren't interested. They obviously lived well on the leavings of the local *taverna*s and nothing I had was of interest. They looked at me in disgust and stalked into the shadows. I was loathe to end the evening, but I had been walking since early that morning and my feet longed for home, so I nudged my way on to the Metro and was soon pouring myself a large glass of restorative wine. I determined to catch the early boat and went to bed, regretting the newly discovered demise of the little travelling alarm clock.

I slept intermittently, waking often to check the time, until I found myself on the first Metro to Piraeus. I was not alone for the children were up too, singing *the Calendar* (a traditional Christmas song), and eagerly collecting the readily given money from me and the other passengers. But it was early and I was only half awake so I wasn't sorry when I finally climbed up on to the passenger deck of the Danae Express and waited for the arrival of the other travellers. After what seemed for ever the boat hooted and we were off, packed with people, stuffed toys and enough cakes to feed the multitude.

The boat was alive with Christmas spirit and mobile phones, but the sea was on its best behaviour, and I could only agree with the man opposite when he repeatedly confided into his mobile phone that there was 'not a lot of sea and everything was fine.'

Once on Poros, I collected my mail, did some shopping and astounded the taxi drivers by taking a car home. Screaming Lord Sutch was asleep on his bag of husks and the flat felt warm and inviting. Later that evening I delivered the rest of the Christmas presents undetected and finally fell into bed exhausted. Sleep came quickly and lasted until the church bells woke me for the last Christmas of the twentieth century.

The Millennium

So it's all over, all the talking, all the speculation, all the videotapes and newsprint, now all part of the past, part of the last century even. But even here in one of the quieter spots in the world, one is left with the distinct impression that something momentous has happened. Somehow there was a great coming together, and for tiny micro seconds here and there it was possible to glimpse the world as it should always be, in all its beauty and variety, celebrating the great delight of being alive.

Of course, the night belonged to television, and it was truly at its best, transmitting moments from across the world and leaving them vibrant and unforgettable in the memories of millions. There were the dawn singers and musicians on the roof of the Sydney Opera House; Kiri te Kanawa singing with the Maori choir at the edge of the sea with the graceful cutters sailing in the background; the Chinese lions, dancing across the sky; the music from Argentina played on a boat at the snow line; Moscow and the Bolshoi theatre, the thrilling Flamenco dancers, and here in Greece, the Parthenon flooded with light as the music of Mikis Theodorakis and Manos Hadjidakis pierced the night air and tugged at the heartstrings. Music – from every country you heard music. The classical orchestras from across the world, and the ancient sounds of ancient peoples brought into the spotlight and enhancing the image of mankind – revealing, for once, everything good human beings are capable of and forgetting briefly the evil which they can also do. From the time of the first midnight until I left the house several hours later, I was awestruck by what had been created across the centuries – and I was often in tears.

Around ten o'clock I put on a warm jacket, unplugged all things electric and, torch in hand, stepped out into the unknown. Uncertain of exactly what midnight would bring, I felt ready for anything!

Fourth-hand British newspapers had kept me informed of the mounting hysteria in America and the UK, but here in

Greece we had stated bewilderedly that the Millennium was not until next year, and then got on with other things. No one on Poros had dug enormous underground shelters or disappeared into the wilderness; instead we gathered this year's small olive crop and waited for the new wine to bubble to maturity.

I wasn't surprised. The Greeks are congenitally incapable of planning ahead though why this is I simply do not know. Whether hundreds of years of occupation have left them without a sense of permanence or whether the energy required is simply too great an imposition remains unclear, but anything in the future is of little importance until it becomes the present. Mind you, things here can happen at the speed of light when someone wants them to.

Anyhow Christmas loomed, and around 20 December the odd decoration appeared in the shops and the T.V. stations changed their logos. Then, one night on the main news, Mega channel started to warn about this thing called Y2K and the possibility of a complete melt-down. The world was trembling, apparently, whilst here on Poros we shrugged and held on to the belief that they had all got the wrong year.

But Mega was tenacious and every night grew more eloquent on the subject. Still I heard nothing about the emergency here and in desperation mentioned the matter to my friends. They seemed unbothered by it all, so we just laughed and made plans to send younger sons fishing and grandmas to the mountains to pick hortas. Had the rest of the Western world got it wrong? Maybe, but I surreptitiously eyed my icon lamps and drawer of hoarded candles, and bought another tin of tomatoes.

Meanwhile, reports came from England of empty supermarket shelves and people queuing to take their money out of banks and building societies. I went down to Stavros's shop and looked in awe at the shelves filled to bursting with tins and packets; no one was stock piling here.

'Are you ready for meltdown?' I asked.

'Don't worry, Anna,' came the reply. 'Just pray for good health, it's all you need. If you want for money I have a little, and if you want food there is plenty here. Just ask for good health.'

I generously warned my friends of the impending disaster. They laughed, but then, after a little thought, conceded that maybe, just maybe, the electricity would go off. But this, they assured me, would only be a minor inconvenience as someone would go and, legally or illegally, quickly get it working again. So I stopped what passes for worrying on Poros and decided to go with the flow. Nevertheless, when I went out on New Year's Eve I left every plug out of its socket and the candles ready for easy lighting.

As I walked along by the edge of the sea following the main road into town, I realised that the wind that had been blowing hard for days now had almost died down. It was cold, the first really cold snap of winter. Above me the sky was filled with stars and I thought of T.S. Eliot's poem *Journey of the Magi*. 'A cold coming we had of it, just the worst time of year for a journey, and such a long journey:'

Thus inspired I strode off into the night until I came across the new fountain opposite the Dionysus Hotel, now playing merrily with a pattern of co-ordinated lights. I was its only audience and it seemed sad that on this, the night of its inauguration, it should not be more generously appreciated. In the middle, a mermaid was poised above the water. She had sat there for several weeks hidden by sacking and brown paper, and many of us were convinced she was a dolphin, but tonight we saw her for what she was – something truly for the new Millennium. Her features were of a magazine prettiness, her breasts large and pointing to the stars, and her neat little behind sat rounded above her fish's tail, a tail that only began around her thighs. Poros, one of only two masculine islands, had his rightful mermaid!

I continued along the harbour towards the crib, worrying rather at the shooting stars that had been mounted on the lamp-posts upside down, thus allowing all the good luck to run out. I hoped briefly, that the gods would be too busy on this special night – or perhaps too preoccupied with the mermaid – to notice.

It was warmer round the corner by Askeli Travel, and there were people in the cafenia and walking along the old marble streets leading to the little square. Here you began to feel the bustle of expectation in the throng milling around the Christmas tree, the *Two Brothers* boat and an Aghios Vassilis, who was beaming goodwill and pouring fizzy drinks for the children. Catherine touched my arm and we stood together listening to the inevitable speeches until our very own Poros band took over and played The Calendar and then the *bouzouki* started and we were off! People moved around the square wishing each other the traditional greetings, '*Chronia polla*' and '*Kali chronia*' (Many Years; Good Years). The *kefi* grew, helped by the local wine and the food until suddenly we were into the countdown. Ten, nine, eight, seven, six, five, four, three, two, one! – and the cheers rose to the sky, which exploded in colour, the fireworks taking our eyes up to the heavens where it seemed all the gods were on duty that night, following man-made time around the world, and benevolent and tolerant for once with these little creatures who wanted so much and gave so little; they were certainly all present on Poros this night.

The square was buzzing now. A group of Scandinavian tourists began a strange sort of conga, and a bunch of ex-pats wearing funny hats broke into 'Auld Lang Syne', but this was a moment beyond national differences and I felt a surge of pure happiness run through me. It wasn't long then before the dancing started and for a brief time it looked as though the square was settling into a night of partying, but alas the *bouzouki* stopped and someone put on some Western pop. Within minutes the square was almost empty, the atmosphere gone and the people drifting off home or to the bars. The moment had been lost.

So I set off back along the harbour front, wanting now to be home myself to share the British midnight with my faraway friends and to open the bottle of champagne that was waiting in the fridge. As I reached the mermaid I realised that all the lights were blazing across the water and that everything was working as usual – we had survived the transition without a blip!

Back in the apartment I plugged everything back in and looked ruefully at the candles; then, with a glass of champagne in one hand and the TV's remote control in the other I was transported on a magic-carpet ride around the world. My glass was raised, toasts were pledged and friends near and far were drunk to until finally sleep became impossible to resist and I crawled into bed.

At dawn I was dragged from my bed by Screaming Lord Sutch wanting his breakfast. This tiny kitten has taken up residence on my doormat, and with a voice as loud as Pavarotti's (although nowhere near as melodious) he succeeds in waking me every morning at first light. But for once I wasn't cross, for as I turned back from feeding him I looked across the sea to Hydra and the first rays of the sun touched the water and turned it into flame. I caught my breath and looked in wonder at the dawn of this new age, and all things seemed possible. It had been a momentous night. And the Millennium? Well, ready when you are, Mr de Mille!

•

The Grand Tour

We set off to walk into Poros town in high spirits, each of us carrying a surprisingly small piece of hand luggage and giggling like over enthusiastic schoolgirls. It was still far too hot to walk that distance carrying luggage, but we had made a pact that we would travel only by public transport and we had just missed the only bus that would get us to the ferry point in time for the Flying Dolphin.

The harbour front was deserted of course, the cafés virtually empty, but we did find two friends there who were greatly surprised at our adventurous spirits and wished us well. We ordered a farewell soda with ice and let the conversation drift slowly across the café table.

I pulled out my Dolphin ticket just to make sure and Sue said, 'You have got mine too, haven't you?'

'No,' I said. 'I gave it to you yesterday.'

'Aagh!' she squawked, 'it's still in the apartment. What shall I do?'

'Go back in a taxi – QUICK!'

The siesta calm was broken. A taxi driver was torn from his game of *tavli*, his mates radioing to the car to discover the cause of the crisis. I looked at my watch. There was still half an hour to go. No problem!

Sue returned clutching the offending ticket, and the heat of the afternoon closed around us. Not an auspicious start, but we decided the taxi ride did not contravene our self- imposed style of travel and the burst of adrenalin had only added to our sense of anticipation.

The Dolphin slid in, taking us by surprise, but we'd already paid for our drinks and were glad that the real start to our journey had finally begun. Well, almost. Half an hour later we pulled into the little port of Hydra, where we disembarked in order to change Dolphins. With an hour and a half to spare we walked around the harbour, past the ever patient donkeys and mules, and headed for the Café Roloi where Vassos and Bernadette were greatly surprised to see us. I collapsed into one of the comfy cane chairs and set about being an idle tourist whilst Sue wandered around the back streets and climbed the cobbled steps of the little town.

I come here every week on the *Anna II* from Poros, so for once it was possible just to sit back and imagine Hydra's rich and famous, past and present, all strolling round the corner on their way to one of the *taverna*s, for the cruise ships had all gone and romance and magic were spreading slowly across the harbour as the sun's rays retreated back to the mountains on the mainland.

'Stay,' said our friends but we had to go for we were longing for unfamiliar sights and sounds and we still had a four hour journey ahead of us. It was to be on one of the little original Russian Dolphins much loved by the tourists, but, I suppose, soon to be replaced by the streamlined Super Cats and Dolphin 2000s. I would not have liked one of those to take us on our adventure, I thought, as we sat back with glee and bounced and rattled, on our way at last, to Monemvasia and the Mani.

Spetses, Portoheli, Tyros, Leonidion, Gerakas, Kyparissis, Monemvasia. After Portoheli we moved forward into the nose of the Dolphin, the only foreigners left aboard and something of a curiosity. The mountains grew taller and came down almost to the edge of the sea, but even in the fading evening light, they looked friendly and protective of the little groups of houses that nestled at intervals along the coastline.

Each little port had a character all its own and we longed to stay. 'We will come back,' we said, and wondered if we meant it.

Three Greek children sat quietly on the ledge in front, checked on from time to time by papa or *papous* (grandad). Just after Leonidion papous came forward and kissed the smallest. 'In ten minutes you will be seeing *yiayia*,' he said. She said nothing but clutched his arm and her eyes grew wide with anticipation; it had obviously been a long time. As the Dolphin pulled into Gerakas we felt ourselves responding to the excitement and we peered hopefully through the window to the people waiting on the quay. Was *yiayia* there? Yes, she was, and the child was moving shyly towards her – but the Dolphin tore us away and they were lost from sight.

Somewhere in the last five minutes day had turned into night and we disappeared into it with only the stars for company. The Dolphin was nearly empty now and Monemvasia could not be far. The escapists' air of detachment that clings to travellers on long journeys was beginning to drift away, and our thoughts were turning towards hotels and food – but the journey had a last surprise for us. The boat slowed until it was barely moving. We looked through the windows but could see nothing until a member of the crew appeared outside on the little front deck shining a powerful torch and then we realised we were surrounded by huge rocks. Before we had time to become afraid, the rocks on the right-hand side fell away to reveal the little harbour town of Kyparissis. Here was a brightly lit *taverna* and a little quay – maybe more in daylight – but for me it was like a glimpse in to a fairy tale, the reflection of the lights in the still water pushing away all reality. We tied up briefly and then reversed slowly out, the lights disappearing one by one until only the torchlight remained. Then suddenly we were out, the mood changed, and ahead of us we saw the lights of Monemvasia gleaming in welcome. For a while, like shy toddlers, they kept their distance, teasing us as they appeared and disappeared in front of the Dolphin. Finally they shone ahead and around us, and the boat slowed down as it pulled into the quay. We stood and began to collect our luggage but suddenly the boat tipped sharply and for a moment it seemed we might go over. '*Malacca*,' swore the man in the seat opposite and Sue and I looked at one another alarmed. But we righted ourselves and all was well. With pounding hearts we stepped ashore, glad of the solid rock beneath our feet.

When writing about Greece it is almost impossible to avoid clichés, and here was no exception. The night really was 'velvet' and it did quite simply 'enfold' us as we stumbled across the bridge into the waiting lights of Gefira, where we had decided to look for a hotel.

It was not difficult to find one and we were quickly settled. Deferring the delights of a shower until later, we set off to find a *taverna*. There were no difficulties about that either, for all along the seafront the *taverna*s were still busy and the Jazz Café belted out the latest Greek pop, somewhat belying its name. We kept on further round the bay, however, and finally settled,

Shirley Valentine-style, for a table on the beach where our toes were almost dipping into the sea. A short while later, wineglass in hand, we looked across to the dark mass of the rock and finally realised that our adventure had well and truly begun.

By the time we had finished our meal the nightlife of Gefira had all but vanished. It was so beautiful sitting at the edge of the sea that after we had paid the bill we asked if we could sit for a while longer to finish the wine. 'Stay as long as you like,' said the owner, adding that they must clear up the kitchen and anyhow they still had to eat themselves; so we sat dreaming of all the delights to come and congratulating ourselves on taking this brief return to the bolder wanderings of our youth. But the *taverna*s were all closing fast now, and even the Jazz Café had shut its doors for the night, so tired but happy we found our way back to our hotel, and we fell into the shower and thence into bed, full of anticipation for the new day.

We were up early. Sue had watched the Flying Dolphin depart as the sky streaked grey across the sea – and already there was traffic in the streets. Greece is one of the noisiest countries I know and no one has any respect or thought for those desperate to hang on to the last vestiges of sleep; but it is amazing how quickly you adapt to this cacophony and learn to ignore it; so it was not the noise but yesterday's anticipation which saw us creeping down the stairs of the silent hotel wondering whom we should tell of our morning's plans.

A *yiayia* appeared from a back room, praised us for getting up so early and assured us it was the best time to visit the old city. 'Pay later' was the familiar injunction, so we smiled assent and set off to catch the first bus of the morning. We had not long to wait and soon we, the first visitors of the day, were entering the old walled town and slithering along its cobbled streets. But history had to wait for we smelled fresh coffee and soon tracked it down to a small café with a tiny terrace overlooking the sea. Miraculously they had croissants too, still warm from the baker's, and we sat feeling, briefly, that life had little more to offer.

From the terrace the sea stretched in ever deepening shades of blue all the way to Africa and with eyes half closed with sleep you could see again the fleets of trading ships and the smaller caiques of the pirates hovering on the horizon, while in the dark interior of the café the barrels of malmsey wine stood waiting for the donkeys to collect. The Greek landscape and seascape are full of ghosts from every period of history. They are mostly friendly and far from oppressive and can be conjured up with ease, but although there once was a Minoan naval base here and there were settlements on the rock from as early as AD 583 it is the Byzantine sailors who come forward to people the atmosphere and cause the rooftop cats to stir uneasily in their sleep. Classical music disturbed our dreams, thoughtful but somehow inappropriate. So we paid the king's ransom demanded and left.

'Think of that as your lunch,' I said to Sue – as guardian of the communal purse I was feeling a miserly twinge. But she just smiled and we both knew it had been worth every cent.

It was fun to play at being tourists and we wandered the medieval streets, cameras at the ready exclaiming at every corner how beautiful it all was. By the time we had determined to climb to the upper town it was nearly ten o'clock and far too hot, but we went anyhow, huffing and puffing our way up until we emerged triumphant at the steps to the little church of *Aghia Sofia*. In truth, it was not as bad as we had thought it would be, but how dearly we regretted not buying a bottle of water before we set out.

I had been here before and had been entranced by the frescoes inside the little church. That time I had only two exposures left in my camera and for eight years I had wanted to return to see if I could photograph them properly. I sat in the shade of the church remembering the delight of that first visit and realising how glad I was to be back.

Greek voices floated up from the steps and two people followed on behind. Being Greek, they greeted us eagerly and then, finding that I spoke something of their language they told us the history of the little church. It was (they said) an exact replica of the great *Aghia Sofias* in Constantinople, the head of the Greek Orthodox Church. This great church took eleven years to build whilst its little twin took exactly eleven months. (Is this true? I can find no mention of it in any guidebook.) My new friends took me inside and explained the icon in front of the iconostasis. It was Mary with three grown children. Not Jesus, they explained, not even real children, the figures stood for love, peace and hope. Were they right? I hope so for that was an icon I could pray to. They went outside and I wandered slowly, gazing back in awe at the frescoes so casually staring down at me from the walls of the church. When I left the church they had gone but the encounter, like so many of the casual meetings that take place in Greece, had left behind a memory which would for ever belong to that time and that place.

It was time for us to descend now but we did so reluctantly, checking first that the images of this amazing place were locked firmly in our minds. The magic evaporated when I came across a Greek sailor posing his girlfriend against the backdrop of the town. Each time I tried to pass, it seemed the moment of perfection had been achieved, so I waited for the click of the camera; but no, still something was not quite right and the positions had to be changed. At some point my Greek side triumphed over my English politeness and I pushed past and went on downwards, but no one seemed in the least put out. Sue was waiting and clutching our desperately needed bottles of water we headed for the tunnelled entrance that had given the old walled city its name – *moni-emvasis* (only-entrance).

We did not have long to wait for the little bus and we were quickly back at the hotel where the receptionist greeted us warmly; our early-morning plans had obviously been faithfully passed on by the no longer visible *yiayia*.

Now one thing only was filling our thoughts. The sea was beckoning like one of the sirens of yore. Having to hobble across the pebbles to get to it somewhat reduced the romance of it all, but the water was superb – so transparent it barely seemed to exist at all and so cool it both refreshed our bodies and cleared our minds. A nearby clock struck the half-hour.

'What time is it?' I asked.

'Eleven-thirty,' came the reply

'Sue,' I said, 'do you want to wait for the two-fifteen bus or shall we go for the twelve oclock, we can catch it easily.'

'Let's go,' she replied, so we started on the great British struggle to climb out of our wet swimsuits and into knickers and bras and when once more decently clothed found ourselves sitting somewhat damply at the bus stop clutching more water and a packet of crisps – the only concession to lunch!

And it was the right decision, the longing to know what was round the next corner was back firmly in place and we soon sat happily in the air-conditioned bus reliving the last few hours and gazing idly at the sights of the Laconian countryside which was passing before our eyes.

We reached a little town and paused to wait for the arrival of another bus. Again we aroused a great amount of curiosity but we had grown used to this by now and had learned that a friendly smile usually succeeded in deflecting the stares away from ourselves on to some unidentifiable object in the middle distance. The town was called Molai, and we had approached it through the hot and arid countryside with which we were becoming so familiar, so it was something of a shock to find ourselves now travelling through rich orchards, the little trees often protected by towering chestnuts. The change was dramatic. In one village square there was a life-size statue of a soldier, but no local hero this, well not Greek anyhow, for he was wearing the round tin hat and the uniform of a British soldier. What story lay there?

After the orchards came a busy dual carriageway and then an army camp looking strangely lush and exotic. The bus stopped and a score of young and hearty recruits came on board, clutching radios and mobile phones. The atmosphere became charged with suppressed energy and the testosterone level on the bus rose alarmingly! Intrigued by our new travelling companions, we neglected to look out of the window for quite a while. When we finally did so, another shock awaited us for ahead loomed the Taygetus Mountains and the sight quite simply took your breath away. I had seen mountains before of course, almost certainly bigger and taller ones, but these were nothing like other mountains. All at once it was quite easy to understand why the ancient Greeks had such a close working relationship with their gods, for looking across to the mountains, the tops crowned with fluffy grey clouds, I was convinced that Zeus and all his cohorts were still up there causing their usual chaos and leaping around from mainland to island and back again. These huge lumps of rock, like the mountains of Parnon, seemed to protect rather than threaten the people living in their shadow.

By now we were entering the hustle and bustle of a large city – at least, large to us who had been so long away from a city of any size. Sparta was one of the greatest cities of the ancient world, and its name conjured up images of violent fighting men and new-born babies left to die on cold mountainsides. Perhaps it was because of all this rich history that we found ourselves less than impressed with what the present had to offer. We climbed down from the coach into the turmoil of a busy terminus, looked at one another and decided to see if we could give Sparta a miss. The timetable was mounted on the wall above the entrance and there I saw 'Areopolis' and the time '17.45.'

'Sue,' I cried, 'we can go to Areopolis tonight. Look it's all possible.'

Areopolis is the capital of the Inner Mani and to visit the Inner Mani had long been a dream of mine and was the most important (secret) aim of this trip. Sue, however, was not strikingly enthusiastic. 'Can't we go to Gytheron instead?' she asked. 'Look the bus goes there in half an hour.' But Gytheron was not quite where I wanted to be.

The Mani is the southernmost area of the Peloponnese and until only quite recently had been isolated by its rough terrain and bad roads. Its people were known to be proud, fighting men and, like Crete, the area had a reputation for blood feuds that were handed down from generation to generation. Traditionally the Maniotes lived in tall towers with only slits for windows – to make it difficult for the flying bullets to enter the living space – and not so very long ago, the people there only ventured out in daytime during the truces that were negotiated at harvest time or for a funeral or wedding. I had long wanted to go there.

I looked across to Sue. 'No,' I howled in anguish, 'it has to be Areopolis. Gytheron is in the outer Mani and there are no towers there. There has to be towers, I have to see a tower.'

'All right,' she conceded quickly for I was getting quite noisy. 'All right we'll go to Areopolis, but what are we going to do for nearly four hours? We can't just sit in a bus station.'

We should have followed the first rule of travel and leapt on the bus to Gytheron, for the bus to Areopolis went via this lovely old seaside town and we could have spent a happy four hours there. But we did not know that then. Instead we leapt on a bus to Mistra only to find when we got there that there was no return bus which would get us back in time for the bus we wanted. So we came straight back again, leaving Mistra for the next day – really this time – for Mistra is perhaps the most famous of Byzantine cities. Once a Frankish stronghold, it later became the last city of the Byzantine Empire and is still standing in ruined magnificence a few kilometres outside Sparta. It also has some of the best preserved Greek Byzantine icons in the country.

Meanwhile, it appeared that we had settled for the option of sitting in the Sparta bus station. Well, I had, but Sue was restless and went for a walk into the centre of the town leaving me behind. She had only been gone a few minutes when from out of nowhere came a black cloud, a clash of thunder and a torrential downpour. I sat smugly with the luggage and watched an almost perfect rainbow arch itself across the hills in front of me.

The sun and Sue were soon back and before long it was time to get on the bus. Everything in Greece seems to happen in a last-minute rush and suddenly the drivers were calling out their destinations and just in time we slung our luggage into the baggage hold and climbed aboard. The inertia of *mesi meri* was over and we were off – back down the road on which we had arrived only a few short hours ago! We made good progress until, temporarily leaving the Taygetus Mountains behind, we moved back into the olive groves and a more gentle rolling landscape.

We arrived in a small seaside town that had about it an air of seedy recklessness – Gytheron! It looked bustling and charming in the early evening light, a real seaside town which made you look around for striped blazers and jaunty straw boaters. Out at sea the big liners and the cargo ships lay anchored, but even they failed to destroy the cheerful image that greeted us. I said little until the bus was moving again, then thought I had better own up.

I think this is Gytheron,' I said. 'You remember; the place you wanted to come to?'

'Yes,' said Sue.

'It's great isn't it?' I continued. 'Look at the lovely balconies and the flowers. We must come back.'

'Yes,' said Sue and it went rather quiet for a while. The next time she spoke it was to point out a sign for a castle and a couple heading off up the track the arrow was indicating.

'Castle?' she said. 'Odd to find one here?'

Now we know it was the Frankish castle of Passava, very famous and linked to the Crusaders, but by now I had other things on my mind and I soon forgot it. The vegetation was changing again. The tiny Vallonia oaks were appearing and the tops of the mountains were exposed rock. A bleakness was creeping into the landscape and we soon saw the first cactus. Then suddenly there it was exactly as I had always imagined it and just as beautiful, my first Maniot tower.

'Arrgh,' I squawked.

'What?' said Sue, alarmed.

'The tower, the tower, look, there, and another one there, and one there. We've done it, we're here in the Inner Mani. Oh gosh, it's another dream come true.'

After that things just got better and better; more and more towers, sometimes single, sometimes in groups and all just as Patrick Leigh Fermor had described so many years ago. Of course it had changed, but somehow the essence, the heart of it was still there. It is indeed a wild place and, understandably, produced wild men.

The bus drew into the square of Areopolis and we got out and rescued our luggage. There was a hotel just behind us but it wasn't quite dark so we decided to be more adventurous and set off down what appeared to be the main street. The old buildings pressed close and there was hardly anyone about. It was easy, though, to imagine men darting about in the shadows, pistoli primed, chasing the Turks or the Germans or maybe just engaged in a simple *vendetta* – one of the blood feuds mentioned earlier and for which the area is famous; and which are rumoured not to have died out even at the present day.

Sue spotted the sign, 'Tower House Hotel'.

'Stay here with the luggage,' I said. 'I'll go and investigate.'

There was a wide cobbled path that disappeared round a corner. I set off down it and turning the suddenly caught my breath. Was it really possible? Yes, like so many things in Greece, yes, it was possible. For, standing there, beautifully restored and magnificent, was one of the very Maniot towers that was (in case you hadn't realised by now) for me anyhow, what this particular trip was all about! Inside it was equally beautiful, the original wood still in place and everything in keeping with the period. A trap-door was open leading to a concealed cellar and a wooden staircase climbed up from the side of a cavernous fireplace.

A young woman came, smiling to greet me and was thrilled when I spoke Greek. Yes, they had a room, yes, we would be welcome to stay for one night. I turned to go back to Sue with this amazing news and almost as an afterthought asked, 'With en-suite bathroom?'

'Ah, no,' came the reply and my heart sank. Sue is a marvellously easy travelling companion but even the easiest has an Achilles' heel and with Sue it was bathrooms. For some inexplicable reason bathrooms, even in the remotest village, are expected to be on a level with those usually found in the Beverly Hills Hotel. No en-suite bathroom? This was a tragedy indeed and required some exceedingly quick thinking. Explaining that I must go and consult with my travelling companion I ran back along the path

'Well?' said Sue.

'It's very nice,' I said, 'but the rooms don't have their own bathroom.'

I saw the glint and continued rapidly.

'Look, go and see what you think.'

She went but was quickly back.

'Oh it's gorgeous, perfect. Come and look. We've got this marvellous room with a gallery in it and the bathroom is next door but it doesn't matter anyhow because we're the only ones here.'

Phew! Life could go on.

And the room was beautiful. There were rough white walls contrasting with the deep-chestnut tones of the wood, the blankets cream and beige and pure wool. I stood gazing from the floor-length windows out across this strange land. The light was fading rapidly and the colour was bleached out. Somewhere in the distance the rising moon caught the edge of the sea and a streak of silver shot across the horizon. I turned to find Sue unpacking, every surface covered with the contents of her bag. I saw I had been allocated one coat hanger but it didn't matter, nothing mattered.

'Go and have the first shower,' I said recklessly, and she disappeared happily in the direction of the bathroom. Several centuries later she returned, moving sheepishly across to the window before she spoke.

'The bathroom's in a bit of a mess,' she said – but you don't want to know any more! As I said earlier, every travelling companion, however perfect, has one fault – and I never did dare enquire about mine!

So, a little while later, squabbling amicably about this and that, we set off to explore the town and find some food. The little town was busy now, though not with tourists, and we seemed to attract a lot of attention. We went back to the square and found a well stocked bookshop with a large poster standing on an easel in the centre. 'Oh look,' I said, 'Petrobey Mavromichaelis – wasn't he handsome?' The shopowner looked astounded and I smiled sweetly. Outside we found a life- sized statue of him standing magnificent and proud, one hand raised as though in welcome. Petrobey Mavromichaelis (black Michael), was one of the great leaders of the revolution against the Turkish occupation and a Greek hero. You can't live in Greece long before you hear his name, but the shopowner must have thought we were tourists and was surprised we knew of him.

It was truly dark now and we were hungry. Tomorrow we must head back to Mistra for we were in Byzantine mode, but the Mani had bitten deep and we swore we would return, next time with no watches on our wrists. Meanwhile we ate in the street itself, the meat grilled on charcoal, and the barrelled wine some of the best ever. The portions were huge and a tiny black and white kitten discovered to its amazement that on certain nights in the Mani bits of chicken fall out of the sky! It ate carefully, its little tummy getting rounder and rounder. Finally it just gave up and staggered home, leaving us to do the same.

We were quickly asleep but woke early before the alarm clocks. Leaving the matter of the bathroom aside, we dressed quickly and set off in the halflight of dawn, back once again to the little square to wait for the early-morning bus to Sparta. We saw with relief that the bus-station café was open. Every outside table had one man sitting at it, and no one was going to move, so I ordered two coffees and asked if there were other tables. 'Yes,' they said, 'across the road.' There we sat comfortably, sharing our breakfast with Petrobey Mavromichaelis and a large cicada that clung to the sleeve of my jacket and would not be dislodged. The bus for Sparta arrived and we climbed in, travelling back along the road on which we had arrived – not always a foregone conclusion in Greece. Too soon we ran out of towers and cacti, but we swore again we would be back and with a last sigh we turned our heads towards the Mistra.

By now Sparta bus station was becoming increasingly familiar. The same smiling girl in the ticket office accepted our luggage and with just time to grab two bottles of water and a packet of cream crackers (who says people don't learn from experience?) we leapt on the bus and retraced our steps towards the houses of the crusaders and some of the finest frescoes in Greece.

We climbed the rough terrain up to the entrance, following a French lady who, for reasons best known to herself had chosen to wear a pair of white stiletto heels that day. Now we were seriously back on the tourist trail and voices from all over the globe called excitedly across the ruins. We sat for a while trying to salvage some atmosphere until, suddenly and miraculously, they were nearly all gone, a crocodile of coaches bearing them away to the next point of their whistle-stop tour. Peace descended and time slowed down to its normal Greek rhythm. We began to enjoy ourselves and strolled off confidently – in the wrong direction!

Eventually we came to an area so untrodden that it was impossible to proceed, so we retraced our steps, finding a gentle old man sitting in the shadows of a building we had so carelessly passed a few minutes earlier. We stopped for a chat and he pointed us in a more conventional direction. We took his advice gratefully, for it was starting to get very warm and our habit of neglecting to read up on the places we planned to visit was beginning to reveal some considerable disadvantages. Now, however, we soon found ourselves in the metropolis that is dedicated to Aghios Demetrios and is the oldest in Mistra, dating from the end of the thirteenth century. This is still a sanctified church with some of the loveliest frescoes in the old city and the taking of photographs is forbidden. In some ways I was glad, for instead I stood there for a long time just looking, and now the images remain vividly in my mind together with the smell of incense and the singing of the birds and the noise of the cicadas outside in the little walled courtyard. It was also deliciously cool but soon we had to move back out into the heat and on to the other churches – *Evangelistria*, *Aghios Theodoroi*, the Vrontochi church and monastery and, finally, *Hodegetria Aphentiko*. Such a feast of Byzantine art, all, miraculously surviving on the Taygetus mountainside.

But there was no time to stand about waxing lyrical. If we were to catch the last bus to Kalamata then we were rapidly running out of time. And there was still so much to see. Reluctantly abandoning Aghia Sofia to another visit, (again, really this time!) we set off at a rather alarming pace to the Pantanassa, only to find it packed with soldiers. We sat in the shade of the northern arcade and sipped thoughtfully from our bottles of warm water. The army left and we took their place, grateful we had at least found time for what is perhaps the most beautiful church in Mistra. The saints here, unlike those in the other churches, all had had their eyes gouged out, and the walls were pockmarked with bullets. Everyone in Greece will tell you that the Turks who, unable to stand the stares of the forgiving saints, scratched out the eyes of the saints to make them blind, but of the bullet holes I could find no mention and there was no one to ask in the church.

Regretfully we set off back down the mountainside, finding it much steeper and treacherous than on the way up. Reaching one bit that seemed to hang out into space, I hesitated. 'Is this the time to tell you that I suffer from mild vertigo?' I said. 'Not really,' came back the reply. 'I was just about to confess the same.' There was a pause, then, 'If the worst comes to the worst, go down on your bottom.'

Happily we made it back down with some vestiges of dignity still clinging and were soon squeezed together in the only small patch of shade left at the bus stop, waiting to be returned to the very familiar shade of the Sparta bus station. Once there and refreshed with ice-cold water and another packet of cream crackers, we carefully photographed the one floor tile that had been put in upside down, in order to carry away with us incontrovertible proof that the journey had been reality and not the result of vivid wishful thinking.

Again we threw ourselves on to our intended bus in the nick of time, this time going to Kalamata, and then sat back in anticipation, ready for the next stage of our tour.

'How long will it take?' asked Sue.

'Well,' I replied, adopting the air of a seasoned traveller and an expert on the Peloponnese, 'it's only forty-eight kilometres so I don't suppose it can take much longer than an hour.'

'Ah, good,' said Sue, 'we should be there in time for an early-afternoon swim.'

'Yes,' I rejoined confidently, 'good idea.'

All right, even Scorpios can be wrong occasionally and I had neglected to notice that in order to get from Sparta to Kalamata it was necessary to cross this large lump of mountain of which I had become so fond – namely the Mount Taygetus! We didn't notice at first, but just bumbled happily through the foothills, through villages and small towns, slowly becoming aware of water, an excess of water. Streams chuckled down from the mountain and were channelled into gullies at the sides of the road. Many of the villages had working fountains and everything was much richer and greener – until we began to climb that is, and then there were other things to catch and hold our attention.

The road snaked ahead and we began to look back on Sparta and the flat Laconian Plain; then there were glimpses above us of road still climbing up into the mountain, a mountain that was rapidly taking over the sky. It was at the first tunnel, I think, that my stomach dropped alarmingly and I looked across at Sue who appeared to be rather paler than usual. For two people who had recently confessed to suffering from mild vertigo, this was obviously going to be something of a challenge; but there was no going back, so we clutched the sides of our seats, closed our eyes from time to time, and expressed great thankfulness that we were going up and not down. Meanwhile the views became more and more spectacular, and gradually the fear subsided and we began to speculate on the lives of the people living in the houses clinging to the mountainside. The chestnut and oak trees gave way to trusty pines, and then they too disappeared and we were left with only the exposed rock; in winter it must be awesome here, truly another habitation of the gods.

One hour passed, then two, and still we climbed. Sue looked at her watch but again, tactfully said nothing. Then, finally, we were on top of the world, and the sky returned to its proper place. The bus began the descent but very soon pulled into a small mountain town – Artemissia, I found out later – and we all got out. We stood on a café terrace while our bus turned round and headed back to Sparta. Sue set off to look round a few corners whilst I stayed with eyes peeled, looking for the connecting bus and worrying that she would wander off too far in the wrong direction and miss it. We still seemed a long way from Kalamata.

All was well, however, and we were soon trundling along, ever downward, but with nothing like the precipitous corners we had so recently experienced. The harsh contours of the rock softened and it began to look very pretty. There were wayside stalls selling fresh herbs and honey, cheese and eggs, and then the summer *taverna*s began to appear, their outdoor tables offering stunning views down to the sea, and their menu boards boasting of the best country lamb in the south. Not for us this time though. Our much-yearned-for swim was fast becoming an impossible dream; hot and sticky, we began longing, at least, for a shower. Then, suddenly we were in the outskirts of Kalamata. The bus stopped every few minutes now, dropping off little old ladies and picking up children returning home from school, the long summer holidays now over. The air became lively with greetings and farewells.

We turned a sudden corner and found ourselves in the bus station, the noisy clamour coming as a shock after the tranquillity of the mountains. We retrieved our luggage and headed to the centre of the town and the railway station. Once there, having looked in vain for a hotel, I asked a friendly looking man on the pavement if he knew of one. He eyed at me a little askance and said, 'There.' I turned just as a large truck pulled away from the kerb and revealed that we had been standing opposite one. With laughter on all sides we picked up our bags and crossed the road. Within minutes, I was marooned on my bed surrounded by the contents of Sue's bag, but this time I fought back and regained some territory and half the coat hangers. When we finally left to go adventuring, the room was festooned with dripping laundry and I did not even want to think about the state of the bathroom; but at least this time half the mess was mine!

Once back out on the street, and convinced that we had yet to identify the centre of town, we made for the sea – and found ducks and a park full of train engines instead. The engines came first, one after the other, all vintage and standing proudly on the original narrow-gauge rails. They were grouped around what must once have been the main Kalamata Station. Enough to make any rail enthusiast's year, they were now sat upon by children and scarcely afforded a passing glance by the adults accompanying them. Well, we loved them and ooh'd and argh'd and took their photographs until they almost seemed to swell with pride and become again the kings of the railway that not so long ago they had been.

The ducks came at the end of the park, a great cluster of them, quacking and fluffing their feathers as they clustered around us, hopeful for bread. But we reluctantly shoo'd them away and set off across a huge triple carriageway towards what we thought was the sea. And eventually it was; a very large marina that was encircled wall to wall, so to speak, with seafood restaurants set in an enormous arc. They were all open too, with bored waiters propped against the bars and not a single customer to be seen. A seafood restaurant had been our aim but we looked at the sad expanse of empty tables and chairs and shook our heads. Maybe there were more traditional *taverna*s in an old part of the town? We really should have read that guide book before setting out! We knew there had been a severe earthquake back in 1986, but only now was it beginning to sink in just how severe it had been. So, when we asked two old ladies where the old houses were, they shook their heads sadly and said there weren't any. We returned to the park and the railway station in order to rethink our strategy.

We decided that two vodka tonics were called for, but the tonic presented problems so we settled for Campari sodas instead. Sitting there in the early evening, with the day's heat fading with the light, we considered the problem from every angle. But one thing was becoming abundantly clear – we were starving! We decided we would retrace our steps in the direction of the hotel and stop at the first *taverna* we came across – only we didn't come across any. So there was only one thing left to do, and that was to go back to the hotel and ask at reception.

We plodded back and turned the corner into the street that housed the hotel – and we stepped right into a vibrant throbbing town centre, with a friendly looking *taverna* right opposite the hotel door; we had been in the centre from the very beginning! The friendly looking *taverna* turned out to be just that, so we looked into the kitchen, ordered far too much food, drank far too much wine, and then slipped back to our beds which were just about visible under the now dry washing. Even the bathroom was slowly drying out.

We crashed into deep sleep, only to be woken time and time again by the bikes revving outside our window, and the shouts and laughter of the teenagers who were packing every one of the countless cafenia that sprawled out along the streets around our temporary home. But never mind, for we knew they would quieten down eventually, and indeed they did, just as the dustcarts started to rattle through the city, and the early workers began to start their cars.

Around half-past seven Sue had one of her not infrequent brilliant ideas. She simply got up, got dressed and went out, returning a few minutes later with two huge plastic cups of coffee and still-hot croissants. I immediately vowed never to mention bathrooms again. And so we slowly came to terms with the morning and then ambled off to sit for ever in the railway café, where a tiny mouse popped out of a plant pot and Sue showed her knickers!

The time meandered slowly across the morning as we waited for the little train that was to take us across the central Peloponnese into Naplion. This was to be one of the highlights of the whole trip, and the arrival of the little train itself caused an outburst of fuss and bother, which only added to the excitement. Whole families arrived from nowhere, every member clutching an item of luggage or the inevitable box of pâtisserie, without which no arrival or departure is complete. There was much toing and froing and changing of seats, but eventually the minute hand of the totally accurate station clock ticked on to the departure time, the engine hooted triumphantly and we were off, bobbing and swaying into the unknown.

The track ran through fields and olive groves and back yards, offering us a glimpse of other people's everyday lives. The train carried on hooting gaily every few minutes as we approached crossings and stations or came across a council meeting of goats standing impassively between the two rails. We called at stations as the Flying Dolphin called at jetties, briefly entering into little human dramas before being abruptly torn away.

Each station had its own station master, resplendent in his red cap, and holding the traditional round wooden signals, red and green, like long-handled table-tennis bats. Everything was so pretty, the stations freshly painted and smothered in bougainvillaea and geraniums, often with huge chestnut trees shading them from the worst of the summer heat. But our immediate travelling companion seemed immune to the charms outside the window. Greeks are notoriously nervous travellers and this young girl was no exception. Indeed, more nervous than most, she jumped and blanched at every noise and came close to total panic when the train braked unexpectedly. We tried to reassure her but it was something of a relief when she reached her destination and shot out of the train and into the safety of the little town of Meligalas (Honey and Milk).

Soon after that, we started to climb, and the passengers became fewer and were obviously more serious travellers. The mountains of Arcadia are softer and more feminine than the slopes of the majestic Taygetus. There is rich vegetation in many areas, the soft greens of a range of deciduous trees add a languid and rather seductive air to the scenery, but the inclines are still steep and must have presented a considerable challenge to the engineers who created this decidedly cheerful little railway. On the whole it was less of a challenge for the mild-vertigo sufferers amongst us. In fact, Sue did rather well and was soon calling out, 'Don't look,' when we came to a viaduct or a particularly precipitous bit of mountain.

As we passed through the village of Anemathouri we remembered friends who had a house there and so we shouted 'Hello!' and waved to them. We must have presented a slightly strange spectacle, but no one in the carriage seemed surprised. Then we pulled into Tripolis and the magic spell was broken; from now on we became just two more passengers on an everyday train and it was quite a relief to glimpse the sea again as we approached Argos. The adventure was now entering into its final stage and we needed the bus to Naplion – but first, the toilet! I left Sue with the luggage and walked off the end of the platform as directed by the sign. When I emerged, she was leaping up and down and gesticulating wildly, pointing to a very small train indeed which stood chuntering quietly to itself on the opposite track.

'Quick, quick, it's going to Naplion.'

'OK, I'm coming, but I'll have to get the tickets.'

'No problem,' said the guard from the train, 'we will wait; of course, we will wait.' And they did, laughing as we scrambled aboard and tooting in welcome once we had made it. Eat your heart out, British Rail travellers.

And so, effortlessly, we arrived in Naplion, a town I knew quite well and one that now marked the beginning of the end of our journey. We found a hotel and woke up the deeply sleeping *yiayia* in order to look at the rooms, but each bathroom appeared to be made out of a wardrobe, which meant instant disqualification. Feeling somewhat guilty we slunk towards the harbour and stopped to think. Here, quite suddenly I experienced a total loss of self-confidence and, somewhat unfairly, sent Sue off to find a room. This she quickly did and so, climbing up into the old town we entered the world of the backpackers, all laden like snails and glued to copies of *The Lonely Planet*. We must have looked slightly incongruous, two ladies of a certain age clutching small items of designer hand luggage, but inside we were still safely immersed in our early twenties and passed, oblivious, through their midst.

It was Saturday so we decided to celebrate with a serious aperitif in one of the sea-front cafés. It was early September and the town was packed with weekending Athenians. All the latest fashion was here and there were beautiful girls to wear it. The Mediterranean evening stroll (the *volta* in Greece), is a source of great delight, irrespective of whether you take part in it or, like us, merely watch. Any attempt at intellectual conversation dies away as some extreme item of designer dress wear passes by, borne aloft on enormous platform soles, or some outrageous snippet of conversation makes you long to dash across to enquire the outcome of what can only be some dark tragedy taking place in Athens. That night was no exception and we sat entranced until hunger forced us along the harbour front to one of the older *taverna*s that I knew, from past experience, to be especially good. Alas, most of the kitchen dishes had been sold out at lunchtime and the waiter was deeply upset at our disappointment. Never mind, we settled for something more prosaic and promised him we would return for lunch the next day. Later we strolled back past the more expensive seafood restaurants, now packed with people and running waiters, and then turned into the tiny roads and squares which made up the old town. Here we browsed through the brightly lit shops and treated ourselves to this and that, all purchases that we were almost certain to regret once we had returned 'home' and grown up!

It was still quite early – well, for a summer night in Greece, so I asked Sue if she would like to go to a music bar or a disco, and was slightly surprised by the reply.

'Actually, I think I'd rather like to go back to the hotel.'

Well, that was fine by me so back we went, ordered breakfast for the next morning and collapsed on our beds.

Quite often in Greece you are awarded unexpected treats, and that night was no exception. We did not go to the disco, so the disco came to us! The music pulsed in through the shutters and bounced across the room, but could not lure us out. We had already missed one night's sleep and were not about to miss another. I stretched luxuriously and fell deeply asleep.

Next morning I woke to find Sue missing and the bathroom un-flooded. Only one thing could have brought about this state of affairs, so I dressed quickly and went in search of breakfast. I found Sue feeding the sparrows that were wobbling fearlessly across the balcony. A steaming pot of coffee quickly arrived and I began the lengthy and complicated process of learning how to open my mouth and string words together. Eventually everything seemed to be back in working order and I successfully started a conversation with Sue about our plans for the rest of the day. As always, they were not complicated.

'We'll just see what happens, shall we?' said Sue.

'Right,' I replied.

That settled we went back to feeding the sparrows.

Later, we strolled back through the little streets of the old town, across the main square and into a café where tables were spread out in the shelter of an enormous plane tree, right at the foot of the nine hundred and ninety-nine steps leading up to the castle. Sue expressed a thought that she might climb the steps. I wished her well and opened, somewhat belatedly perhaps, my recently purchased book on the Byzantine churches of Mistra and Monemvasia. After all, someone had to stay with the luggage.

After a while I looked up the steps leading to the top of Palmidi and tried to remember something of its history. It was built in the seventeenth century by the Venetians and used as a prison after they had left. Kolokotronis, the Klepht hero of the revolution against the Turks, was incarcerated there after he had objected to being told what to do by the new government; to the extent that he had kidnapped four of them and tried to hold them to ransom. That much, I remembered, the rest I had to look up later. Then I found that the town had been originally founded by Nauplius, the son of the sea god Poseidon and Amymone. The Mycenaeans appear to have been there, and also the Argives, but that great jet-setter Pausanias found it abandoned when he visited there in the second century AD, and it doesn't seem to have got going as a city again until the Byzantine period. In 1210 it was captured by the Franks, and in 1389 ceded to the Venetians. After that came the Turks.

Sue's return brought me back to reality. She had not after all climbed the steps, but had wandered around chatting to people instead, and was now eager for a rest and a long, cold drink. It was my turn to go exploring, but the morning was passing quickly and it would soon be time to go for the bus. Regretfully we decided we could not return to the *taverna* for lunch. Breakfast had been bigger than we thought and we were not in the least hungry. I promised to make our apologies next time I was there.

I wandered off away from the fashionable bits of Naplion and found another disused railway station, complete with magnificent engine. There were some pretty good statues too and then, more alarmingly, a miniature version of hot-rod racing. I wandered around in a wide circle and then sneaked up on Sue and grabbed a surprise photo, much to the amusement of two men sitting at the opposite table.

'Come on,' I said, 'let's go and do one of the things we've become really good at.'

'What's that?' Sue enquired.

'Sitting in Ktel bus stations,' I replied.

And so we did exactly that.

The rest of the travelling now was on roads familiar to both of us, the flat plain, the little villages, and then the tiny Mycenaean bridge, with its new 'Official Historical Site' sign standing proudly beside it. Lygourio was soon reached and then, briefly, Epidaurus. Next two marble centres and the much advertised, but still unopened, 'Byzantium Bar', and then finally we ran into Ano Fanouri, turned the corner and found the whole of the Saronic Gulf spread out before us. The sea was a million shades of blue and the dark shapes of the islands floated free, Poros was there, and Aegina, and Angistri. The Methanan peninsular stretched before us, and the little shrine near Vathi where, some say, the water turned to wine was clearly visible on the headland. To the left you could see Piraeus and far, far ahead the misty shape of Cap Sounion, all so comfortingly familiar, but still breathtaking in the early-afternoon light.

We began our descent down the twisty, precipitous road which led to Poros, but there was nothing scary here for two people suffering from mild vertigo, and we were soon on level ground and running into the outskirts of Galatas. Here the nearly perfect timing that had accompanied us throughout our trip sadly deserted us and we just missed the car ferry. Eager now to be home, we crossed to Poros in the little water taxi and just missed the little bus! We shrugged resignedly and set off to walk, for taxis were still not allowed. It wasn't long before Sue stopped in order to cross the road to her apartment.

'See you in the *taverna* later then?'

'Yes. Er – Sue, it has been great, hasn't it? Can we do it all again soon?'

'Oh yes! Said Sue, and we went off to our separate bathrooms.

I walked along the road and climbed my mountain to my front door. 'Maybe next time we should take the bus to Naplion first, the train to Kalamata and then the bus to Kardamili and then…

It is the end of October now and some days the wind that comes down from the mountains has the taste of snow on it. Winter is coming and it is time to store away the summer memories. Now is the time for log fires, roast chestnuts, thick quilts and long, tall stories in the *cafenion*. Then one day you wake to find the sun that bangs at the shutters outside your window is bringing with it a brightness and a clarity you have not seen for weeks. There is the promise of summer in it and you realise with a burst of happiness that the journeys can start again. But then, again, why wait for the summer?!

•

The Trip to Northern Greece

The idea had first been mooted sometime towards the end of last summer. We would go on a trip during the winter, up into northern Greece. The cast list varied slightly, but it was always basicly Andreas, Maria and me. Sometimes a Yiannis was added, though whether it was the small one or the big one was never made entirely clear.

In the event it snowed. All autumn it had rained, rain like we never usually see here except for a few days in October and February, and it was cold, bitterly cold. Then, just before Christmas, the snow came – and came and came, all over the holidays and all over Greece. Sometimes it seemed that Poros was the only place in the whole of Europe without snow, for only the tops of the mountains on the mainland wore white in sympathy with the rest of Greece. The television news showed nightly pictures of a snow-covered Acropolis and, more disastrously, oranges frozen into the heart of an icicle. The trip was never mentioned and I assumed it had passed into history like so many things here. Meanwhile I got on with Life – Life with a capital L.

In the early days of January there was the big souvenir exhibition held in halls all over Athens. Takis was back in Piraeus after the enforced and unpopular move to the north of the city. Last year I was in London so had been unable to help, and by now he and Giorgia had become confident and experienced enough to do the stand on their own. I was left behind as they braved the still icy weather and headed for the late-afternoon ferry. I understood, but had to be involved a little, if only as a visitor. So I rose early on the Friday morning and, half asleep as always at 07.20 I slithered on to the second Flying Dolphin of the day and almost immediately lapsed back into the half-land of sleep.

We were quickly into Piraeus and near to the exhibition hall but there were other things to do first. I caught the train up to Tavros and walked to Kleopatra's studio. It was still early and I didn't expect to find her there but I had a parcel and was hoping to leave it for her in the shop upstairs. Despite a sign saying the shop should have opened (at the long ago hour of eight-thirty), the door and windows were barred and there was no sign of life. I wandered off into the side streets to enjoy the welcome rays of the newly returned sunshine and collected a few more phone numbers from lamp-posts, for this is the area I plan to live in for a while and I hope to find a flat there soon. About an hour later I returned but there was still no sign of life, and it was far too early to phone Kleopatra, so still clutching my heavy package I headed towards Monastiraki and a brief wander round the shops. But Sue's recent visit had filled me to the brim with 'shopping' and I was quickly bored, so I bought a beautiful bouquet for Takis and Giorgia and walked back for coffee in the Plaka. By now the sun was really warm and after all the days of winter it was good to wriggle out of my coat and sit back to watch the constantly changing scene in the road in front of me. But not for long! I was quickly embarrassed by the insistant bleeping of my newly acquired mobile phone. Not, alas, Kleopatra replying to my query as to her whereabouts; no, these were rather snide messages from England implying that life must be extraordinarily difficult under such adverse weather conditions! I achieved considerable satisfaction from drafting my replies and then, finishing my fresh orange, I made the short but hazardous journey down the street to 'my' *taverna* and a warm welcome.

A huge bowl of freshly made meat soup was placed in front of me and a glass of white wine materialised from thin air. I sat, a snow-covered mountain before me and a still white Acropolis to my right, and fell into philosophical mood – until, that is, I was joined by the owner, and we embarked on a catching-up session on our respective lives and times over the holiday period. Then, as the power of the sun faded with the afternoon, it really did become time to head for the exhibition hall in Piraeus.

I was greeted warmly, handed a glass of Ikarian *Tsipouro* (Greek fire-water!) and sent out to walk the dog! The *periptero*, or stand, looked great and business was brisk. I accepted my redundancy with good grace and spent a happy hour with friends. Later the six o'clock Dolphin left on time and found me safely on it. My feet ached and I was determined to have a taxi home but there were none waiting, and so, almost without thinking, I set off to walk. As I turned into the Neorion road I met Nikos, Andreas's uncle, and then Andreas.

'Ah!' said Andreas, 'When are we leaving for our holiday, tomorrow or Sunday?'

'Sunday,' I begged, quickly trying to adjust to the idea of packing and closing the flat.

'OK. We'll talk tomorrow then.'

But of course we never did, there was just one phonecall to

tell me to be ready for eleven-thirty or twelve on Sunday morning. And I was!

The weather was still behaving, at least temporarily, and we left Poros in warm sunshine. Uncertain at this stage whether we were bound for Rome or the ski slopes of Northern Greece I settled back to watch the world go by, happy to be travelling again after the enforced politeness of an over-sociable Christmas and New Year.

So we climbed the oh-so-familiar road up the mountains and then down to the little port of Epidaurus, the views spectacular as always and, for once, the road empty of cars. We sped along the Corinthian Highway and then, suddenly, we were in the outskirts of Piraeus and the pace quickened even more. Without my noticing, the decision between Greece and Italy had been made. Patras and the ferry to Italy faded away and thoughts of Northern Greece filled the horizon. But somewhere we must have taken a wrong turning for we found ourselves winding through a sprawling settlement of temporary shacks and Portacabins. Well, temporary once maybe, but these had been there for a long time, the people who lived in them Greek but of Russian origin, their faces Slavonic and their Greek heavily accented. Only last year I had sat in a cinema and seen homes like these flash upon the screen. Then the camera had credited them with a simple beauty but now they had an untidy permanence that none had intended. The people who lived here were warm and friendly but nevertheless it was a relief to leave this urban sprawl behind and reach the National road that was to take us north.

We had been travelling for hours and I was hungry, so I was happy when Andreas mentioned stopping for food – but not at all happy when I saw where we were stopping! We pulled into one of a chain of fast-food depots (there is no other word!) where whatever you buy tastes of nothing, unless smothered with the tomato ketchup and mayonnaise so wisely provided free of charge and in unlimited quantities. Well, it filled a gap and it was quick too, but I was glad to leave.

Night was falling rapidly now, for there is little twilight here, even in summer, and with the growing shadows the conversation inside the car had slowed and died as the minutes sped by. We turned off the National road and began to climb. The snow, confined to the edges of the road hitherto, now spread across the whole countryside. We reached a small village but still continued to climb until ahead of us, in the lights from our headlamps diffusing through the mist, we began to make out the outline of a large building. It was our hotel and we were relieved to be there. We found it quiet after a busy weekend and delightful, its walls hung with delicately woven antique fabrics and on the floors and tables huge pots with flower arrangements and dried grasses; this promised to be a pleasant stay!

We were tired that first night and ate quickly in the hotel restaurant. The food was good – and in the case of Andreas's fassoulada and my prawns, very good. Maria chose some safely grilled beef that looked pleasant enough but held no surprises. Conversation was sparse for we were hungry, and I think we were all a little surprised we had actually embarked on the trip that had been a part of so many summer conversations. Well, hungry I may have thought myself, but I was horrified to find that there was no way I could eat my fourth prawn and it had to be left lying on my plate, for doggy bags seemed rather inappropriate in this hotel! We sank briefly into some vast, comfy chairs by a log fire, but sleep became so hard to resist that we soon left for our rooms, safe in the knowledge that we had made an excellent start and could look forward to the next day with that advantage firmly in mind.

Alas, the next day did not start off quite as well as I'd hoped. A tiresome cold that had merely threatened in Poros now all but overwhelmed me, and I began the day sneezing for Greece. Worse was to follow, when Andreas and Maria ate a hearty breakfast and pestered me to do the same. I resisted and finally fled to the hotel porch for some fresh air. The hotel was overheated anyhow and I was longing to see what daylight had done to the outside world. Well, not much actually, for a thick mist swallowed up the view and only a smattering of snowflakes filled the space directly in front of me. I beseeched help from Poseidon and went back inside to see what had been planned in my absence. There I found that it had been decided we would go farther up the mountain on to the ski slopes. This we did and it was beautiful.

The snow was packed firmly underfoot, except where it had drifted in undulating lines across the mountain tops – for we really were on top of that particular bit of the world. Not too far away, and on pretty much the same level, was Mount Olympus, home of the gods. Easy to imagine that we and they were neighbours, if only briefly, and easy too to imagine they really were there, these gods. Like the Taygetus Mountains in Southern Greece these mountains were a fitting background for the ancients and lent themselves easily to myth and legend. When we first arrived we were wrapped in low cloud and visibility was limited, but Poseidon did not let me down and soon the sun broke through and the 'whoosh' of the first skiers came drifting across the slopes. Then the ski-lifts jerked into life and music forced itself from the high-mounted speakers around the ski-station. Across on the opposite slope a little stone house appeared and disappeared as the mists swirled round it. When the music stopped abruptly there was the sound of silence, something so concentrated that you felt you could reach out and touch it. But Andreas was disappointed, he had wanted to hire a snowmobile but there were none available and by now we were beginning to feel a little silly walking alongside the pistes; so we returned to the car and headed off to find an ancient monastery that he remembered from a previous visit.

We quickly dropped below the snowline and found ourselves driving along roads crudely cut through the jagged mountains. This, said Andreas, was the home of the *Andartes* (Resistance fighters) during the Second World War. No Germans or Italians came here, they were too afraid. And it was easy to see why.

We turned a corner and came across a miracle shrine – patterns in the rock had formed the face of the Virgin Mary and there were tiny steps leading up towards the sky. This natural curiosity had triggered off stories of miracle cures and good fortune and now there were icons along the rock ledges, some of them expensive ones, and candles and votive offerings and money, quite a lot of it. My Northern European mind marvelled at the possibility of such things being left there unattended, the petitioners secure in the knowledge that they would not be stolen.

By now the mists had closed in again, weaving like chiffon through the treetops, and the colours were the drained greens and greys of winter, so the monastery came as a welcome slash of honey-coloured stone and maroon and gold decoration. We were the only people there that day and the tiny church was opened specially for us – by an Albanian! The icons were superb, pockmarked again by what I took to be more bullet holes alas, but in their muted blues and gold they retained their haunting beauty. For a thousand years they had been there and I lingered inside the church for a long time, conscious, I think, that this was probably one place to which I would never return. When I came out Andreas was talking to one of the two resident monks, a friendly, chatty one, seemingly glad of some fresh company. An old woman, maybe a nun, hurried across the courtyard with something in a saucepan for the ever present cats, each of whom wore a tiny blue cross around their necks, even the kittens. We lit candles, I for one feeling that God would have more time to listen in this peaceful backwater. Then we headed back the way we had come in search of more material comforts.

It was slowly dawning on me that there is a considerable advantage in visiting famous beauty spots in the heart of winter, especially after a bout of really bad weather, for you are made especially welcome and few of the unattractive tourist trappings are yet in evidence. So when we stopped for lunch at a café-bar labelled 'The Saloon' and pretending to be in the American Deep South, I was nowhere near as horrified as close friends would have supposed. Andreas had confessed to a longing for a Jack Daniels but, strangely, drank only a coffee. I embraced (almost literally, for I was shivering) a glass of hot Tsipouro with honey and cloves that made a welcome attack on my increasingly oppressive cold and Maria settled for her usual hot chocolate. After that some of the passion seemed to have gone out of the day and we returned to the hotel to sleep, first arranging to meet at the indoor swimming-pool at six o'clock.

I am no fan of swimming pools, having nearly drowned in one as a child, but I had every intention of keeping my promise to be there at the appointed hour, so there really was no need for Maria to arrive at my room and rush me into my swimsuit! Anyhow, we arrived at the pool together to find Andreas already in the water and we joined him quickly before our resolution failed. It was actually pleasant once we were in, the water was warm and it felt good to be there, with the snow piled outside the French windows and the occasional snowflake fluttering past.

Later that night, after nearly ending up back at the monastery owing to a small oversight on the part of the driver, we eventually made it to the village of Karpenisi and one of the local *tavernas*. Robust country cooking this, with a far from subtle local wine, but it went down well after the day in the open air; back at the hotel we drank hot chocolate by the fire and then were away to bed. The next day we were to leave these mountains and be on our way.

'Where to next?' I asked of Andreas.

'We'll see tomorrow,' came the reply.

How like my Greek friends not to plan ahead, I thought, and yet I somehow felt that this trip had in fact been very carefully planned indeed and that only I remained ignorant of the itinerary!

After the usual battle over breakfast, we piled into the car and left the ski slopes behind, plunging down through the mists and then back up into the mountains again. The road wound below us for miles, twisting and turning through rocky outcrops and rough scrub. An occasional group of pine or spruce broke the even lines of the horizon, but of houses there were none.

'I need petrol!' said Andreas and as the car started its descent he cut the engine.

Below us, climbing slowly towards us and appearing and disappearing from view, there came a large mechanical digger. As he plodded ever upwards and we coasted silently down, our meeting became inevitable. There was something epic in the event, all that space and only the two vehicles in sight; one needing petrol and the other, hopefully, possessing the information as to where we could buy some. Would we make it to the next petrol station? Inside the car the tension grew, but, when we both pulled up side by side, our query was met only with the reply: 'Maybe thirty kilometres,' and the driver continued on his way.

'I don't think I will do it,' said Andreas, thoughtfully, and a weighty silence descended as we carried on our journey.

Some may believe that it is better to travel hopefully than to arrive but there was considerable relief all round when a small village with a petrol station appeared round a bend in the road. Now all we needed was for it to be open and have petrol, not always a foregone conclusion on these remote roads after appalling snowstorms such as they had had over the last few weeks. But it was and it did and we drove away in some considerable style, our tank full to the top.

After that the atmosphere in the car lightened considerably and everyone began talking at once. Houses and small villages now appeared at regular intervals, clinging to the mountain and precarious in their tenure, for they were threatened by frequent rockslides. One house in particular caught my eye. It stood in a small field of green with huge boulders littering the tiny cultivated patch; it was old and must have stood fast for many years but on stormy nights I think its owners must long to light a million candles as they lie shivering beneath their blankets.

We now had a view over quite a large part of north-west Greece and so far ours was the only road in sight, but still Andreas stopped to greet the occasional villager and ask if we were going the right way for Arta. I'm sure it was a politeness but I'm not sure it was appreciated, for our greetings were met only with the briefest of acknowledgements and I got the impression they were regarded as an intrusion. Any car on these roads must have constituted an event but not necessarily a welcome one. The people here seemed closed and wary of anything unexpected; living in villages, shut off for several weeks each winter by the snow and pretty isolated all the year round, they had clearly developed a resistance to outside interference, and the usual Greek eagerness to chat and exchange gossip was not evident here.

I vividly remember one old lady we found standing on the road outside her house. She could have been over eighty years old. Clad all in black but making no attempt to hide her face she seemed reluctant to acknowledge our existence at all. She must have been beautiful as a young woman for her face was still clearly defined, with high cheek-bones, soft lines and a full mouth. When she eventually spoke she gave us only the briefest affirmation that we were on the right road and her eyes never left the ground. She simply could not or would not look at us – perhaps conditioned by tradition and upbringing against such brazen behaviour. As we drove on I realised with a shock that here was someone who had almost certainly never left her mountain home. This was a lady who had lived through almost all the history of modern Greece, and through events that had changed the world in so many ways, but how much of it had touched her in these remote mountains? It was a staggering thought.

Still rejoicing in a full petrol tank we quickly descended to the valley floor and found ourselves now in an area rich with streams and the deciduous trees of a softer clime. We were entering one of the main citrus-fruit-growing areas of Greece and as we drew ever nearer to that National road we came across more and more trailers packed tight with oranges and mandarins, for it was harvest time. They made a colourful background to our journey but, unfortunately, represented a tragedy for the local farmers. Here the a-typical winter storms and sub-zero temperatures had resulted in the ruin of the whole crop, and these trailers were not waiting to go to market as they had done year after year. Instead they were awaiting the destruction of their loads. There were roadside stalls too, packed high with fruit and vegetables, but no one was stopping to buy and, like everyone else, we too hurried by, feeling guilty that we could do nothing to help. At least the Prime Minister has declared a state of emergency and we could only hope that financial help would be forthcoming from the government.

Then, suddenly, we were on the outskirts of Ioannina and passing a large house. This turned out to be the Vrellis Museum. 'We must see this,' said Andreas. 'Let's do it now, why not?' And he reversed back down the dual carriageway and into the car park. We only had half an hour before it closed, but in a way it was enough. One man had been responsible for its creation; it had been his dream and he made it all come true, even building the house that accommodates the exhibits. He is shown at the end of the exhibition, immortalised in wax, creating himself. The other tableaux each show a scene from various historical moments of Greek history. There are scenes showing life during the Turkish occupation – children being taught in secret schools, scenes of torture, a priest having his hair and beard ripped out, and the death of the local Turkish tyrant Ali Pasha in his house on the island in Lake Pamvotis in Ioannina. More recently there were scenes from the German occupation and the liberation of Crete. The exhibition left a vivid impression and we were quite relieved to re-emerge into the afternoon sunlight.

A group of well-fed cats posed artistically along the museum steps and included a very beautiful and friendly Siamese. The reason for their presence became clear with the arrival of an avuncular figure clutching a bulging plastic bag. We left them to their late lunch and walked quickly to the gates of the museum. There we found two more cats waiting patiently. We explained that lunch was being served up by the main house but they seemed unperturbed and one began washing himself in that scornful way cats have when they know better than you, so we retreated to the car and headed off into the centre of the town.

Ioannina is a town with a vivid history, one that centres mainly round the time of the Turkish occupation. The most notorious figure of that period is the tyrannical Ali Pasha who ruled over the area in the nineteenth century. At that time Ioannina was the capital of southern Albania and its inhabitants lived in terror of their capricious ruler, whose harem, it was rumoured numbered over five hundred of the local girls. Today his name still colours local history, the mosque is still standing and the old part of the town conjures up pictures of armed men and veiled and cloistered women, but Ioannina is now a modern city with three universities and a fashionable centre full of expensive shops.

Before we knew it, we found ourselves on the lakefront. In the distance towered the mountains, white with snow almost down to the edge of the lake itself, a lake that was frozen over with thick ice. To my left we could now see the outline of Ali Pasha's mosque and the cluster of houses that made up the old town. It was bitterly cold, and although in the distance lay the little island and Ali Pasha's house and a hundred stories, all that must wait for tomorrow. We needed a bed for the night and some hot food.

We settled in the village of Perama on the far side of the lake from the town. No five-star hotel this but clean, warm and comfortable and I, for one, did not miss the swimming pool! An hour and a half later found us in a large supermarket buying tins of milk and packets of pampers for the baby Andreas and Maria had left behind with grandma and grandpa in Poros. In an attempt to enter into the spirit of things I bought a small milk saucepan and a notebook, and then we went to eat in a restaurant by the lake. The food was good and the service pleasant but all thoughts of any further exploration disappeared in the warm glow that followed; it was raining now anyhow, and we were happy to end the day.

It carried on raining all through the night too, but as we left the hotel next morning the sun broke through and was to stay with us as we headed for the Perama caves. Here we solved the tricky problem of parking by buying a *komboloi* (a string of worry beads), and a silver-and-agate necklace from the shop directly opposite the entrance to the caves.

'There is no problem,' said the owner of the shop, 'leave the car where it is.'- and indeed there wasn't despite all the No Parking signs. There was a slight problem at the caves, however, for the custodians showed a great reluctance to open even though it was long past the official opening time. But Andreas chivvied them along and Maria and I yawned and twitched expressively and eventually we set off into the bowels of the earth. There are almost two kilometres of cave and a rough path that falls and rises many times. Formed from limestone like those of my childhood in Castleton in Derbyshire, they are indeed impressive and very beautiful. Alas, my persistent cold spoilt most of my time below for the humidity varied between eighty and a hundred per cent and at one point I could scarcely breathe. I was relieved to get out but still congratulated the little fox that is reputed to have shown the entrance to one Yiannis Kontoyiannis in 1940, just in time for the villages to shelter there when Mussolini started bombing Northern Greece at the start of World War II. There were few other historical facts to be gleaned, though it is thought the existence of the caves was known back in the nineteenth century.

With oxygen restored to my grateful lungs, we continued on to the lake, courtesy of the taxi-boat service to Ali Pasha's island. The lake was still frozen and it was bitterly cold again at the water's edge. Something had kept open a channel between the island and the mainland but must have had difficulty for the ice was at least four inches thick on either side of us and our water taxi crunched through the newly formed top layer like an ice breaker. We left the shadows cast by the old town and the sun warmed us a little – or perhaps only gave the impression of warmth, for the temperature was still below freezing.

I think we were the only strangers on the little ferry; everyone else was clutching supermarket shopping and swapping tales from the mainland. As we stepped off the boat we were greeted rapturously by the two open *taverna*s on the harbour front. But I was disconcerted to see tanks of fish and eels beside the tables and chairs and we walked quickly past and into the village. I am a complete hypocrite about my food. I eat most things but prefer them to arrive in anonymous shapes already cooked and on my plate. Any prior acquaintance kills my appetite completely and in this case the tanks contained large goldfish.

Surely they didn't…?

Again it seemed that Andreas had been here before, for he led us directly to Ali Pasha's house and up the wooden steps into the museum. He reminded us of one of the scenes from the Vrellis Museum, depicting the death of Ali Pasha and his Turkish retinue. It took place here, he told us, and suddenly it was easy to see it for real. I had imagined it on a larger scale than this but it was chilling to realise that I was standing on the very same wooden floor where the blood had flowed so freely.

In one of the glass cases there was a dress belonging to Vasiliki, Ali Pasha's favourite mistress. Although he ordered her killed just before his murder, she was spared and lived until 1835, one of the few survivors of the Turkish tyrant's rule and more fortunate than the seventeen young women he drowned in the lake for displeasing him!

I stopped in the museum shop and bought a little olivewood duck for my mother-in-law and then we wandered back through the tiny streets, almost able to see again the rich Turkish costumes of the men and women who had lived there.

Hunger forced us into what looked like someone's front parlour but was in fact a restaurant. There was a tank outside there too, but I firmly averted my eyes and left Andreas to order a *mezere* (hors d'oeuvre) to go with our ouzo. This, when it came, was not like anything I had eaten before. There was crayfish, I think, and duck, and what Andreas asserted rather too firmly were duck's legs. But I am sure they were frog's legs for they are a local delicacy and one that he had been talking about for days. So I tried hard not to think of that large tank just outside the door. In fact it all tasted rather good but I wasn't very comfortable and quite happy to leave for the four o'clock ferry, secretly hoping that trade would be slack and that the unfortunate occupants of the tanks could enjoy a few more days in safety.

On the way back we sailed through a series of landscape paintings. Tall reeds fringed the lake, with sun-bleached boats hidden in their midst. Fishing nets were spread to dry at the water's edge, backed by the stone cottages and the greens and greys of their front doors; a different Greece this, without the exuberance of the blue-and-white decor of the Aegean. Wild life abounded and the air was full of the cries of ducks and cormorants and moorhens – and others I could not name. There were fish in the lake, and long dark shapes I took to be the famous eels. Framing it all the snow-capped mountains completed the picture.

By the time we reached the mainland, the last rays of the sun had disappeared and it was even colder than the evening before. The skim of ice was already thickening on the once half-thawed water channel and we clunked and snapped our way back to the moorings. No one wanted to linger or to go exploring in the old town so we headed back to the hotel, Andreas had a date with a football match, Maria wanted to sleep and I was thinking of an early coffee. We arranged to meet later for one of the great loves of Andreas's life, Pasta! And this we did with considerable enthusiasm and no worries about lurking fish tanks.

From Ioannina we were ideally placed to visit many well-known places like Igoumenitsa and Corfu, Florina, the Meteora and Metsovo. We settled on Metsovo, but I couldn't help admitting to a long held desire to see Albania.

'OK, we will go to the frontier tomorrow,' said Andreas. 'I promise.'

So the next morning I was ready long before the other two and excited, like a small child. I don't know why Albania had always intrigued me. Maybe it was because access had been impossible for so long, maybe it was because the name of ex-King Zog sounded like something from a fairy tale, but I was longing to go there. Over the summer I had spoken to Albanians working on Poros and they had talked of a country with a great natural beauty and a way of life that had not been so bad. The churches had been open, the education excellent and no one had gone hungry. As Angelos said, there are freedoms other than the freedom to travel, and in many ways life was more difficult now than then. He had a large family and a big house in Albania, but there was no work there and he didn't have the freedom to live there – ironic, but true. So, perhaps some of the mystique had been taken away, but I continued to be intrigued.

Once the car was loaded we soon found ourselves speeding towards the frontier. The road was a good one with most of the traffic coming into Greece. Andreas began counting the Mercedes cars dating from the 1960s and the 1970s, all with Albanian number plates, but gave up when he reached thirty in only a few minutes. There was a small military presence which was much more low-key than I had expected. After about half an hour we turned a sharp bend and the Albanian mountains filled the horizon. We were so close now that when we passed a small museum on our right I was reluctant to stop, but Andreas pulled into the car park and I bit back my disappointment and scrambled out of the car.

Across the road there stood a large memorial to Metaxas and King George and someone else too far away to recognise. A solitary soldier was on duty inside the museum, and, like the monk at the monastery, was glad to see us I think, for he couldn't have had many visitors over the last few days. It was not very big inside and the main exhibits were Second World War guns in display cabinets, but there were photographs on the walls and in three albums, and a list of statistics that showed just how outnumbered had been the Greek soldiers and the men and women of Epirus. It must have been impossible terrain in which to fight, the mountains huge and the narrow tracks dropping sheer into the valleys below. Even inside the museum that day it was freezing and the conditions in the mountains must have been unbearable. But in the photos they were always smiling or dancing, proud to be Greek and fighting for their homeland. It was the women who mainly pushed the heavy guns up the mountain tracks and they often fought alongside the men. Inside one of the albums I found a cartoon cut from an English newspaper of that time. It showed a group of Greek statues labelled 'Heroes' reaching out their hands to greet the *Evzone* (Royal Greek) soldiers as they arrived in the land of heroes.

It was such a simple exhibition of heroism, but the contribution to the outcome of the war by these relatively few people was incalculable. By defeating first the Italians as they invaded Greece from Albania, and then delaying the second invasion of Germans, they bought essential time for the Allies at a critical point of the war. I had read of all this of course but standing there I began to understand what a terrible price had had to be paid, and the tears came to my eyes. This was the site of the famous '*Oxi*' of 28 October 1940, the day the Greek government said 'No' to the Italians and the whole of Greece sided with the Allies for the rest of the war. An heroic and truly noble '*Oxi*' this and I couldn't help wishing that all the people responsible for that other 'No', namely the refusal to return of the Parthenon (Elgin) Marbles to Greece, were standing next to me now and were seeing what I was seeing. Maybe then they would begin to understand something of the sacrifices that were made here, and throughout Greece, sacrifices that helped to give both them and me a future free from occupation and oppression. And once they had seen that, surely the return of the marbles would seem a very small way of acknowledging that debt and of paying back something of what is still owed. There would be no precedent here and it would mean so much to all the Greek people. It would be such an honourable thing to do.

As we turned to leave the museum I crossed to the present-day soldier and thanked him on behalf of all the people of Britain, though I couldn't help wondering how many people today knew anything of what had taken place here. We left then and sped on to the Albanian border and it was quiet in the car for a long while. At last Andreas spoke. 'The last romantic war,' he said.

'No,' I almost shouted, still moved by the pictures I had seen. 'No wars are romantic, or at least only in hindsight. What happened here was the death of thousands of people who would have lived if it had not been for the decisions of a few mad men.'

There was no reply from the front of the car and I had no idea whether he agreed with me or not so I let the matter rest.

After a few minutes we reached the Albanian frontier post. A group of men stood waiting, for lifts into Albania I suppose. As a race they are quite different from the Greeks – they seem smaller and their faces are coarser and more heavily featured. Their language sounds guttural after the softer and more familiar sounds of the Aegean, but it is an ancient language and the language in which some beautiful poetry has been written.

I longed to go across, if only for a few minutes, but I knew that any such suggestion would only produce an outraged protest so I contented myself with looking at the mountains that seemed even higher and more forbidding than those closer to us on the Greek side of the barrier. And I thought of all those thousands of people who had crossed over them in peace and in war, mostly on foot and often without shoes, and I shuddered. But then I remembered too that only a very few decades ago, these lands were Greek and so perhaps they were not so vastly forbidding as I had thought.

A man came forward to the car, to ask for a lift I suppose, but Andreas shot the car into gear and we drove off back the way we had come. We drove into a small village and stopped at the bakery for bread. I got out of the car and stood for a while savouring a last glimpse of the mountains until, probably as a ploy to get me back, Andreas promised we would return and spend time exploring that enigmatic country that had been isolated for so long. Later Albanian friends were to tell me that we should have crossed the border and seen something of their country for, as they said again and again, it is so very beautiful. But for the moment I had to content myself with one last look before I got back into the car and Albania faded into the morning mists.

Very soon after that we passed a tall hill with the word '*Oxi*' carved into its side. Another memorial to the war dead, but also the site of some of the worst fighting in the civil war that followed the defeat of the Germans. Shortly after that we turned down a side road and came across a shepherd grazing his sheep; he seemed glad to see us and happy to talk, so we exchanged all the information so vital to Greeks when they first meet strangers – how old were we, how much money did we earn, how much had we paid for our home, and, finally, where were we from! To confirm that we were now on the edge of one of the great national parks, we drove on to the riverbed and the eighteenth century stone bridge crossing it. Here, we were welcomed by two large but extremely friendly dogs, and on reading the notice by the bridge found that dogs were not the only things that might come to greet us. Here also lived wolves, brown bears, deer, and a wide range of smaller animals, together with insects and reptiles. Not all of them friendly either! In addition, the skies were the home of eagles, including the golden eagle, and some of the rarer hawks. It was pretty there, very pretty, and it would have been easy to spend the day walking the mountain trails, but it was already past midday and we were supposed to be bound for Metsovo. So, instead, we returned to complete our chat with the shepherd, and set off along the National road. But not for long. Andreas soon turned off again on to another narrow track that wound ever upwards.

'Er, do we have petrol?' I enquired, but my question was met with silence, so I shrank back into my corner and stared fixedly at the passing scenery. And so it was that I caught my first glimpse of the Pindus Mountains, and just said, 'Oh!' For that which filled the windscreen was a king and queen of mountain ranges, beautiful, but awesome too, and my thoughts went back briefly to the men and women of Epirus and World War II. There are many photographs of these mountains and they are good photographs too, but nothing comes close to catching the reality. No wonder the gods chose them as yet another of their sacred places – they would have been crazy not to.

We were back now in the park that laps their feet, still very beguiling in an English or Pyrenean sort of way. Many streams chattered over white pebbles, the water a pale-blue crystal. Even in winter the leafless trees stood in carefully arranged groups, and in summer, with the sunlight filtering through the green leaves, it must be close to the Illyrian ideal, wanting only nymphs, satyrs and a few vestal virgins to complete the scene – for shepherds there already were!

The road wound and narrowed and we were soon above the snowline again. We stopped for a snowball fight, and then drove on into a stone-built village for coffee. No breeze-block accommodation here. The new houses matched the old and there was a sense of pride and well-being. It would have been good to explore a little but the afternoon mists were already closing us off from this mountain world and Metsovo was still a long way away.

We headed back, skirting Ioannina and Lake Pamvotis and plunging back yet again into the mountains. Andreas had some sort of football chat show on the car radio, hosted by one of those interviewers who are in love with the sound of their own voice – so much so that they never listen to what their guests have to say and keep interrupting in all the most interesting places. This one also seemed to be under the impression that the phrase 'Have a good afternoon,' was a more than adequate substitute for anything even approaching intelligent conversation. It was annoying but somehow fitting for there was a drastic modernising programme going on all around us, with bridges being built over the valleys and tunnels being dug through the mountains. 'Like Austria,' gloated Andreas, whilst I shuddered with horror.

The landscape was strange, with rough, low vegetation, and then groups of skeletal trees standing like ghosts. I was very happy to reach Metsovo. The guide books say of Metsovo that it is the most attractive town of Epirus, and they are probably right, but for me the main attraction lies in its ancient history, for this little town is like no other in Greece. The people of Metsovo are descended from the Vlachs and were once nomadic shepherds. Their language has its roots in Latin and is thought to have been acquired during the Roman occupation, when, one theory has it, they were used as guards and sentries in the high mountain passes. Until recently they were thought to be unique, but, when the borders with Russia were opened ten years ago, a remote village in Siberia was found to have an almost identical vocabulary. How or why has not yet been established.

First impressions of this little town are nothing but good. The houses again are all of stone, rather squat and solid but sitting cosily into their surroundings and many with wooden balconies. Wood has been used everywhere and even the newly opened Alpha bank has been clad in it, ensuring that it merges inconspicuously into its surroundings. Our hotel was quite old I think, but offered all the modern comforts, except, that is, for the electrical sockets that were of the old three-pronged variety and thus required some lateral thinking on my part before I could operate my faithful electric kettle.

There was a large reception area, furnished with huge sofas covered in blankets and embroidered tapestries, all in the traditional style – deep reds and bright woven flowers. Antique copper pots and trays stood on the wooden coffee tables and a huge log fire burnt in the fireplace. It was all very welcoming and made me think of old hostelries with horse-drawn carriages waiting outside their doors.

We left our bags and went exploring, listening for examples of the ancient Romaic language. It wasn't difficult to find. The central square was busy still and although many people were speaking Greek, many others, the older generation in particular, were obviously using this other language. Many years ago, when I was trying to be an actress, I went to a voice coach who told me that all accents reflected the terrain in which the people lived, and this certainly seemed to be borne out here. The sentences ran in jagged ups and downs, and there was a hard quality to what I took to be the vowels; but it was pleasant to listen to all the same.

Later, when we walked around the side-roads, we saw that most of the older women still wore the traditional costume (a long, heavily gathered skirt of navy blue or red, together with an embroidered shawl across their shoulders), and there was an air of quiet affluence about the place, and a feeling of solidarity. Later that evening we drank a bottle of the local red wine; it was rich and full-bodied, an appropriate wine for the surroundings.

Down a side-street we found an antique shop, fatal for me, and went inside to see what was on offer. Outside I had already seen an old coffee pot, with the sloping Turkish spout, and I had thought to buy it as a souvenir, but once inside I could have bought a dozen things. One in particular caught my eye: at first glance it looked almost like a model of a minaret, with a round bowl as a base and a long, sectioned tube ending in a brimmed hat-shaped top. I was intrigued and felt that instant tug which usually ends up in a purchase! But I had no idea what it was. An enquiry elicited the information that the base was for perfume or sweet-smelling herbs. The top had three holes that allowed the scents to escape and sweeten the air around it. I knew I wanted it, but it was expensive, and Andreas persuaded me to 'think about it'; so I reluctantly followed him and Maria to a restaurant, where I managed to sit and eat without rushing back to the shop before it closed. Alas, the image of it stayed in my mind and, despite the price, I grew determined to go back the next day and buy it. Nothing new there then!

On our way back to the hotel we crossed the busy central square where groups of men stood smoking and talking and teenage boys in jeans mingled in groups. This was obviously the social centre of the town, the equivalent of the smokey cafenia of the islands, and important matters were being discussed at length. But it was bitterly cold and we could only admire their hardiness. We didn't linger for long.

Next morning I persuaded Andreas that we had to go back to the antique shop, but when we reached the town centre we found that the shops were only just beginning to open and ours showed no sign of life at all. Plan two seemed the obvious option and so we climbed up to the Averoff house, breakfast in hand. Evangelos Averoff is famous throughout Greece. The family is an affluent one and influential in the political life of the country. They came from Metsovo and in the 1930s, when, having noticed that his home town was rapidly losing its people to the big cities, Mr Averoff decided to do something to try to stop the exodus. He hit on the idea of tracing the Tosita family and discovered that the only surviving member was a wealthy banker living in Italy. The Tosita family had been a prosperous family of Metsovo who had sheltered a Turkish refugee from the local sultan's rule way back in the seventeenth century. Once the survivor was back in favour he returned to the town to repay his friends and asked them what they wanted as a gift. The Tosita family requested the freedom of the town from Turkish rule and this wish was granted. From then on Metsovo flourished and kept its own identity until the early 1900s. To cut a long story short, Evangelos Averoff got his substantial financial help from Italy and set up several local cottage industries and kept the people away from the cities. The old Tosita family home became a museum, restored as a period family-mansion. It is an impressive house, furnished in the traditional manner and giving a clear picture of an old but comfortable lifestyle. The rooms on the ground floor could be sealed off during the bitter winter months and a small stream had been diverted into an inside source of running water. Large divans are still grouped round huge fireplaces and there is a smoking-room for the men and a sewing-room for the women. The rooms are filled with personal possessions, some antique and some belonging to Mr Averoff. There are stunning icons and traditional costumes in the wardrobes. The glass-fronted cupboards are filled with old china and glass and there are swords and guns and ladies' purses and fans. It is a place that lives, and I for one wouldn't mind moving in tomorrow!

Coming out of the Averoff house into the warm sunshine and finishing off the last bit of my *spanokopita* (spinach pie), breakfast that had hastily been consigned to a pocket before we entered, I now only had one thought in mind. I dragged Andreas and Maria back to the shop. We found it open but with no one inside.

'Let's go then,' said Andreas, but I dragged my steps and before we had gone far we saw the owner returning with his morning coffee.

'Say nothing you,' muttered Andreas, and he bargained hard. But the man knew I wanted it and he remained unmoved. Maybe if we had stayed for longer and entered into a serious round of bargaining; well, who knows? But the morning was slipping away and I was determined not to leave without it. We won five thousand drachmas off the price for cash, and I paid in euros and we left, Andreas disappointed, I delighted.

'Where to now?' I asked.

'The Meteora,' came the reply, as we climbed high up the

mountain and into the most beautiful snow. Now everywhere we looked was like a scene from a Christmas card, the snow frozen thick on the branches of the pine trees, and lying deep on the ground in unmarked waves of white. We were still in wolf-and-bear country and looked hopefully for tracks, but there were none. The sun sat in a deep blue sky and the trees threw strong shadows across the snow, but the valleys lay still shrouded in mist and there were no other cars on the road.

'Oops, I need petrol,' came from the front of the car, but I refused to make any comment. Then the road started to descend and we left the bright sunlight behind, running into the thick fog that was to stay with us for five hours. I had visited the monasteries of the Meteora with Sue, during the summer, but I was happy to return.

The monasteries of the Meteora are unique in Greece for they were built on the top of rocks that were formed twenty-five million years ago. The first thing you see are high, jagged shapes standing in the shadow of the Pindus mountains, only on closer examination can the monasteries be seen crowning virtually every peak; it is an extraordinary sight.

The first monastery was established by Saint Athanasios in the fourteenth century, though quite how he climbed alone to the top of a sheer rock four hundred and thirteen metres high remains a mystery to this day. Once the monastery was established, however, things became a little easier – well, relatively that is. Until the 1920s access to the monasteries was provided by either a rickety wooden ladder, or by a net that was winched up with its human cargo crouched inside. The winches are still in use, but nowadays the nets hold only provisions for the monks. On the rock surface below the monasteries you can see many shallow caves where monks were known to live in solitude for years at a time. Their aim was to gain a state of religious ecstasy through an absolute belief in the presence of God, rather similar to the Stylites who sought the same experience by sitting on top of a pillar in the deserts of what is now the Middle East. By the sixteenth century there were said to be thirty monasteries in the Meteora, but today, alas, only a few still remain, and only a very few of those are open to the public. These are well worth a visit however, for they contain original, breath-taking frescoes, mostly of the saints who died for their faith. Oh, and by the way, access has been considerably improved!

This time, however, I did not find the Meteora of my first visit. Coming to it from the Pindus Mountains instead of on an organised tour from Athens, it all seemed to make much more sense. The weird rock shapes with the monasteries on their peaks belonged to the area in a way that I had not appreciated before. Instead of basking in the brilliant light of the summer sunshine they were covered in thick mists that swirled around them, making them invisible at times. One or two were open, but there were no visitors, no cars and no coaches. I stood in the car park in front of the Great Meteoron monastery, exactly where Sue and I had stood only a few months ago, and it was a strange feeling. Four souvenir shops were optimistically open and we tried to buy something from each, but the rain, that had merely threatened half an hour ago, now started in earnest and it seemed a depressing place. We ran for the car.

'Do you want to stay, or shall we drive back to Athens tonight?' enquired Andreas.

For some reason it was a startling thought. I examined it carefully. If we drove back it meant the end of our travelling, the end of our escapist interlude and part of me longed to keep going, but in so many ways it seemed the obvious thing to do. I mentally changed gear and agreed to the drive back. It was not a particularly pleasant drive, especially for Andreas, but by the time we pulled into the car park of a hotel in Piraeus I had become reconciled to returning home.

Next morning, the sun now back, we went to the hypermarket in Glyfada where Andreas and Maria celebrated a return to the commercialised side of life by buying vast quantities of household goods and I bought a camera to replace the one that had, literally, fallen to pieces during our travels. We then caught the two-thirty ferry back to Poros surrounded by familiar faces and a buzz of local gossip.

Back in my apartment I unpacked with that initial sense of pleasure that is part of coming home from any trip. I cleaned my Metsovan souvenir and discovered it to be silver-plated, I then found it a home on the chest of drawers in my bedroom where I can see it first thing every morning, a state of affairs that gives me enormous pleasure. Then a few days later, as I walked towards the Neorion road, my neighbour asked if I had spent a pleasant winter. So, I can only assume that winter is past and spring is here. Soon it will be time to begin preparing for this season's tourists. The winter journeys will fade into the smoke of the cafenia and from there into the past. But as the sun climbs high and the temperatures soar, they will provide a memory of stillness and quiet and cool havens. Enough, anyhow, to last until next year!

•

A September Return to the Mani

This time it began with a text message on the mobile phone. 'If I come to Poros, can we go back to the Mani?' wrote Sue. The answer to this question, unlike so many in my life at that time, required no late-night agonising, no packets of cigarettes or thoughtful glasses of wine. I replied immediately, 'Book flight now.' So she did.

In fact it all came as rather a surprise to both of us, for all summer Sue had been categorically stating that she had no intention whatsoever of coming to Poros this year. Turkey had been mentioned and together we had scoured the travel agent's notice-boards when I had paid a flying visit to England in August. But nothing was so tempting that it couldn't be resisted; so I had left London convinced that I would not see her again for at least another year; and that conclusion had been reached barely a week ago. Now I was faced with packing another bag, and working out a route that, if possible, avoided too many hours sitting in Sparta bus station!

It could all have been a big mistake, returning to the Mani, but once we had hit on the idea it seemed the right thing to do, and we soon became agog with the sheer anticipation of it all: the open road and two ladies of a certain age, eager for another adventure.

Here on Poros the thought of the Mani soon began to work its usual magic, the map of the Peloponnese reappeared and Patrick Leigh Fermor's book was removed from its easy-to-find place on the bookshelves. The images of two years ago swam to the forefront of my memory: the Mani towers, the rampant cactus cloaking the derelict buildings, and the glimpses of the sea tumbling across the rocky coastline. We were going back! But this time we were going back better equipped for the journey, physically, mentally and emotionally.

The first improvement came with our choice of luggage. Designer hand- portmanteaux were out, and in their place we expressed a preference for 'something small on wheels'.

'And don't bring all that make-up,' I stipulated.

'What make-up?' came the anticipated reply.

Our mental improvement came with the news that Sue had finally started to read her copy of P.L.F.'s book. This, bought as a present after the last trip, had been barely opened for two years. Now, maybe, it would come into its own. Emotionally? Well, we were both by now really in love with the place. My original dream had more than survived its journey into reality, and Sue had joined me in my delight in it all.

I think there was one long-distance phone call and then she arrived on the wrong Flying Dolphin and we set about the intricate final stages of our intensive pre-planning.

'Shall we take the eight o'clock bus on Thursday then?'

'OK. that sounds good.'

We were up and running!

Well, sort of! There was a slight last-minute hitch when Sue's pre-booked taxi didn't turn up and we nearly missed the bus, but somehow or other we made it, and eight-fifteen found us sitting complacently towards the back of the Naplion bus as it drove through the outskirts of Galatas and began its inevitable steep climb up to Aghios Fanari. Now the breathtaking views once again tumbled down the mountainsides and lay in fantastic azure patterns at their feet. The tensions of the early morning start tumbled with them and delight took their place.

'Where exactly are we going after Naplion? questioned Sue.

'Well, we can take the train to Kalamata, or maybe a bus somewhere.'

'Not Sparta.'

'Not if we can possibly avoid it, and I think we can.'

We settled into a long, comfortable silence.

Maybe breakfast in Naplion?'

'Yes,' said Sue.

And it all worked out very nicely, though somewhere in the midst of breakfast, the railway got forgotten and we decided on the mid-morning bus to Tripolis instead. From there, we reasoned, we could go on to Kalamata and then…? But first a toasted sandwich and a fresh orange juice at the foot of the old fort, the sun dappling the ground through the eucalyptus trees and thoughts and daydreams drifting in and out of the conversation from the neighbouring tables, bringing a hint of other lives, fascinating but remote from ours.

Then it was time to go, so we headed for the bus, Sue's borrowed suitcase sounding like an approaching tank as she rattled it, oblivious, across the uneven road surface. The bus to Tripolis took us past the Argos railway station and we experienced a momentary pang of regret, but we were committed now, and anyhow had no idea of the train timetable. 'Never look back,' we admonished ourselves – and then proceeded to do just that as we watched people descend from the bus high in the mountains with no sign of habitation anywhere. Still, if we hadn't ignored our own advice we would never have seen, revealed behind us, a fair-sized town clinging to the mountainside and providing the explanation for the recent mass exodus from the bus. Then we pulled into the busy streets of Tripolis and finally into the dark interior of the bus station.

'I'll go and get the next lot of tickets,' I said and crossed to the busy ticket desk. There, looking surprised but relieved that I spoke Greek, a charming, elderly man explained that the bus to Kalamata left from another place, five hundred metres down the street. So we set off and thundered our way across the cobbles, clearing all before us. But when we reached the place where the second bus station should have been we found only empty streets and a very enthusiastic taxi driver. He spoke to me in English, though later he was to deny he could speak any at all, and he began extolling the advantages of taking a forty-euro taxi ride to Kalamata instead of the bus. It all sounded very reasonable, and, having learnt by now that such offers in Greece mostly turn out to be genuine and are made for a good reason, I turned the conversation into Greek and made some more enquiries. Meanwhile, Sue was getting impatient.

'What's going on?' she demanded.

'Just a minute,' I replied.

'Just tell me what is going on!'

So I interrupted my conversation with the taxi driver, saying 'Give me a minute?' where-upon he walked away and dramatically turned his back on us.

I found myself laughing and I think that did it; a few minutes later, after waiting for a letter and passing on a few parcels for local delivery, we were off, Greek music on the radio, the sun shining and a new tarmac road stretching straight ahead. Any reservations we may have had quickly shot into the past. Our new friend was a good driver and a delightful travelling companion.

In no time at all, or so it seemed, we found ourselves at Kalamata bus station, a sleepy, relaxed place at this time in the afternoon, for even buses seem to stop during *mesi meri*. But there was a bus to Kardamyli at five o'clock, one we would have been far from certain of catching if we had waited for the bus in Tripolis, and so all was fine. We collapsed yet again into a *cafenion* and ordered omelettes, salad and a beer. While we waited for them to arrive, I wandered across to the bus-station shop and bought some requested *pastelli*. A local delicacy this, made from sesame seeds and honey and much enjoyed back on Poros.

For some inexplicable reason time never seems to drag at a Greek bus station. Try sitting for two hours in Leeds or Sheffield and you are soon reduced to a seething mass of anger and frustration, but outside a K-Tel depot even Sue assumes the patience of a saint and is content to drift in and out of conversation as the minutes slide by. The bus came and we jostled our way on to it and then settled back to enjoy what was the real start to this year's adventures!

For most of the journey we ran alongside the sea, the landscape quickly changing from town suburbs to more rural vistas. Small houses now with gardens, bougainvillaea masking the golden stone and geraniums a bright splash of colour everywhere. Eventually I spotted the sign for Kardamyli and nudged Sue awake. We got off at what luckily turned out to be the right place, and rattled off to find somewhere to stay. Rather to the surprise of both of us I had read up a little on Kardamyli and remembered the name of a *taverna* with studio apartments overlooking the sea. It turned out to be exactly where I had thought it would be and was delightful. There was one apartment empty. We took it. It was light, cool and friendly. Lemon trees framed the back balcony, while at the front the rocks grouped themselves round a small bay, the swell of the sea a constant sound as the waves rolled over them.

'I think we're going to like it here,' I said.

'Yes,' said Sue, busy unpacking copious jars that looked suspiciously like make-up.

But joy of joys, there were two wardrobes and plenty of coat hangers! We showered, delighted to find the bathroom surprisingly large and the plumbing capable of absorbing large amounts of water. There were no arguments and we soon found ourselves exploring the now darkening streets of a pretty little rural town. In the bookshop we found copies of that day's London Evening Standard and looked at one another in amazement but resisted the temptation to buy. We wandered on, leaving the major sight-seeing for the next day, and then returned to 'our' *taverna* to eat. We found it packed with people, not surprising really for the blue-gingham-clad tables looked appealing beneath the trees at the very edge of the sea. Still our luck held, however, for there was just one vacant table. We sat filled with satisfaction at the day's events, content to be exactly where we were, now some good food and a little wine was needed to complete the day; the only things awaiting our immediate attention. Later we sat on for a while talking of this and that until sleep crept around the edges of our conversation and drove us upstairs to bed.

Next morning my little travelling kettle provided us with that essential first coffee of the day and put us in an exploring frame of mind. But the day proved to have a slow start to it after all, for we had only got as far as the bus station café when a longing for fresh orange juice overtook us and it became necessary to watch the world go by for quite some time.

Eventually, however, curiosity overcame inertia and we set off up one of the little side-streets and began some serious exploring. It really was very pretty there and I soon began recognising houses and gardens from a recent television series. I also remembered that it was the place where Patrick Leigh Fermor now lived, so we stopped for a moment in the middle of the street and said our thank yous for all his much loved travel books, trusting that the message would reach him somehow! Then Sue found a signpost to the old town and a sliver of excitement entered our explorations.

Like most of the medieval sites in the Peloponnese it was set back from the sea. The ancient sites usually bordered the coastline, but in later times marauding fleets and pirates created a need for greater security, and the old town of Kardamyli was no exception.

Although not one of the greatest historical sites in Greece, it nevertheless afforded us an enjoyable solitary hour scrambling over the ruins and recreating for one another the lives of the long gone inhabitants. There were no ghosts here though, no disturbed spirits troubled our wanderings and it was only hunger that finally drove us down and back into the centre of the modern town.

We next explored a supermarket, came away with an unlikely selection of bits for lunch and then headed for the beach. Well, the large pebbles that passed for a beach that is – they were remarkably uncomfortable to sit on and impossible to hobble across to reach the sea. Optimists as always, however, we enjoyed having the bay to ourselves, and the view across the sea towards 'wherever' pushed us into philosophical mode and relaxed us completely. When we ate our lunch, the avocado pear proved to be something of a challenge, but hunger triumphed and we finally declared our improvised picnic to be the best yet! We then moved on to try and find a less painful path into the sea. We settled eventually on a group of rocks where Sue revelled in the sun and I huddled into a corner where one large stone partly protected my head. At least we were now able to bathe, and so we idled away a few more hours until it was time to return for our suitcases and the evening bus to Areopolis.

Back at the *taverna* there were signs of life as they began to set up for the evening. The *Kyria* (lady owner), was sitting outside peeling the small onions for the *stifado* (a type of beef stew) and we stopped for a while for a chat. She asked where we were from and then went on to say how many people she had met in the last few years, people from all over the world. She seemed unsurprised by it all though she, herself, had never been farther than Kalamata. They were open all year, she told us, a huge log fire replacing the heat of the sun in the winter months. She was good company and we experienced a pang of regret that we were leaving, we even thought briefly of returning to sit in front of that blazing fire one day, but for now we were keen to move on. Kardamyli was in the Outer Mani and we longed to be amongst the Maniot towers and the stark silhouettes of the Inner region. We wished one another well and headed back to the bus-station café.

We found it surprisingly busy.

'Shall we sit on this wall here, Dave?' said an unmistakable English voice cutting through the tranquillity of the sleepy town centre. This was followed by the more guttural sounds of Swedish and German. It was some time before we realised that we were all waiting for the same bus! It arrived pretty much on time and I handed our suitcases to the conductor.

'Where are you going?' he asked.

'Areopolis.'

He nodded and we scrambled aboard. A little while later he came round with the tickets.

'Two to Areopolis,' I demanded confidently.

'We don't go to Areopolis,' he said, and handed me two tickets. I looked at Sue and we both shrugged. I paid.

'Where are you going?' I enquired, curiously.

'Oitylo,' came the reply, and he moved on.

Out came our maps.

'Ah, there,' said Sue, 'it's not far from Areopolis.'

'Well, we'll see what happens then.'

'Yes,' said Sue, and we settled back to enjoy the journey.

For a time we ran along the coast and through a series of pretty fishing villages grouped round tiny bays, but when we arrived at the tourist resort of Stupa, modern apartment blocks and fast-food restaurants clustered round the edge of the road instead. We stopped and parted from most of our travelling companions, losing all the intriguing snippets of conversation that had been coming our way since we left Kardamyli. Only a few local Greeks, two Polish girls and Sue and I still sat hopefully on the bus.

Once out of Stupa we quickly changed back to the rhythm of rural Greece. The bus started to climb now and the softer landscape was replaced with low scrub and stumpy, wind-blasted trees. The sea re-appeared from time to time, a blue carpet far away, glittering now and again as the setting sun caught its surface and sprinkled it with a million fragments of golden light. By the time we dropped into Oitylo the light was fading fast. We got out of the bus – Sue, I, and the two Polish girls – and stood looking hopefully along the empty street. The bus turned and left. Silence fell and the two Polish girls walked on in to town.

At the bend of the road there was a small *cafenion* where two or three men sat by the door and watched us carefully. No one moved.

'I'll go and ask about a taxi,' I said, and parking Sue and the luggage at the side of the road, I walked up to the group and smiled sweetly. 'A taxi?'

They nodded.

'Stelios, where is Stelios?' the name leaked round the bend of the road and disappeared down the sloping street. I heard no reply but there must have been one for after a few minutes I was regretfully informed that, unfortunately, Stelios was not working that day, and silence fell again.

'Maybe we could have one from Areopolis?' I ventured.

'Ah yes,' they said, 'go to the *cafenion* round the corner.'

So I went. As I turned the corner I looked back. Sue was standing in the middle of the road in a long, shocking-pink dress and a silk, lavender pashmina was now draped across her shoulders. At the little café every eye was upon her but she stood oblivious, like a diva.

I smiled and crossed to the second café. Yes, they would telephone, and then, later, yes, the taxi was coming, and no, they did not want any money for the phone call. Hands were placed on hearts and smiles travelled from table to table. I turned to leave.

'But stay here' they went on, it's beautiful here.' And indeed it was and worthy of further exploration, but we had already determined to visit the famous caves at Dirgos the next day, and were unsure of the times of the buses from Areopolis. With our penchant for lazy starts to the day it seemed silly to take the risk, so, pleading the half truth of a rendezvous, I regretfully declined the invitation and returned to Sue with the good news.

I found her 'talking' to a small, elderly lady in black.

'Help!' said Sue, so I joined them to discover the problem. It was no problem, only that the lady wished to invite us to her house for a coffee, or something to eat, or to stay if we wished. There was to be no question of payment. I translated for Sue and we were both touched by her generosity, but I explained about the taxi and that, regretfully, we had to decline the hospitality. She returned to her house and we moved back to the suitcases. But a few minutes later we turned to find her crossing the street again, this time with a plate of biscuits. They were the ones baked for special occasions and often taken to the church.

'Please take one, each of you,' she said. 'I am a widow, but yesterday would have been my husband's birthday and I baked them for him. I live by myself now and it is lonely without him. It has been so nice to talk.'

We found ourselves close to tears for it was impossible to imagine her life as a widow now in this small town deep in the Mani. Maybe for one brief moment we almost understood, but it would be a life so different from any that we had known that we could not hold on to that understanding. I think part of us wanted to stay then, but in truth it was with something approaching relief that we saw our taxi twisting its way down the mountain road. We said our second goodbyes and got in but our driver was in a convivial frame of mind so we stopped for several chats with the villagers before we finally shot off to Areopolis.

We were quickly there and it felt good to be back. Once in the main square, we saluted the statue of Mavromichaelis and walked down to the hotel where we had stayed before. We had long been savouring the thought of two nights in our Maniot tower and we strode confidently up to the door. The young man was as charming as before, but he was sorry to have to tell us that the hotel was full for the whole week! He mentioned accommodation behind the church, and so, once again leaving Sue with the luggage, I set off to see what I could find.

I found a sign saying '*Rooms and Museum*' and suitably intrigued I opened what seemed to be the main door and went in. Sitting opposite me was a lady on a mobile phone surrounded by the most amazing collection of old Maniot furniture and antiques. I was considerably taken aback. I don't know what I had expected to find, but it was certainly not this. The phone conversation continued and I looked around the room. At either end were two enormous glass cases, packed with guns of all shapes and sizes: pistols with inlaid mother-of-pearl, sporting rifles and others of a more substantial nature. In the bottom of each case there were hand-grenades and other bits and bobs of a lethal kind. I stood transfixed until the phone conversation came to an end and I was greeted warmly. Yes, there was a room would I like to see it? I would. I was taken across a small paved courtyard, fringed with lemon trees and flowering shrubs, and shown a large room with a television, fridge, phone and huge bathroom. Would I like to take it? I would! And I set off back to retrieve Sue.

We took it for two nights and quickly settled in, experiencing again that warm sense of security that surrounds all travellers once they have arrived somewhere and found an agreeable place to stay.

We showered and changed and crossed back into the main room. Our landlady greeted us cheerfully and showed us round her collection. It was all from her family she hastened to assure us and she knew the history of everything. On a more practical level, she also knew the times of all the buses and exactly where they went, so our next day's adventures were easily sorted before we left to eat.

We went back to the same street *taverna* as before and were joined by a large, complacent tom-cat. We fantasised that it was the little kitten from two years ago, and then decided that it was quite possible that it was. I don't remember what we ate, but it would have been something off the grill. I think Sue was disappointed that there were no stuffed tomatoes, for they had temporarily become the latest fad. It was busy there and at the next table was a group from a television series; obviously they were filming in the area, which explained why the hotels were full. Again the food and the wine made us sleepy and we quickly returned to our beds, inadvertently waking up our landlady in the process.

Unusually, we both slept fitfully, taking it in turns to wake up and creep off to the loo! It was a relief when dawn elbowed her way through the shutters and we could plug in the electric kettle and make a very early cup of coffee. We had another slow start to the day for our bus for the caves did not leave until eleven o'clock; this meant that when we finally left the apartment our washing was hanging tranquilly on the line in the courtyard and our room was uncharacteristically tidy.

Back in the square a busy Saturday market was in progress. For a while we went our separate ways and then met up again to enjoy the drama – provided, we felt, for our entertainment and delight – as we sat drinking another fresh orange juice and waited for the bus.

When it finally arrived and we were comfortably ensconced, we were treated to another unexpected pantomime. This time it was provided by our driver who had decided to ignore the accepted method of turning the bus around and go for a circular trip around the four sides of the square instead. This started out as a successful venture until we turned the third corner and disaster struck. We became inextricably enmeshed in the strings tying the awnings to the market stalls and were forced to a halt. All work stopped abruptly and many willing rescuers ran towards us proffering a wide range of advice. For a time there was chaos, voices became raised, hands waved in all directions and the stall holders' language became bluer and bluer. After some attempts at negotiation our driver finally grew tired of it all and simply drove off, breaking the strings and leaving one stallholder enveloped in his own awning. There was a wave of laughter as we sped out of the square and into the countryside.

We reached the caves and were soon balanced precariously

in one of the flat-bottomed boats that was to take us on our tour. Alas, we had not been seated diplomatically weight-wise, and the boat rocked alarmingly. As there were only about two feet of water between us and the floor of the cave I was not too worried, but Sue was less than happy and clutched me every time we turned a corner. I pointed out the depth of the water, but this did little to reassure her and I began to be as nervous as she was. Our boatman and guide showed little enthusiasm for his work and shouted at us constantly as he bounced the boat off the sides of the caves. The stalactites and stalagmites were indeed spectacular but nevertheless it was a great relief to reach terra firma once more and head out into the sunlight.

We wandered down to the beach and sat alone under one of the beach umbrellas. The weather turned cloudy but still we sat on, looking like something out of an Italian Art House movie. Eventually it dawned on us that we were not really enjoying ourselves, so we returned to the ticket kiosk where they kindly phoned for a taxi.

Back in Areopolis it was the middle of *mesi meri* with only one *cafenion* open to provide us with a toasted sandwich and a shared beer. We sat next to a group of itinerant Albanians and provided them with a topic of conversation for a while, and then, embracing the principle of 'when in Rome…' we tottered down the street bent on a siesta of our own. On the way, we passed an open pâtisserie and decided to treat ourselves to something really sinful for later. After a lengthy conversation covering all the usual topics of 'where', 'how' and 'when', we emerged from the shop clutching our two purchased cakes and two others as gifts. We pondered for a while on what passed as commercialism in the Mani, but soon gave in to the demands of sleep, leaving the cakes sitting, untouched, in the fridge!

By early evening we were refreshed and off out to explore the parts unknown of Areopolis. We were in for a surprise, however, for there was a large area we had not seen before – beautifully restored hotels and modern shops selling hand-painted glass and other up-market souvenirs, all in sharp contrast to the still rural part of the old town that embraced the more traditional small houses and farms. Then hunger overtook us and we returned to the restaurant we had chosen earlier, only to miss the last vacant table by seconds. So it was back to one of the older *taverna*s in the square where, happily, there were some fine-looking stuffed tomatoes and Sue declared herself content. Then it started to rain, seriously, so it was back to bed for our early start the next morning.

It was still raining when we awoke, and our landlady was most upset on our behalf. We professed not to be too put out ourselves and explained that our British background encouraged fortitude in these situations. Then we paid our bill, spoke enthusiastically of a return visit, admired the guns one last time and, sharing our sole umbrella, mine, set off for the main square yet again.

We were heading for Gerolimenos, a small town on the bottom of the Mani, on one of those three fingers at the end of the Peloponnese, and we hardly expected the bus station to be busy, but it was. We also noticed a marked change since our last visit. People talked to us and were delighted when I spoke Greek. Information and advice were quickly forthcoming, often unsolicited. The Mani had had a reputation of being closed, unfriendly almost, and indeed we had found evidence of this the last time we were there, but now things seemed different. Tourism was obviously bringing changes – or were there just fewer Maniots in the Mani? I was once told that I would find more in Kolonaki Square in Athens than in the Mani itself. I simply didn't know, but the influx of foreign residents, especially German, seemed to be reaching alarming proportions and there were certainly more souvenir shops. But surely those vendettas were not really lost for ever, buried amongst the cares and tribulations of new tax systems or the arrival of the tourists and affluence inconceivable only a few short years before? I didn't think so. The Greeks are a passionate race and jealousy is a fatal flaw in all of us. Perhaps there was some sort of truce, but somehow it was easier to imagine everything still smouldering below the surface; sudden deaths, though infrequent now, are not unknown there even today.

'Would you like to live here?' asked Sue.

'It would be impossible,' I replied. 'You would never be anything other than a foreigner here.'

'Yes,' said Sue, 'I can see that'.

In the paper shop we found that day's British Sunday papers, the more popular ones anyhow, containing pages and pages of celebrity gossip, and self-righteous reports on so-called scandals. Somewhere around page 24 there was a small article on the 'imminent' war with Iraq. It all seemed remote and unreal – the Americans now anxious to remove with the 'utmost prejudice' the man they had helped to power only a few short years ago; Bush continuing his own personal war against terrorism and ignoring America's dubious activities throughout South America and Asia. And Blair trotting after him like a puppy dog. From a small Greek *cafenion* the world seemed an unnecessarily tragic place, unnecessarily complicated too.

Our bus finally opened its doors and in the flurry of activity that followed we pushed such considerations into the background and concentrated on finding our seats and settling in. Finding specific seats had never been necessary before, but when we looked at our tickets we saw that they had numbers on them that corresponded to the numbers on the seats. We looked around the bus. Some people were taking this seriously, others not. What to do? We adopted the Greek solution, did nothing and remained in our seats undisturbed as the bus pushed its way through the rain and sped off down the newly tarmacked road that had not existed when Patrick Leigh Fermor wrote his book.

Again we were the only foreigners aboard, and very soon virtually the only passengers; only two Greek men rode with us now and no one spoke.

The rain continued to pour down, the colours so drained

from the landscape that even the groups of towers, usually so dramatic on the skyline, seemed barely visible. There were some new buildings, all constructed in the traditional manner but looking sadly in need of mellowing. Once I glimpsed a group of towers, the sea their background and with a solitary shaft of sunlight lying across them. I heard myself gasp as I saw them and one of the Greek men saw my reaction and smiled to himself. Then suddenly we were in Gerolimenos and decisions had to be made.

The rain had eased slightly but black storm clouds stretched way out to sea. The bus (the same one) would leave for Gytheion in two hours, and Gytheion was where we next wanted to go. So reluctantly deciding against staying the night there we left our cases on the bus and headed for the sea-front *taverna*.

Inside it was full of groups of men eating roast pork, so we settled for one of the outdoor harbour tables, protected from the rain by large plastic awnings. One or two other tourists sat there already, and we were joined by the man from the bus who listened to my Greek and then proceeded to speak fluent American! He sat briefly on one of the chairs and then suddenly picked up his belongings and disappeared. We never saw him again.

As our food arrived, so did the wind on the edge of the storm. Tables blew over, awnings pulled at their strings and chairs danced across the street. We fled inside, taking our food with us, and settled at a small corner table. The food was delicious, the weather whetting our appetite and sharpening our sense of taste.

The *taverna* appeared to be run by two brothers. There was no sign of a woman anywhere. Once our presence had ceased to disturb the easy flow of male conversation we all relaxed. Sue and I chattered between ourselves, but watched slyly as the people at the other tables swapped tales and arguments. At one point something deeply offensive must have been said, for people started shouting and one brother was extremely upset.

It was a while before it was smoothed over and the atmosphere in the *taverna* returned to normal. As our bus driver was involved we were more than usually interested, but he was sitting far away by the door and we failed to discover what it was all about. The *taverna* was also the ticket office for the bus so we had a preview of our future travelling companions.

For nearly two hours the rain streamed relentlessly down, but I was loath to leave the little town without seeing something of it, so, on an impulse I grabbed the umbrella and walked around the edge of the bay into what must have been the original centre. Here the houses were in good repair, small and clustered together – though only two storeys high for the winters are wild down here. But glimpses through the shutters showed huge fireplaces and rich curtains and hangings. The old furniture of the Mani was still in use and I wouldn't have been surprised to see more cases of guns, pistols and hand-grenades! Meanwhile, glimpses of the sea revealed an angry grey swell, and as the sky was dark too, it was almost impossible to see where one ended and the other began. I turned and walked back to the bus. Sue joined me and we climbed aboard as it turned and headed back along the way we had come. There were few other passengers and again, unusual for Greece, no one seemed disposed to talk. Sue snoozed quietly and I searched greedily for a sight of the Maniot towers that I had missed on the way down. The rain showed no inclination to stop.

We, however, did. An old man stood at the side of the road with a woman and a dog beside him. The bus came to a standstill and the woman got on. You knew there was a tragedy here, for the woman was nervous and ill at ease and the atmosphere on the bus changed dramatically. I could not hear what was being said and I never learned her story but another passenger spoke to her and she seemed reassured. She was dressed in black, the clothes new, so I guessed at a death of some kind, but as the miles sped by I lost interest in her and almost dozed myself.

The journey took on an unreal quality, the scenery blurred through the rain- splattered windows and the light was that of an English winter evening. Seconds ran into minutes, then into hours, and then we started to leave the rain behind. Not long after, we reached the outskirts of Gytheion. The road now ran alongside the sea, a straggle of houses and holiday apartment blocks on the other side. I saw one with a sign advertising '*All Rooms with a Zimmer*', and pointed out to Sue that that might be for us before long! In the event we settled into the Aktaion Hotel not far from the bus station. It was rather upmarket for us on this trip, but we felt we deserved it, for storm clouds still rolled along the edges of the sea.

Our balcony was on the front, overlooking the bay, and when the sun briefly put in an appearance, we sat aloft watching the busy sea-front and the fishing boats heading out of the harbour. We could see a street market behind the bus station and finally curiosity pulled us out and into the street to check it out. It was a big market, selling everything from clothes to household goods to toys, but many of the things were imported and most of the stallholders were Bulgarian or Ukrainian. Unlike the country markets in Athens or Piraeus there was little atmosphere, none of the *kefi* that makes shopping such fun. The stallholders talked amongst themselves, and when we tried to buy something they showed little interest in encouraging our custom. Only the gypsies called after us, their brightly coloured rugs and carpets piled across the street, though why they thought two such obvious tourists should wish to burden themselves with heavy things of that kind remained a tribute to wild optimism!

We sat for a while eating banana ice-cream and drinking coffee and then returned to the hotel to plan our evening. Later we set out in good heart only to have our progress somewhat curtailed when we came across an antique shop and decided, recklessly, to 'just have a look'! Still, I was delighted with my purchases! Two new copper mugs, unlike anything I already had – one was shaped like a large teacup, the other like a beer tankard, and they look very nice on my coffee table as I write this. There was also a silver-plated bracelet, circa 1900, genuine according to Takis who knows about these things, though probably made in Ioannina in Northern Greece, but never mind. Buying them took some time, however, as we had to wait while the shop-owner read a large selection of his poems to two visiting friends, so it was already dark when we finally started to climb one of the side-streets to see what else we could find.

The road we chose ran steeply up-hill. On one side there were fine old houses three or four storeys high, all with their original iron balconies. On the harbour side of the road, the ground dropped sharply, the houses there low and sprawling, often on two or three levels. Sue was greatly taken with the tall balconied houses.

'This is where I'm going to buy my house in Greece,' she said, and so we spent a happy hour deciding which one she would buy, how she would restore it (most of them needed a lot of work), what colour she would paint it and how she would furnish it. We were laughing a lot, rather to the amusement of the local residents passing us in the street, but no one seemed to mind and they often called out a greeting or smiled to themselves as they walked on.

Finally we grew tired of our game and we walked back down to the harbour in search of an *Ouzeria* (a bar selling a wide variety of ouzos and snacks). This, never being difficult to find in Greece, was soon spotted and we sat high above the sea watching the little coloured boats bobbing below us. It started to rain again, but only lightly, so we sat on under yet another awning and enjoyed our *mezere*. Then, just as we were finishing eating the rain came back in earnest. We paid and hopped, skipped and jumped our way over the flooding streets and back into the hotel.

We were both dozing nicely when my mobile phone jolted us awake. 'When are you coming back?' it said. Poros, already on the edges of our minds, pushed its way into the present.

Next morning found us early at the bus station. Our bus was, we thought, going to Athens via Tripolis, but it appeared to be full of students returning to university and families heading back for the new school term. We were put on another. 'No problem,' they said, but you must change at Sparta!' Sue and I looked at one another and started laughing. There was no avoiding it after all, the Sparta bus station was back as part of our itinerary! In a way it all seemed quite fitting. We were not there for long, there was just time to check on the one upside-down tile in the foyer and then they were calling our bus. We were among the first on and sat chatting away until a Greek lady marched up to us and informed us we were sitting in her seat. She waved her ticket and pointed at the number it bore. We produced our numberless tickets, apologised and moved. She settled herself down importantly, obviously feeling she had won some sort of major war. After a few minutes two more travellers arrived and the scene was repeated. At this point a charming and extremely good-looking student explained that most seats were pre-booked and we must wait until everybody was on board and then take two of the still empty seats.

'Ah!' I said. 'A new system.'

'No,' he replied. 'A Greek system.'

So we stood chatting, both Sue and I wishing we were at least twenty years younger, for he was a delightful young man!

Eventually, seated comfortably, we were off, but before very long we were pulling up at the stop in Tripolis. We said a reluctant goodbye to our student friend, who now spoke fluent English, wished each other a good winter, and descended the steps of the bus directly into the arms of our earlier taxi driver!

'Ah!' he exclaimed, recognising us instantly. 'Where are you going now?'

'Naplion.'

'Come, we go together for twenty euros.'

There seemed no point in arguing, and, pausing only to collect another passenger, we were soon speeding on our way. Now we had to tell him where we had been and what we had done and the time passed quickly. Then the mobile phone rang. It was another friend wanting to know when we were coming back. Poros was really re-entering our lives, the little holiday was coming to an end.

The taxi climbed up the mountain road and turned a corner. Now the bay of Naplion lay at our feet, the sea stretching to infinity and giving us one final new image to take back with us for the winter. Then we dropped into the town. Once in Naplion we said goodbye to 'our' driver, resisted his offers to take us back to Galatas, and returned yet again to the café by the old fort. Then it was the now familiar journey back to Galatas and Poros. It was all over for another year.

That evening the *pastelli* was received enthusiastically. We ate enormous platefuls of fried prawns and spaghetti marinara. Someone was glad we were back. And so was I. To quote Frank Sinatra, It's nice to go travelling, but it's oh so very nice to come home!

Chapter Five

TRIPS ON THE *ANNA II*

•

I don't remember exactly how I came to be working on the *Anna II* cruise boat but I do know that before long I was thoroughly enjoying myself and feeling very much a part of the family who owned and ran her.

From the very first few trips we got on so well, which was nothing short of a miracle really for I spoke no Greek and they spoke no English. I did eventually teach Eleni to say 'mineral water' and 'vegetarian' and the captain finally came up with quite a number of nautical terms, but I think what really bonded us together was the fact that we were all blessed with a highly developed sense of the ridiculous and if in doubt we simply fell about laughing – and there were quite a few opportunities for that.

Inevitably, working on the boat, we quickly created little rituals and one of mine was to sample a roast potato whenever they were brought up from the ovens prior to serving. This particular day in Spetses was no exception but rather than getting my hand slapped as usual I found three pairs of eyes anxiously watching my reaction.

'Are they good Anna?' asked Eleni, somewhat over casually. I took a careful bite.

'They've got sugar in them,' I said.

'Sssh!' came the reply. 'What can we do? Mitsos put sugar in them instead of salt and we have only just found out.'

'O.K.' I said, laughing 'we don't say anything. They won't hurt anyone, so we'll just wait and see what happens.'

We served lunch and then I walked around the boat to see if the passengers were happy. We always got one or two requests for Eleni's potato recipe but this day we were overwhelmed. Everyone loved them and thought they were the most amazing-tasting potatoes ever. I just smiled and agreed that Eleni was a very, very good cook.

As you have most probably realised by now Eleni is not exactly a stereotypical Greek wife. She is full of fun and between us, as the captain often complains with a twinkle in his eye, we succeed in making his life very difficult, especially in mid-summer when we are all very tired and irritable. We, however, think that he is a very lucky man.

The first time we made the trip to the Corinth Canal from Aegina we were all a bit nervous and very much on our best behaviour. We left Poros at six-thirty in the morning and arrived exactly on time to pick up the passengers at Aghia Marina. From there we proceeded in stately fashion to the Isthmus of Corinth and then through the canal. We went on to dock in Loutraki for a while before sailing back effortlessly through the canal to the isthmus again. From the isthmus we went to Angistri, from Angistri to Aegina and from Aegina we set off back to Poros; everything had been perfect.

As we sailed back into the harbour at Poros, I woke up the sleeping Eleni and said, delighted to be back, 'Look, look, Poros.'

'Poros?' questioned Eleni. 'Oh, Praise the Lord, he's found it at last!'

Surprisingly, perhaps, it is rare for any of our passengers to get drunk on the boat though they obviously enjoy a few beers or some wine during the day, but on one particular occasion there were three Scandinavian men who started drinking before the boat left the harbour and went hard at it all the way down to Spetses. They were absolutely no problem, and apart from a tendency to lurch as they walked around and a penchant for falling on the other passengers from time to time, they were perfectly well behaved.

I happened to be sitting by the bar when one of them arrived, propped himself up and ordered a coffee and a sandwich. I smiled in encouragement, thinking that it was a sensible move – and then watched in amazement as he took the coffee and sandwich, lurched heavily and sent them spiralling down the hatch into the kitchen. I grabbed him just in time to prevent him following and then heard a horrendous series of crashes followed by total silence. After what seemed an eternity, Eleni appeared half-way up the stairs covered in coffee, an empty cup in one hand and a broken saucer in the other.

'Oops,' she said, 'what's happening?'

The tourist fled. In his inebriated state he must have thought her to be some ghostly apparition come to haunt him, for he was remarkably quiet for the rest of the day and never came near the bar again.

As far as I can gather, by far the biggest problem the tourists encounter on their fearless sallies abroad is the troublesome question of toilets. Basically in Greece there are few, if any, public conveniences of the type known and loved by the Northern European tourists. If any do exist they tend to be of the 'hole in the ground' variety so deeply abhorred by our foreign visitors. I must confess myself to be perplexed by this attitude. But over the years I have been forced into admitting that it is a genuine anathema

We do have lavatories aboard the *Anna II*. In fact we have two, one on either side of the entrance to the bar. For quite a long time there was nothing to indicate which was for the ladies and which was for the gents, and I thought this perfectly sensible, for the toilets were identical and as far as I was aware the foreign visitors did not have signs on the relevant doors in their own homes. Anyhow, weren't the Scandinavians supposed to be pretty open about sex, etc? Well, sex maybe, but seemingly not toilets.

So eventually two little signs were bought and screwed on and all was well. The next season, on the first trip, I checked our signs were still in place, found they were and congratulated myself on starting the new season in what looked like a highly organised boat. Alas, the gods must have been listening for we were hardly out of the harbour when a lady came to me with tears in her eyes.

'There are no locks on the toilet doors,' she said.

My heart sank for I knew the captain and his family had been working on the *Anna* all winter. As far as he was concerned the boat was finished. Getting locks on the lavatory doors was not going to be easy and I wasn't even sure my Greek was up to it. I assured the lady that the matter would be dealt with as soon as possible (liar!) and spent the rest of the voyage with my fingers crossed. All went well till we got to Hydra, but there disaster struck.

Hydra has a very small harbour and these days we are only allowed in it for two or three minutes in order to let off the passengers. That particular day we were being severely pressed by the Port Police to get out of the way for a large ferryboat was heading rapidly towards us, bent on coming into the same mooring. I always warn the passengers that they must be ready to disembark and I thought that they were all off. Tassos ran round checking the boat and, just in case, banged open the toilet doors – only to find a very large lady sitting there, her knickers around her ankles. To say that he was deeply shocked would be an understatement and the next day the locks were on the lavatory doors. It's an ill wind, so to speak.

One of the nice things about the *Anna II* enterprise is the chance it gives us to meet so many different people. Of course, we don't like everybody and there are some days we heave a sigh of relief as the last tourist walks down the ramp and off into Poros. But mostly we all get on fine. A vast number of people really do come back to Poros year after year and most make it on to the boat. Indeed, sometimes people come back especially for one of the trips and that gives us a great boost. Our biggest fan, I think, is Howard. He loves the *Anna* above all things and his dream is to buy her (and us!) and take her back to Liverpool and put her on the Mersey. He hasn't managed to do it yet but he hasn't given up hope. Howard is confined to a wheelchair but he and his mum come every year with a selection of friends and relatives to help with the complications of getting here. He says the *Anna* gives him the freedom to do things he never thought possible – and to see him at the back of the boat watching the dolphins play or the seagulls sweep past the stern is to see someone pretty close to paradise.

He is also extremely fond of Eleni's cake, though he's not the only one. On the days she bakes it (especially if she knows Howard's in town) it always disappears very quickly and I have to move very fast if I fancy a piece myself. Time after time it arrives on the *Anna* a veritable perfection of a cake, filling the air with the smells of home-cooking. But there was one particular morning when something was wrong. We don't talk much on the *Anna* for the first hour or so but Eleni's eyes were doing a very good job of warning of some disaster or other (though not, I felt, life threatening, for there was a hint of laughter there too).

'What is it?' I asked.

'Eleni's cake is not good,' she replied. 'Eleni's cake is flat.' She was not wrong. In looks it resembled more a slab of shortbread than a cake. 'What shall we do, Anna, we can't sell it.'

I thought long and hard and then broke off a piece and ate it thoughtfully. It tasted great.' This,' I said, 'is obviously an island speciality cooked to an ancient recipe passed on from Eleni's grandmother. Of course we can sell it.'

So we did.

And now it's time to pick up the microphone and say, 'Good morning ladies and gentlemen. On behalf of Captain Kiriakos and the crew, I'd like to welcome you aboard the *Anna*. Sit back and relax. It's time for a little history. Don't worry, it won't hurt!'

The section that follows consists of some of the talks I gave on the *Anna II* as we were sailing around the Saronic Gulf. They stand out a little strangely from the rest of the book but are included because so many of our passengers have asked for them to be made available. In fact it was on the insistence of these same passengers that I started to write the book at all, and then found myself staring in amazement as, like Topsy, it just 'growed and growed'!

•

Around Poros

The *Anna II* is not the only Poros boat to offer trips around the island, indeed the other two, the Two Brothers and the Giorgia Star are perhaps more suited to this trip, for they are traditional wooden boats and rather more romantic. But we use our trip as a chance to slow down the new arrivals, put them on to Greek time, and also give them a taste of the local history and a feel for the island which is to be their home for the next few days. We usually go on a Monday, all freshly stocked up with Eleni's hamburgers and oven-roasted potatoes. It's an easy laid-back, five-hour, trip and the people love it.

Anyhow, as we sail slowly alongside the harbour front towards the old abattoir it gives me a chance to tell people that the ancient name of Poros was Eirene, or Peace, and this was the name which survived until eighth or ninth century BC. Later the island adopted the name of Poros or Passage, possibly after the water strait between the island and the mainland. This water strait was so shallow until the last century that it was possible to walk across it from Galatas. In the early part of the twentieth century however, it was dug out to accommodate the big passenger boats, and so nowadays we must use the little water taxis if we want to go to the mainland. Poros is in fact two islands. The smaller one, that has on it the present-day harbour and old town, is known as Spheria and is said to be named after King Spherus who is thought to have been buried here. The second and larger island is called Kalavria, which translates as Fair Breeze, and is a name which may be linked to the pastoral god Kalavrian Apollo, who carried a shepherd's crook and was known to have been worshipped on the island. But whatever the sources of its names there is no doubt that Poros, together with the city state of Troezen (more later), was an important site in ancient Greece, and the area has continued to pop up throughout history right up to the present day.

As we leave the harbour behind and turn the corner (if one can do that on a boat), we see the trees of the Lemonodassos spread thickly across the lower reaches of the mountains of the mainland. This is the biggest lemon-growing area in Greece and lemons were until quite recently an essential part of the local economy. With the advent of tourism the importance of the region has declined and instead it has become a delightful excursion you can make for yourselves. Take a taxi boat across to Plaka or Aliki beach or stroll out along the coast road from Galatas. Eventually the road winds inland and begins to go uphill. Carry on walking until you come to a small church on the right-hand side of the road and there you will find a donkey track disappearing into the lemon groves. There may well be a signpost saying '*Taverna*' but even if this has blown down or is not in evidence you should follow the donkey track up the mountainside and then, just as you are beginning to get really thirsty and wish you had stayed on the beach, you will find yourself on the threshold of a *taverna*. Ah, you think, water.! But no, you want lemonade, for here they make their own lemonade from the local lemons and it is delicious. Before the arrival of electricity they used to cool it under the waterfall but nowadays it is kept in the fridge. The waterfall is still there though and also some mysterious caves where the partisans are said to have taken refuge from the occupying Germans during the Second World War. Ask anyone in the *taverna* and they will show you to where they are. When you have eaten and drunk to your satisfaction come back down the mountain and collapse into the welcoming sea until it is time to catch the little boat back to Poros, taking with you some delightful memories of views across the Saronic Gulf and the friendly family who run the *taverna*.

But the *Anna* has sailed on by now, passing the little island of Bourtzi on which are the remains of a nineteenth century Venetian fort. There is something vaguely sinister about this island and hardly anyone goes there. It is rumoured to be full of snakes but there are other rumours too for Greece has a turbulent history and Poros is no exception. Appearing on the left-hand side of the boat we can see Askeli Bay, now in summer bustling with tourists, and its sea-front *taverna*s just opening for the first of the mid-day customers. Only a few years ago this was a tiny fishing village with shepherds and their flocks roaming the mountainsides. I was told that, also during the Second World War, a group of five women ran the only radio station for the Allies in the area. I met one of them in Spetses; another was Metaxas' daughter who lived on Poros until her death quite recently. There are ghosts there too, a band of troubadours who tread the coast road playing their music and singing gaily; and up the river-bed road and way into the pine trees there is said to be yet another ghost, someone who was murdered and wanders unhappily, seeking the peace he cannot find.

But the sun is shining too brightly for ghosts so from the deck of the *Anna* let us follow the coast road up to the Monastery of Zoodochos Pigi. This is a lovely walk and one you should do by road, walking in the footsteps of George Seferis, the Greek poet and Nobel Prize winner for literature in 1963, who was a frequent visitor to the island. Before his death in Athens in 1971 he claimed that the walk to the monastery was his favourite on the island and was one he never grew tired of making.

The original monastery was founded by the Metropolitan of Athens in the mid seventeenth century, after he was cured of gallstones by drinking water from the sacred spring; the spring is still to be found by the little church of *Aghia Anagiri*, just outside the monastery grounds. It is also claimed that a silver icon of the Virgin Mary was found here and provided the exact location for the larger church. Inside this church is a fine wooden screen, said to have been carved in Cappadocia in

Asia Minor, and some fine icons of the Virgin and Child thought to have been painted by the Italian artist Raphael Ceccioli in 1853. Rumour has it that the bones of the ancient orator Demosthenes (more of him later) were moved here from the Temple of Poseidon at the top of the island, though they are now lost without trace.

As you stand outside in the little courtyard, look up into the giant cypress for during the Second World War some intrepid Greek resistance fighters hid in its branches while the Germans searched fruitlessly below. As they searched they probably trod on the tombstone of one Bradnell J. Bruce, a foot soldier who accompanied His Majesty's Ambassador to Poros during the Greek War of Independence. After travelling all this way, the poor man had the misfortune to die of a local fever on 8 October 1828. I often pause at his grave to assure him he is not forgotten.

As you leave the monastery, look across the sea and down to the beach *tavernas*; it is easy to imagine the excitement caused by the arrival of the boat from Piraeus that used to dock here daily, bringing people and goods from Athens on a voyage made pleasant by the live orchestra on board which played classical music. Ahead now is little Modi or Lion Island. From here it looks like a lion couchant – hence, its name. It is said to be the site of a powerful Mycenaean naval station but it is so small it is difficult to imagine how this could be true. Nowadays, like Bourtzi, it is also said to be over-run by snakes.

The *Anna* turns another corner now and there is Aegina silhouetted against the lighter shapes of the mainland. We are sailing at the back of Kalavria past a series of rocky inlets covered in the rough scrub that loves to attack bare legs. The mountain above us is Profitis Ilias and is the site of the ancient city of Poros. This area was first inhabited in tenth century BC.

The ancient city was actually built on the slopes of Mount Profitis Ilias and extended down to the bay of Vaygonia. The Temple of Poseidon was its crowning glory and stood on the summit of the mountain above the ancient harbour. This

Doric temple was built around 520 BC, originally with twelve columns. A limestone stoa was added in 420 BC and this was followed by others in 370, 350 and 320 BC. It was well known throughout ancient Greece and scholars have made frequent reference to it over the centuries.

In the mid-seventh century BC the Council of Kalavria was formed. Also known as the *Amphictyon* of Kalavria, its seat was in the eighth century temple. It was a naval, religious and political federation that sought to control a large area of the Saronic Gulf. Among its members were Athens, Aegina, Epidaurus, Ermione and Naplion. It reached its zenith around 459 BC but continued to function until the third century BC.

At the beginning of the fifth century BC, the Persian invasion began and the citizens of Troezen sent five ships to the Battle of Artemesian. This city state of Troezen was situated on the mainland opposite Poros and is known to have given shelter to the women and children of Athens during the Persian Wars. In 431 BC the Peloponnesian war began between Athens and Sparta. Now the Troezinians sided with Sparta against Athens and took part in the attacks on that city. This war lasted until 404 BC and virtually destroyed the magnificence that was at the heart of that great city of ancient Greece.

By this time the Temple of Poseidon had become something of a sanctuary, and was well known throughout the area. In 322 BC Demosthenes, the great orator, sought refuge here after he had been implicated in a bribery scandal in Athens, though there is considerable doubt as to his guilt. The situation at the time was so serious that when they came to arrest him he committed suicide by swallowing poison concealed in his pen, first leaving the temple in order to avoid desecrating the sanctuary.

Demosthenes was one of the great orators of ancient Greece. Afflicted with a terrible stutter, he walked along the seashore as a young man, shouting above the waves with his mouth filled with pebbles. He continued doing this until he overcame his handicap. Pausanias recalls seeing his tomb in the temple in the second century, but now it is difficult to place for, alas, little remains of this important site today. In 1760 most of the stones were removed to Hydra on the authority of the archbishop there and used to build a monastery. It is also rumoured that quite a few of the stones helped to build some of the older houses in Poros town – which is quite likely.

There is a bust of Demosthenes opposite the petrol station where the three roads meet. Unsurprisingly, there is a story about this statue! After I had visited Poros for the first time I was clearing out a high shelf in my flat in London getting ready for some building work. This shelf held a number of books I had inherited from my grandmother and included some rather nice early editions of novels like Jane Eyre – books my grandmother had declared to be 'racy', thus engendering in my breast an early and abiding interest in the classics. Amongst these novels was a largish book entitled *People of Poros*. I nearly fell off the stepladder and was soon sitting on the floor engrossed in this find of which I had no previous recollection.

It was indeed about Poros, the Poros immediately before the start of World War II. An American had visited there for the second time and this was an account of his visit. He left as war was declared and must have missed meeting Henry Miller by months. How my grandmother came to have it I don't know, for she never went farther than Sheffield and never talked to me of Greece. Anyhow, in the pages of the book is an account of an evening in a little town *taverna* on Poros when some of the young bloods of the town came in carrying the bust of Demosthenes. They had been celebrating rather too well and, finding him on his pedestal looking cold and wet, they had decided to bring him to the *taverna* for some good company. However, once inside the *taverna*, they had grown impatient and hit him with a glass to make him drink. They knocked off part of his nose, and if you look at the statue today you will see that he is still missing that bit of his nose – and not a lot of people know that!

This whole area ceased to be inhabited in AD 395 when the Goths invaded and sacked it. Anything that was left standing was destroyed by an earthquake that was probably also responsible for the ancient harbour and town being engulfed by the sea. It is sometimes still possible to see parts of the buildings and the harbour wall along the sea bottom.

Leaving ancient Greece behind for a bit, the *Anna* calls in at Beesti Bay with its fish farm. This is one of the new rural industries that have been introduced since Greece's entry into the EU. The fish are exported mainly to Italy though some find their way onto the *Anna* if Mitsos and his brother Yiannis are in the mood to go snorkelling with the gun. And for our guests too, it's now time to plunge into the beautiful clear water and drum up an appetite for lunch.

Lazing back on the *Anna* after two and a half hours of swimming, eating and relaxing on deck, and by now half asleep, we set off on our round tour once again. As we emerge from Beesti Bay and look down towards Aegina we see a tiny flat island and near it a group of rocks sticking jaggedly out of the sea and providing a permanent nuisance for boats of all sizes, especially on moonless nights. Tall stories are connected with these sharp rocks. The flat little island is always referred to on the *Anna* as Kiriakos's island, and I'm not sure if it even has another name. One day several years ago we arrived at Beesti Bay to find the water full of rubbish and looking extremely unappetising. We tried several other small bays but always with the same result. So in desperation we set off to this small lump of rock that, although covered with seabirds, somehow caught the imagination of our passengers. They insisted on staying and proceeded to have a great time there. Later I was asked the name of the little island and, never one to disappoint, I informed them that it was called 'Kiriakos's Island' after our captain who had been the first man to step on it in recent times! This delighted both the passengers and the crew – who consist entirely of Captain Kiriakos's family! A few days later I came across one of the families who had been on the boat that day and they expressed their disappointment on having purchased a map of the Saronic Gulf and failed to find any trace of Kiriakos's Island. They cheered up considerably when I explained that the island was too small to be shown on ordinary maps and they would have to purchase one of the special sea charts on their return to England. This they swore to do, so it is perhaps just as well that this particular family has not reappeared among our annual visitors! – though they would still find Kiriakos's Island as popular as ever and now referred to as such throughout Poros!

The dangerous group of rocks has collected a romantic story concerning a sea nymph and the moon. The local fishermen say this sea nymph lived around here many years ago and was an excellent swimmer. She was probably the best swimmer of any sea nymph known to man but, alas, she knew it too and took to boasting about it. The moon overheard her and took her to task, but she would not stop, and finally, believing herself unbeatable, she challenged the moon to a race around the world. The moon told her not to be silly. He explained that he travelled through air and was much faster, but she refused to listen and went on and on. In an attempt to stop her, the moon finally agreed but insisted that if she lost she would be turned to stone for a thousand years. He expected that to settle the matter but she still refused to back down and eventually the race took place. She swam and swam, going faster than she had ever done before, but it was all to no avail and she lost and was turned into stone, and there she sits, a hazard to everyone and hated by most sailors. But the local fishermen feel sorry for her, for they say that on a moonless winter night they can hear her sobbing and pleading to be a sea nymph again.

I used to tell this story when we had a lot of children aboard the *Anna*, but now I am a little more careful, for one little boy became so worried about the sea nymph that he spent his entire holiday trying to think of a way to help her, searching the sea in the belief that the thousand years were up and she was back as a nymph.

By the time the story of the sea nymph has been told we have reached a point where Methana has come into view. This little town is situated on a rocky peninsular off the mainland and is best known in Greece for its once live volcano and the thermal springs which this volcano bequeathed to the area. The volcano is long dead and it is possible to walk to the edge of the crater through a village surrounded by the lava dust. The thermal springs, however, are still very much in evidence and are said to be beneficial for both arthritis and rheumatism. The baths that house the springs are to the right of the harbour and people come from all over Greece to take the waters. On a day when the wind is blowing from the northwest, the smell of sulphur gets everywhere.

But Methana has a history too. Remains found on Mount Helena tell us that the peninsula was inhabited from the earliest times. During the Peloponnesian War, the Athenian General, General Nikias occupied Methana and established a garrison on the isthmus. After his defeat in 421 BC Methana was linked with Sparta. Then in AD 273, according to the French geologist Fougue (1867), the Methana volcano erupted for the last time and changed the shape of the gulf. Pausanias describes the eruption quite vividly and also tells us for the first time of the hot springs which began to flow. Strabo, in his account, adds that after the eruption the area was unapproachable for days due to the great heat and the smell of the sulphur. It is said that Methana was used by Patrochus, a commander of the Egyptian fleet. He renamed it Arsinoe and made it into an important commercial port. It stayed under the rule of the Ptolemyies for a hundred years and when they left they handed it on to the Romans, at which point the seas became thick with Sicilian pirates.

But I think Methana has not given up all its secrets yet, for only a few years ago a local priest started to dig the foundations of a new church and came across an ancient grave with some fine artefacts in it. Now the archaeologists are taking a new interest in the area and this is good news for Methana and bad news for the priest, for he will have to wait a number of years before he can go on with the building of his church. It is early days yet but evidence seems to be emerging of links with the Minoan period and this is causing small shock waves to pass through learned circles for the Minoans were not thought to have travelled this far.

Just hoving into view on the mainland is the modern village of Trizinia, or Damala as it was once called. It sprawls way up the mountainside nowadays but still to be found just outside the village centre are the remains of the city state of Troezen. And it is impossible to tell the history of Poros without continually referring to this city state and its history. In ancient times the citizens of Poros were almost always part of the state of Troezen, though in many aspects of everyday life they retained some independence. This great city state was originally inhabited around 3000 BC.

According to tradition the first king was named Orus, a name derived from that of the Egyptian god Horus. After Orus came King Althippus who was thought to be the son of the god Poseidon and Orus' daughter Liees.

I always think claiming paternity on the part of a god is so sensible. After all, if I were faced with the task of telling my father that, although unmarried, I was pregnant, and had the choice of naming a local farmer or a god, I would certainly go for the god. It would make my life a lot less unpleasant I'm sure. And this seemed to happen quite a lot in ancient times, with Poseidon being very popular in the surrogate-father stakes. Poseidon was certainly often around these parts for he and Athena had been quarrelling a lot about the land in this area and Zeus had had to intervene and order them to share it. So Poseidon had his temple on Kalavria and Athena had hers under what is now St George's church in the old town of Poros. This duality is confirmed by coins which have been found here dating from between the fifth and third centuries BC and bearing the head of Athena on one side and that of Poseidon on the other. Anyhow, walk up to the temple at the top of Kalavria one day and then tell me that Poseidon isn't still around. I always take him flowers or a gift of some kind and on the whole we're good friends; I'm convinced he has a great sense of humour, because very strange things sometimes happen while I am up there. But no more, I must keep my counsel.

So, after Althippus there was King Saron, who drowned in the sea when out hunting and gave his name to the Saronic Gulf – a most unfortunate way to achieve immortality, I always feel, but anyhow that's how he did it. History seems to have drawn one of its net curtains over the next bit, at any rate until the Achaeans invaded the area led by King Pelops and his two sons Trizin and Pitheus. They eventually ruled here and the area became known as – yes – the Peloponnese. And this brings us to the birth of Theseus who was to grow up to be the second most famous Greek hero after Hercules.

Theseus' story is a long and fascinating one – some say there were even three Theseuses – and you must turn to more learned pages than these for a detailed account of his life, but briefly the story goes as follows. Aegeus, King of Athens, had no heir from two wives and, desperate for a son, he left Athens to visit the oracle at Delphi. On his way back to Athens he called in at Corinth and bumped into Medea just prior to her expulsion from that city. She made Aegeus swear a solemn oath that he would shelter her from all her enemies if she ever sought refuge in Athens, and in return she undertook to procure him a son by magic. Somewhat heartened by her promise, for he had only received an uninterpretable message from the oracle at Delphi (all about not untying the mouth of his bulging wineskin until he reached the highest point of Athens lest he die one day of grief), he then embarked on another detour to Troezen. Here he met up with Trizin and Pitheus who made him very welcome and ordered a great feast in his honour. Pitheus was renowned as one of the learned men of his age and he was said to be pretty big on friendship, being often quoted as saying, 'Blast not the hope that friendship hath conceived but fill its measure high.' He founded what is thought to be the oldest shrine in Greece at Troezen, dedicated an altar to the triple goddess Themis and taught the art of oratory in the Muses' sanctuary there. Three white marble thrones, now placed above his tomb, used to serve him and two others as judgement seats.

At the time of Aegeus' arrival Pitheus' daughter Aethra was rather down in the dumps. Her fiancé Bellerophon had been sent away in disgrace and she was left languishing as a virgin, with seemingly little hope of attaining the marital bed. The welcoming party for Aegeus obviously turned into quite a rave and during the evening her father got drunk and started to come under the influence of Medea's spell. Moved with pity for the loveless state of his daughter he more or less threw her into bed with King Aegeus and left them to enjoy themselves, which they apparently did. Later that same night the goddess Athena started meddling on behalf of Poseidon and she sent instructions to Aethra in a dream, telling her to wade across to the island of Spheria and meet up with him there.

Being a good girl – well, in one sense anyhow, Aethra complied and Poseidon found her and had his wicked way too. You must have begun to realise by now that Poseidon is a great one for the ladies and pops up in the role of suitor/rapist time and time again. It will come as no great surprise to many female readers to learn that next morning King Aegeus remembered urgent business in Athens and began preparations for his departure. But he was not a total cad; on waking up in Aethra's bed he told her that if a son were born to them he must not be left on the mountain to die or sent away but should be secretly reared in Troezen. Poseidon was obviously consulted at some point for he is reported to have agreed that any child born to Aethra in the next four months (don't ask!) should be known to have Aegeus as its father.

Before King Aegeus sailed back to Athens he hid his sword and sandals under a hollow rock telling, Aethra that when the boy had grown sufficiently strong to move the rock he was to take them and travel to Athens where Aegeus would recognise him as his son. And the rest, as they say, is history, for, as many schoolchildren know, Theseus became one of the most philanthropic kings of Athens and is famous for his slaying of the Minotaur of Crete. The stone he had to lift is still there today and going to find it on the local bus and then shanks's pony makes for a very pleasant day out indeed.

There are many other stories about Theseus and it is well worth reading them up in greater detail. Here on Poros he is also well known for being a leading figure in the myth of Phaedra and Hippolytus, for this too largely took place in Troezen. After his traumatic trip to Crete, Theseus married Phaedra, daughter of Minos, and they had two sons, Acamas and Demophoön. But Theseus also had an illegitimate son by Antiope. This son was called Hippolytus and had been sent to Troezen to live with King Pitheus, who adopted him as heir to the throne of that city state, thus conveniently leaving the throne of Athens for his two more legitimate siblings.

All should have been well, but of course it wasn't. When Phaedra came to Athens she brought with her the cult worship of Aphrodite. Before that, however, Antiope had encouraged the worship of Artemis, and Hippolytus and had built a new temple to this goddess at Troezen. Aphrodite took great umbrage at this and to punish him she made Phaedra fall in love with Hippolytus when he attended the Eleusinian Mysteries while Theseus was away in Thessaly. This love quickly turned into an obsession and Phaedra, taking advantage of her husband's absence, followed her passion back to Troezen. There she built the Temple of Peeping Aphrodite, siting it so that it looked into the gymnasium where each day a naked Hippolytus would keep himself fit by running, leaping and wrestling. It is said that Phaedra would jab the leaves of a nearby myrtle tree in frustration while she watched unobserved. Later she followed her love to the All Athenian Festival and spied on him again. She told no one of her passion but she ate little and slowly wasted away; her old nurse guessed what was wrong and urged her to write to Hippolytus before she grew too sick to do anything. This Phaedra did, proclaiming her love, her conversion to the cult of Artemis, and further urging Hippolytus to revenge the murder of his mother by paying homage to Aphrodite and coming to live with her, Phaedra. Hippolytus, being one of the few Greek princes possessed of honour, was horrified by the letter and went to Phaedra's chamber to remonstrate with her, but she tore her clothes and rushed through the palace shouting for help and claiming that she had been ravished. When Theseus was given the note he ordered Hippolytus out of Athens never to return and then he remembered that Poseidon had given him three wishes, so he wished for the death of Hippolytus – a death that he wanted to take place that very day.

One must be very careful about wishes that have been granted by the gods for they tend to have a rather fast and literal result. Hippolytus left Athens at full speed. His chariot and four horses raced towards the Isthmus of Corinth. Here he was engulfed by an enormous wave and from its crest there sprang a great dog seal (or it may have been a white bull) which caused the four horses to swerve towards the cliff. Hippolytus managed to prevent them all from going over the cliff and raced on pursued by the monster. The horses were terrified and swerving wildly, and they headed unseeingly towards a wild olive tree. The reins caught in one of the branches and the chariot turned over and was shattered on the rocks. Hippolytus was helpless; caught in the harness, he was thrown against the tree, then on to the rocks and finally dragged to his death by his horses. By this time the monster had vanished. Legend has it that Theseus travelled to Troezen at the speed of light and arrived in time to be reconciled with his dying son. Meanwhile, back in Athens, Phaedra, overcome with remorse, hanged herself.

It is said that the tombs of Phaedra and Hippolytus lie side by side in the temple at Troezen near the myrtle tree with the pricked leaves. It is a beautiful spot to visit in the spring, the whole area rich with wild flowers and rare orchids peeping from behind the palace stones. But the atmosphere is heavy and however bright the sun a long shadow seems to fall across the place, as though there has been one tragedy too many within its rich and honoured walls. Unlike the Temple of Poseidon on Poros it imparts no sense of life or laughter and it is with a feeling of relief and a small shudder that you climb out of the valley and head towards the Devils' Gorge. Here you find dramatic scenery, rushing water and a bridge held up by three perfectly normal devils!

Leaping forward to the Byzantine era, Emperor Leon VI renamed Troezen and called it Damalas; after the fall of Constantinople to the Turks in 1453 the Greeks ceded three castles of the Agolid to the Venetians, and the castle of Damalas was one of these; it remained in Venetian hands until 1531.

While we have been treading through ancient history, the *Anna* has been sailing slowly on, leaving Trizinia to disappear behind the boat and Poros and its little blue-domed clocktower to appear ahead of us. We are nearly home but first we must pass by Russian Bay with its little island of Daskalio. The bay and its crumbling buildings always provoke a string of questions, of which the first is, 'Why Russian Bay?'

Well, Greece has a tradition of trading with Russia that goes back to the reign of Catherine the Great and is still continuing to this day. The first president of Greece, appointed after the successful revolution against the Turks, was one Capodistrius. He was serving as foreign minister in the court of the Tsars when he was summoned back to Greece in 1827. He came back to tales of heroism and great sea battles, for during the Turkish occupation (roughly 1470 to 1821) Poros had, like Hydra, amassed a good-sized commercial fleet and this was well equipped to play a substantial role in the war of independence. Poros's ships were moored in the natural harbour on this side of the island and you are now sailing over the site of some pretty ferocious sea battles and the graveyard of many fine ships.

After independence had been declared Capodistrias stayed on Poros from April until June 1827, and in September 1828 the ambassadors of the three Great Powers, (France, England and Germany), met on Poros before conferring with Capodistrias on settling the boundaries for the new Greek state.

Later, as part of a thank you to the Russians for allowing him to return to Greece, and also for the more practical help they gave Greece in the fight against the Turks, Capodistrias built the trading station. It was destroyed once during the continuing fighting but almost immediately rebuilt. It ceased trading in 1917 when the communists took control of Russia. At that time there were two Russian ships in the harbour whose crews were in sympathy with the revolutionary cause. When they heard of the successful overthrow of the Tsar they made preparations for a fast return to Russia and as they left, the Greeks say, they fired their guns in celebration and knocked down half the trading base, leaving it in much the same condition that we find it in today.

The little island of Daskalio has on it a tiny church dedicated to all schoolteachers for it is said that there lived on Poros a lady teacher who fell madly in love with one of her male colleagues. Alas, he did not return her affection and one day in despair she rowed out to the island and then walked into the sea and drowned herself. Her parents built the little church on the island and dedicated it to her and her fellow teachers. This small island was also used during the Turkish occupation as a secret school; the local children were smuggled across and taught their language, traditions and history, often at the risk of imprisonment or worse.

Next is Love Bay – a name that needs little explanation, for it is a bay that holds memories of many a secret rendezvous from both the past and, I'm told, the present! The *Anna* is going faster now, anxious to be home, the bay of Neorion lies sleepy on our left for it is mesi-meri – siesta time – and all sensible people are asleep building up energy for the long evening ahead. Neorian's pretty little bay is one of my favourite places on the island. I wave hopefully to friends in the seafront *tavernas* and think of Yiannis Ritsos the poet, who comes often to Poros and loves it here too.

Ahead of us stands the naval station, originally a royal palace and once the main base of Greece's professional navy. Now it is used mainly to train its national-service boys before they are returned to their families a little fitter and more independent than they were when they arrived.

Before the *Anna* settles gently back into her moorings there is one treat left in store for our passengers, and that is the house of Galini. It is the Italian style red brick house standing on the Neorian road that I described earlier in the book. As I confessed, I fell in love with it the first time I saw it. It was built by an Athenian family with a strong interest in the arts and was once well known for the fame of its visitors. Alas the guest-book has disappeared but certainly Lawrence Durrell, Henry Miller and Georges Seferis stayed here before the Second World War. But there were many more names in that book for Poros has many exotic visitors and quite recently has played host to Prince Charles, ex-President Bush and Edward Kennedy. Closer to home, the list is endless.

The *Anna* is resting at her moorings now and it's time to head for home. The little harbour front is almost deserted but I glimpse a movement out of the corner of my eye. Something moved towards the edge of the old town. I look again but nothing stirs. Was it perhaps Athena seeking the remains of her ancient temple?

Maybe, because one thing is certain, anything is possible on Poros!

•

Spetses

If it's Tuesday it must be Spetses and Hydra! On the *Anna II* we all have varying estimates as to the number of years I've been helping out as a guide, but however many it is, Tuesday and Spetses and Hydra are one of the constants.

So we leave at nine in the morning, on the dot, and head down to Spetses – the island of the group that is farthest from Athens, unless you count Kithira which really isn't in the Saronic Gulf. Writing in the second century AD, Pausanias – that early jet setter – referred to it as *Pityousa*, the Pine Tree Island, and at first glance, that name appears to be justified, but at the beginning of the eighteenth century a flourishing ship building industry was to cut down many of the trees and the island lost many of its pleasant woods; with goats and forest fires doing their best to help.

In 1913 Sotiris Anagyros, a local man who had made his fortune in America, came back and set about changing the island's fortunes. He bought up large areas of the island and replanted the ubiquitous pine before going on to introduce tourism to Spetses, one of the first islands to enjoy this dubious privilege. He built a luxury hotel here in 1914; named the Poseidon, after the god of the sea, it was something of a high spot for the first international travellers and it still stands on the harbour front today, hinting at a high life filled with scandalous secrets that, alas, has long departed.

The island has probably been occupied for more than four thousand years; historic remains have been found dating back to around 2000 BC, but only much later on, around the eighteenth century, when refugees from Turkish rule came over from the Peloponnese mainland and settled, did Spetses begin to have a viable community.

Greece is of course the home of democracy, but throughout its history it has been occupied by foreign powers. Perhaps the most hated of these occupations was that of the Turks, which lasted around four hundred years. Somehow or other the Greeks kept their language and their traditions alive. Children were awakened in the middle of the night and taken into caves where they were taught by the priests and the schoolteachers. Somehow communities survived until finally, outside of

Greece at first, a resistance group was formed and gradually these ex-patriot Greeks returned to their homeland and the rebellion grew. It started in the Mani, that southern-most area of mainland Greece renowned for its fierce fighters and its fearless sea captains. It spread slowly northwards and into the islands, and became a veritable war of independence. And it was during this time that Spetses began to find a place in history.

In 1822 the successful capture of Naplion from the Turks was finally accomplished by the lady admiral, Laskarina Bouboulina. Bouboulina is very well known and much loved in Greece. She was born in prison in May 1771 when her mother was visiting her father there. The family came originally from Hydra but moved to Spetses on the death of her father. She was married twice, both times to sea captains, and both times her husbands were killed in battles with the Algerian pirates who constantly threatened this whole area. She was nevertheless left with a considerable fortune and she used this money to build the first Greek warship of the 1821 revolution, namely the Agamemnon. She armed this ship, hired the crew and then fought alongside her men at the victorious battle for Naplion. She survived the revolution but was murdered in 1825 in an argument with the Koutsis family after one of her sons had eloped with their daughter. Her statue by Natalie Mela, a famous local artist, stands in front of the Poseidon Hotel today and her house is being restored and is open as a museum, with many of her personal belongings preserved and displayed inside. It's a beautiful house and gives some idea of the style of living that was enjoyed by the well-off nineteenth century islanders. If you visit the house and find yourself being taken around by a charming young man, it will almost certainly be Bouboulina's great, great, great grandson, for the family still owns the house and is understandably proud of its famous relative.

Fans of the author John Fowles will know Spetses from his book *The Magus*. Many strange things happened to the leading character in the book which its author has always maintained were pure fiction. But certainly the *Villa Bourani* existed, for the Villa Yasmina on which it was based can still be glimpsed at Aghia Paraskevi on the far side of the island. The school, too, was a reality until 1984. Opened by Sotiris Anagyros in 1927 and soon to become the best boys' private school in Greece, it employed several English teachers who were sponsored by the British Council. John Fowles was one of these. The school buildings still stand, set in magnificent gardens by the edge of the sea, and it is easy to stand in front of the main gates and transport yourself into the pages of *The Magus*.

There are few motorised vehicles of the four-wheeled variety on Spetses and most private motor cars are banned but the motorbike or *mykhanaki* is alive and well, its noisy presence giving a life and bustle to the little harbour town centre. A more romantic way to see something of the island is to take one of the horse-drawn carriages and travel in style. These are the original carriages that have been used down the years as the local taxis. The drivers are characters themselves, entertaining you with tales of the past, proposing an unlikely marriage and presenting the ladies with exotic sweet-smelling bouquets. But it is well to negotiate the price for all this before you get in as it can be alarmingly variable from driver to driver. Still, romance never does come cheap and I usually find experiences of this nature to be worth every far-fetched euro.

There is a museum, which not only contains many local exhibits from Greece's turbulent past, but is also reputed to house the very bones of Bouboulina, though I must confess I have never actually seen them for myself. Its collection of nineteenth century guns is impressive, and some of its traditional antique clothes have been beautifully embroidered. To the west of the museum is the Monastery of Aghios Nikolaos in a cell of which the body of Paul Bonaparte, brother of the Emperor Napoleon was preserved in a barrel of rum for five years after he had accidentally been shot on the flagship of Lord Cochrane. A most unfortunate death I always think – to be stuck in a barrel of rum for five years and not be able to drink it!

There are some fine naval captains' houses along the seafront and a walk around the little town reveals some of the fine pebble mosaic floors which are a tradition of the island – and very slippery too. Follow the coast road farther west and you will arrive at the old harbour where the shipyards are still busy building the traditional fishing boats. All in all Spetses has enormous charm. Many of its houses stand in pretty little gardens and its bar and *taverna* signs have been recreated from the originals. It still attracts an international clientele and if you really want to be exclusive you can always try and get yourself invited to Spetsopoulos, the little island that nestles close to its big sister. This is one of the few privately owned islands in Greece and belongs to the Niarchos family, the shipping millionaires – well, you can dream!

•

Hydra

'Traditional arch rivals and neighbouring superpowers in the maritime affairs of pre-revolutionary Greece, Hydra and Spetses could scarcely be more different in aspect. Spetses is as gentle, fragrant and self-effacing as Hydra is rugged and confrontational.' (*The Which Guide to Greece and the Greek Islands.*)

When describing Hydra on the *Anna II*, I usually refer to it as 'a lump of volcanic rock', which it essentially is. But it is not without a history of its own, for the island's ancient Mycenaean name was Hydrea; in ancient Greek a word meaning water, for many years ago, the island had many freshwater streams and was a rich grazing ground. Alas, there is little trace of these freshwater streams today and the name has become ironic, for most of Hydra's water is brought to the island by boat from the mainland.

Today Hydra's economy is based firmly on tourism, but the earliest traces of human occupation actually date from the period between 3000 – 2600 BC and we know that during the thirteenth century BC Hydra was linked to the kingdom of Mycenae – though later it was attacked by armies from there.

Around 528 BC it was sold to the Samians who kept it until they departed for the island of Crete. Subsequently the island came under the protection of Troezen, the city state situated on the mainland opposite Poros and very famous in its time – as described before. During the Persian Wars it is believed that Hydrea took part in the famous battle of Salamis on the side of the Athenians, though later, during the Peloponnesian War, it sided with Sparta against them.

Then, for many centuries Hydrea disappeared from history until AD1200 when it reappeared as Hydra, an island ruled by the Venetians then so dominant in this area. In 1460 Hydra passed into Turkish hands and out of the limelight again, so much so that it was widely believed to be uninhabited. In 1715 however, when a Turkish fleet under the command of the Grand Vizier anchored off the mainland, all on board were surprised to receive a delegation from the Hydriotes. The islanders would have done well to stay at home that day though, for after that they were visited once a year to have their taxes collected. In 1774 Russian ships were given permission to sail through the Bosphorus and Hydra seized the opportunity to sail her trading ships under the protection of the Russian flag. It was then that many of the island's great sea captains gained their reputations. The Hydriote ships all had small canons aboard for protection against the ever-present pirates and they began to use these guns in hit and run operations against the Turkish fleet. They had some success, and these skirmishes gradually grew into the War of Independence with the Hydriotes becoming expert in the ancient technique of fire ships.

During her comparatively few years of trading Hydra had become extremely rich. Her merchant inhabitants built large and beautiful stone houses, landscaped around the harbour, but her involvement in the War of Independence was to all but bankrupt her. Undoubtedly her participation played a vital part in the outcome of that war and today the island has many statues to its famous sons – notably Admirals Miaoulis and Kolotronis – but by the time of independence her fortunes were gone. She settled back into the shadows of history.

After the Turks were expelled from Greece the island declined. Its main industry was sponge fishing and life was hard. Then, in the 1960s, Athens's thriving film industry discovered the island and the holidaymakers began to follow. It became the second most popular island after Mykonos and the big yachts began to pack its little harbour. Next came the international playboys and the island became famous for its jet-set lifestyle. But, inevitably, in time they moved on and now Hydra relies mostly on the one-day cruise ships for its living. The island is worth far more than a two-hour visit, however, for the little old town has been beautifully restored and there are no motorised vehicles except for a rubbish-collection cart, a fire-engine and a tractor. Transport is by donkey or water taxi and temptingly visible on its mountain tops are some lovely old monasteries.

Many famous people have visited or lived here and their ghosts still haunt the shadows of the little cobbled streets. Once the cruise boats have left, Hydra reveals its true charm, one that is all its own. I have visited it so many times now that I tend to sit drinking coffee on the harbour front and chatting with friends who work there, but occasionally I take a walk round the back streets and glimpse something I have never seen before. Each summer I promise myself that I will go back during the *halcyon* days, days that arrive every January, giving a brief glimpse of the spring to come and I will walk my way round the monasteries. Yes, maybe this year!

•

Aegina

If Tuesday on the *Anna* means Hydra and Spetses, then quite often Thursday means Aegina and Angistri, the other two main islands in the Saronic Gulf. But, for some reason this trip does not seem to catch the imagination of the tourists in the same way as Hydra and Spetses.

Over the years we have arrived on various days and at various times, sometimes in the evening. I'm very fond of Aegina town. It's really just a basic working town and gets on with life, leaving the tourists to join in as and when they wish. The main tourist centre is at Aghia Marina on the far side of the island and we've done various trips from there too, but it is Aegina town that is our main port of call.

As the boat pulls into Aegina town you glimpse the tiny church of Aghios Nikolaos that nestles amongst the fishing kayaks and the private yachts. Once on the quay you are quickly absorbed into the island life, with the busy harbour cafés on one side of the road and the yachts and fruit boats selling local produce on the other. Between them runs a dual carriageway with horse-drawn carriages trotting along it, holding up the impatient taxi drivers. Do all taxi drivers have to be born impatient in order to qualify for the job, or is impatience acquired or thrust upon them? Anyhow, at the end of the harbour just past the big church of *Aghios Nikolaos* (yes, he is the island's patron saint) the road curves away from the sea and heads through the pistachio trees and into the interior of the island. It climbs slowly until it delivers you at the top of the island and the Temple of Aphaia.

This temple is an important one and one of the best preserved in Greece. It has quite recently been discovered that the Temple of Poseidon at Sounion, the Temple of Athena in Athens (i.e. the Parthenon) and this Temple of Aphaia form an equilateral triangle almost exactly. It was then further discovered that the Temple of Aphaia, the Athens temple of Athena and the Temple of Poseidon on Poros form an almost perfect isosceles triangle. Coincidences? I don't think so somehow.

Unsurprisingly, a legend surrounds this temple on Aegina. The lady who was worshipped here is said to have been a friend of the god Artemis and thus part of the Cretan/

Mycenaean pantheon. While on Crete it seems she provoked the passion of King Minos, but, not wishing to be a part of his court, she fled the island and in doing so fell into the sea. She was then rescued by fishermen who brought her to Aegina, but alas, such was her beauty that one of the fishermen got amorous and she ran off into the woods of Artemis and suddenly disappeared (*aphaia* means invisible). The islanders then dedicated a temple to her, proving that virtue can sometimes be more than its own reward.

There is more to the island of Aegina, however, than the Temple of Aphaia. The island lies about 30 kms to the south west of Athens and in ancient Greece it rivalled that city in wealth and influence. It is the largest of the Saronic islands and historically, the most interesting.

Legend has it that Aegina was the loveliest of twenty daughters born to the river god Asopos. Zeus fell in love with her, and to protect her from the anger of his wife Hera, he took her away to the island of Oinone. This island then took her name and became Aegina. Remains have been found dating back to the Neolithic age, around the ninth millennium BC, and there have been rich finds from the Mycenaean period around 1450 BC. Later the Dorians invaded the island and it from then on its fortunes were to rise and fall dramatically. By the sixth entury BC Aegina was an important trading state and had a trading post on the Nile. It was the first Greek state to produce its own money – a silver coin bearing the image of a turtle. These were used for generations throughout the Greek world and have been found in excavations all over the eastern Mediterranean.

Rivalry between between Aegina and Athens eventually resulted in a war that was declared in 498 BC. Later, however, Aegina changed her mind and sided with Athens against the Persians at the famous Battle of Marathon in 480 BC. But once the war was over relations got even worse and Pericles was soon urging the Athenians to rid themselves of 'this sore spot in the eye of Piraeus'. This wasn't quite as easy as he thought, but in the siege of 458BC Aegina fell to Athens and from then on its fortunes declined.

Although subsequently portrayed mainly as an outpost of the Athenian empire, it was not without its literary connections, for Aristophanes is said to have lived on the island as a young man and to have written several of his earlier comedies here. Its literary connections were revived quite recently by the contemporary writer Nikos Kazantzakis (he of *Zorba the Greek* fame), who had a house here where he lived until his death in 1960.

In the fifteenth century, and like most of Greece, Aegina came under Turkish rule. This domination lasted for around four hundred years and was the most hated of all the foreign occupations. The Greeks, however, rose up and during the struggle for independence Aegina became increasingly a haven for refugees and (like Spetses) a communications conduit between Greek patriots on the mainland and the other islands.

Two of the great revolutionary leaders, Petrobey Mavromichaelis and Konstantinos Kanaris, lived for a while on the island, and (between 1827–1829), Aegina became (briefly) the capital of the newly formed Greek state. It was here that Ioannis Capodistrias was sworn in as the first president of the newly freed Greece, and the pink tower still standing in the centre of Aegina town housed Capodistrias's government in the early days of his appointment. I love this little pink tower and often go to visit it. I was told that the island was covered with them during the Turkish occupation, but once the Turks had been sent packing, all the others were quickly pulled down, leaving this solitary one as a reminder and a piece of history.

But Aegina's fame was brief and in 1829 the capital was transferred to Naplion and the island slipped back into obscurity. Nowadays the tourists are its main source of income, though inland the ground is richly fertile and extensively planted with pistachio trees. These, together with almonds, figs and olives are grown for export – look on a packet of pistachio nuts on your local supermarket shelves when you get home and often you will find Aegina written there. The island also produces its own wine – well worth a try as you relax in the harbour *taverna*s or sample the freshly caught fish, tucked in with the local fishermen round the little tables in the fish market. Take the opportunity to have a look at some of the local pottery, actually made on the far side of the island but selling here in the shops of the main town.

Halfway back along the road from the temple (or halfway towards it if you prefer it that way) is the monastery of Aghios Nectarios and the hill of the Paliochora. The monastery was built in 1904 and was presided over by the Bishop of Pentapolis. During his lifetime he was responsible for many miracle cures, and it is said that he continues to answer the prayers of his supplicants even up to the present day. He was canonised Aghios Nectarios in 1960 and is the most recent of the Greek saints. His relics repose in a casket inside the monastery where his skull lies in a golden crown set with precious stones. As Aghios Nectarios, his name day is on the 3rd of September, and each year on that day the island is flooded with people seeking to pay homage or request a miracle. For this purpose a huge modern church has been built by the people of Aegina but the ancient monastery it dwarfs retains for me greater beauty and charm.

Behind the church and the monastery lies the hill of Paliochora. In the ninth and tenth centuries AD, Arab pirates, operating out of Crete, became a major threat to the people of Aegina. The main town on the island was resettled on this hill after a particularly bloody raid in 896. After 1800 however, the people began to move back to the coast and the hill city died. Today it is like a miniature Mistras. Twenty- five of its tiny churches remain, some with the original wall paintings still visible on their ancient walls. You can glimpse them from the road though it is also possible to visit them. An official of the archaeological service has the keys of a few of the churches and is on the site every morning except Tuesday.

The hill of Colona, which is situated at the edge of Aegina

town, was the home of the prehistoric inhabitants of the island and it is on this site that finds have been made dating back to the early Bronze Age. Pausanias, travelling in second century AD, described a large theatre here similar to that at Epidaurus, but no trace of it has yet been found. All that can now be seen of the ancient settlement is one column and a fragment of a platform belonging to the Temple of Apollo and believed to date from fifth century BC. In the grounds of the site there is now a small museum. Nestling under the pines and equipped with air-conditioning, it makes a welcome haven from the midsummer heat and contains interesting archaeological finds from the island and its rich history.

I really enjoy our visits to Aegina for there is so much to do and see and the little port bustles with the everyday business of the islands and is very Greek.

•

Angistri

The *Anna* often visits Angistri either as part of the trip to Aegina or as a welcome swimming stop on the way back from the Corinth Canal. Whether we arrive there in the early morning or quite late at night we are always assured of a special welcome, for the captain's wife comes from the island, as did, originally, the captain's family. It's a small, uncomplicated island with just three roads to take you around it and one tiny little bus. The *Anna*'s passengers love it for its sandy beach at Skala – a rarity in the Saronic Gulf – and also for the quality of the sea that really is as clear as crystal. Until recently it was a closely guarded secret, but inevitably the package-tour operators latched on to it and the traditional yellow headscarves are no longer seen on its little country roads. It is still charming, however, especially once you get away from the tourist area facing Aegina. There are lovely long walks under the pine trees and long lazy lunches to be had in quiet tucked-away *tavernas*.

As far as I know it has no claim to fame, but it really is none the worse for that; I have spent countless happy hours lying in the sea there, dreaming my latest daydream, until the hooter on the *Anna* drags me back to reality and reminds me that, technically, I am working, and it would be decidedly odd if I were the one to miss the boat.

•

The Cornith Canal and Salamis

I used to imagine sailing the Corinth Canal and I used to wish for it to happen. Well, as I keep reminding you, you have to be a bit careful about wishes in Greece! '*O ti thelis esi*' they say. 'Anything you want!' and then things tend to go a bit crazy – so perhaps that is why I've sailed the Corinth Canal – over two hundred times!

We started the trips one summer and within about three weeks we were booked solid. It turned out to be an amazing success, with Eleni's moussaka rapidly becoming one of the highlights. It was a long day and we never knew what was going to happen. Sometimes the boat was so full we had to link up with Andonis and the *Anna I* at the mouth of the canal and do most of the trip in two boats. Sometimes one of the bridges stuck in the up position so we circled round and round or let down the gangplank and sent everyone down it for a swim. Sometimes we had to wait for a huge liner to come through and sometimes we sailed through as though it had all been meticulously planned.

So now, as I imagine us sailing towards the canal across indigo seas under cerulean skies, it seems the perfect moment to mention the last of the Saronic islands – namely Salamis – which we are passing on our right.

Salamis sits cosily in the shelter of the mainland only a few kilometres along the coast road from Athens to Corinth and is clearly visible every time you enter or leave the port of Piraeus.

It is now the home of a large part of the Greek navy, which is fitting as it has been associated with naval activities since ancient times. It is particularly famous for the Battle of Salamis, which was fought in 480 AD against the invading Persian fleet and was one of the great sea battles of ancient history.

At the beginning of 480 BC the advancing Persians controlled all of Attica, only the Acropolis in Athens held out against the advancing armies – a heroic act on the part of a few old men. The Persian fleet, newly spruced up after several earlier battles and some particularly inclement weather, was drawn up on Athens's Phaleron beach (you pass it on the way to the airport). The Athenians had pretty much abandoned their city and taken refuge in Salamis and Troezen. Xerxes the Persian King was confident of success.

For a battle that took place two thousand five hundred years ago, it is remarkably well documented. Eye witness accounts are available because battle-watching was something of a national sport – a bit like football today. On this occasion Aeschylus the famous playwright was there, and it is his account on which historians draw for most of their information.

He tells us that most of the Greek fleet was assembled off Salamis, for they had recently helped with the evacuation of Athens. Xerxes' inclination was to bottle them up and hold them there until the shortage of supplies forced them to disperse. But events did not quite fit in with the king's plan, for Themistocles, the Athenian leader, decided to force the issue. To this end he leaked a message to the Persians that the Peloponnesians were about to retreat. Thus it was that on the night of 20 September the Persian fleet put to sea, Xerxes set up his silver throne (which he just happened to have with him at the time, and I for one, admire his foresight) high on Mount Aiglos and settled back to watch a great Persian victory. Alas for him, it was not to be, for as the king sat there the Corinthian contingent faked a retreat and the Persians, believing victory to be within their grasp, pressed forward until they found themselves trapped in the narrow strait between

Salamis and the mainland. The Persian ships foundered in the shallows and the Greeks wrought havoc. King Xerxes found himself watching the total destruction of his navy.

Looking at the densely populated island now, it is difficult to imagine these historic scenes. Although its links with the navy remain, there is little else of interest to the tourist, though it is a pretty enough place if you fancy a visit.

Sailing on past Salamis and through the myriad tiny islets of the diaspora, you search fruitlessly for the opening of the canal. It teases you by refusing to reveal itself until you are quite close, but at last you catch a glimpse of a break in the land mass and realise that you are approaching it at last.

All along the coast now are remains of the two ports which served ancient Corinth and you must surely explore them one day, but today you are here for the canal and that belongs to the modern world. Still, it is worth half closing your eyes and imagining, if you can, the sight which would have met the eyes of those aboard the ancient sailing ships as they headed for a safe harbour at last. Remember that the whole of this area was covered in buildings. Round the ports were the warehouses and then, set back a little, were the temples and bath houses, palaces, theatres and sports stadiums. Statues filled the public squares and most buildings were decorated with gold, silver and lapis lazuli, whilst the stonework was painted brick red. The first port was known as Cenchrea, whilst next to it, but closer to what is now the canal, was the Sanctuary of Poseidon where the Pan Hellenic Isthmian games were held every two years. It must have been an extraordinary sight for the sailors of seventh century BC, as they sailed in from the far reaches of the Mediterranean, bringing their cargos of spices and exotic oils.

But by now we are at the mouth of the canal itself and the atmosphere on the boat is electric. Somehow this gap between two lumps of rock has caught hold of people's imagination and for many sailing it is a cherished dream about to come true.

The idea of cutting a canal across the isthmus exercised minds from the beginning of time until 1883 when the work finally got under way. Periander the Tyrant, the founder of Corinth, is known to have considered the possibility. The logistics and costs defeated him, however, and instead he built the paved slipway or *diolkos* along the length of what is now the canal. Blocks of stone were sunk into the earth and two parallel grooves were cut into the surface of each. It was these grooves that guided the wheels of the platforms on to which ships, lifted from the sea on one side of the isthmus were loaded in order to be hauled across and returned to the sea on the other. This slipway was used until the thirteenth century AD. After Periander, both Alexander the Great and Caligula toyed with the idea of a canal, but it was Nero who actually started digging in 67AD. Using a gold pick he struck the first blow himself and then imported six thousand slaves to do the rest of the work for him. At the western end of the canal you can see a small wall sculpture said to mark the very spot where Nero struck his first blow. Alas the work did not get very far and was stopped completely when the Gauls invaded the area in the third century.

After that nothing was done until the French engineer Etienne Tyre tackled the challenge in 1883. Using local workers this time, he worked on the project for ten years. When it was finally completed, the canal was opened by the man whose enthusiasm had been responsible for getting the project off the ground, namely Capodistrias. In 1893 Capodistrias, as the first president of the New Greek state, stood and watched as the final piece of land was dynamited away. It must have been quite a moment and there was perhaps relief in some minds that the island of Aegina was not, as had been feared, instantly, engulfed by a tidal wave. The Gulf of Corinth was believed to be higher than the Saronic Gulf and despite the calculations of modern science some of the old misgivings had lingered on.

The tidal wave was a very real possibility to some of the people watching that day and to be honest, as you sail along the canal towards Corinth, it does look as if you are sailing uphill. It was and is an amazing feat of engineering for its time. It is just over six kilometres long and twenty-five metres wide. Its sides rise ninety metres above sea level and drop thirty metres below, and most of the work was done by hand, though they did have the use of dynamite – it was pioneered on the canal – and simple steam diggers, of which there are photos

At either end of the canal is a road bridge that sinks below the water to allow the ships to sail over. The Corinth highways are suspended over the top and there is a separate rail bridge. Below the bridges little has changed since the canal was opened. Herons and kingfishers fly along its banks and it is incredibly beautiful.On the most sheer rock surfaces you can see the footholds cut into the sides of the canal for the use of the workers when, with the aid of ropes, they climbed out at the end of the working day.

Apart from short periods for general maintenance, it has only been closed once in a history spanning well over a hundred years, this was at the end of the Second World War when the Germans closed it by sinking ships at both entrances before they left the shores of Greece in 1944. It was reopened five years later.

After so many years of sailing with the *Anna II* my head is packed with many brilliant memories, but I think the most vivid of these are those of the times we sailed the Corinth Canal. They are something very special indeed.

Chapter Six

Finale

•

If you have read this far I hope you will have begun to see the charm and understand something of the magic of this tiny island in the Saronic Gulf of Greece. I came, fell in love with it and made a life here and it has been, and still is, one of the best decisions of my life. As I said at the beginning, here is not Paradise, and in the midst of the laughter there have been tears and desperate times; but somehow we all pull through and tomorrow is always another day. Many people really do come back year after year, a few arrive to live, and maybe one or two find they do not like the island at all. The reality of Poros is here to be discovered, so come if you will, for you are assured of a warm welcome; but if you decide to stay away I hope that you have, at least, spent a few happy hours with us through the pages of this book.

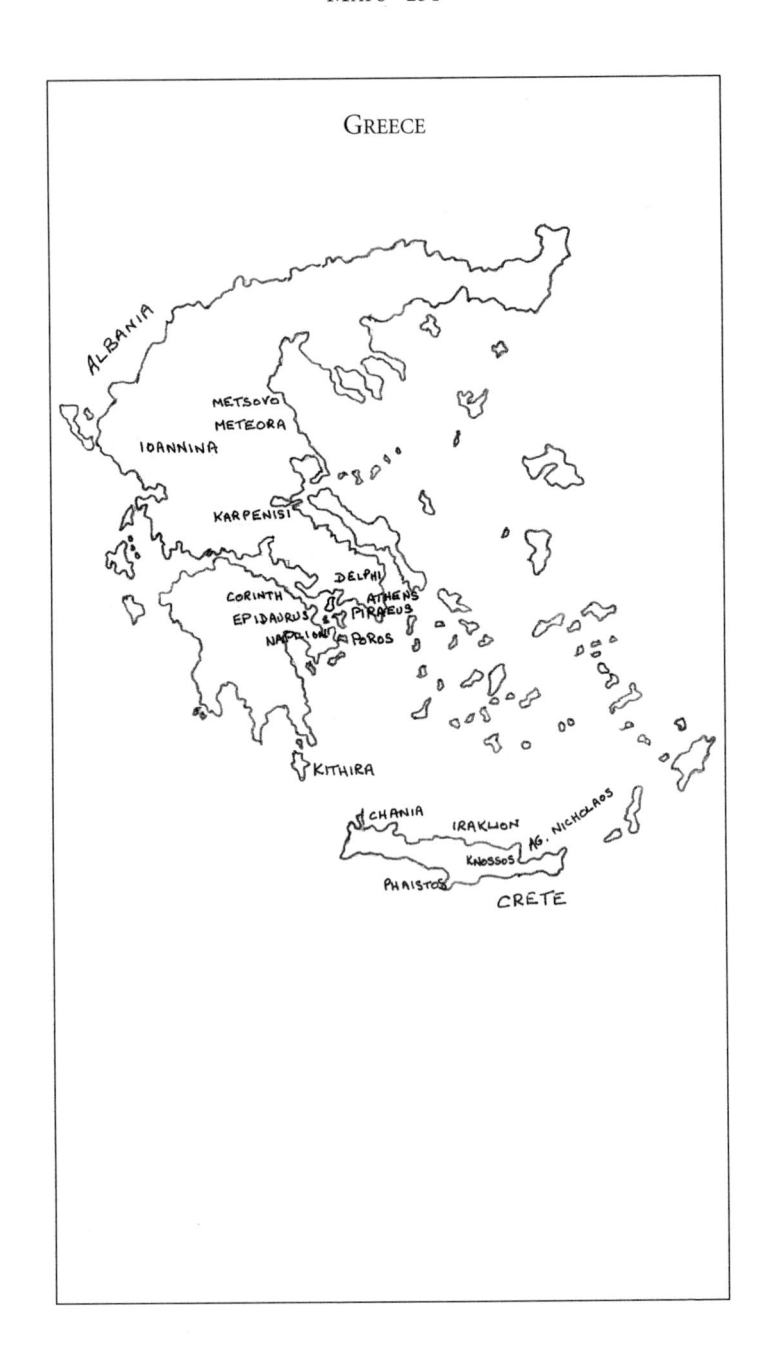

GREECE

MAPS · 255

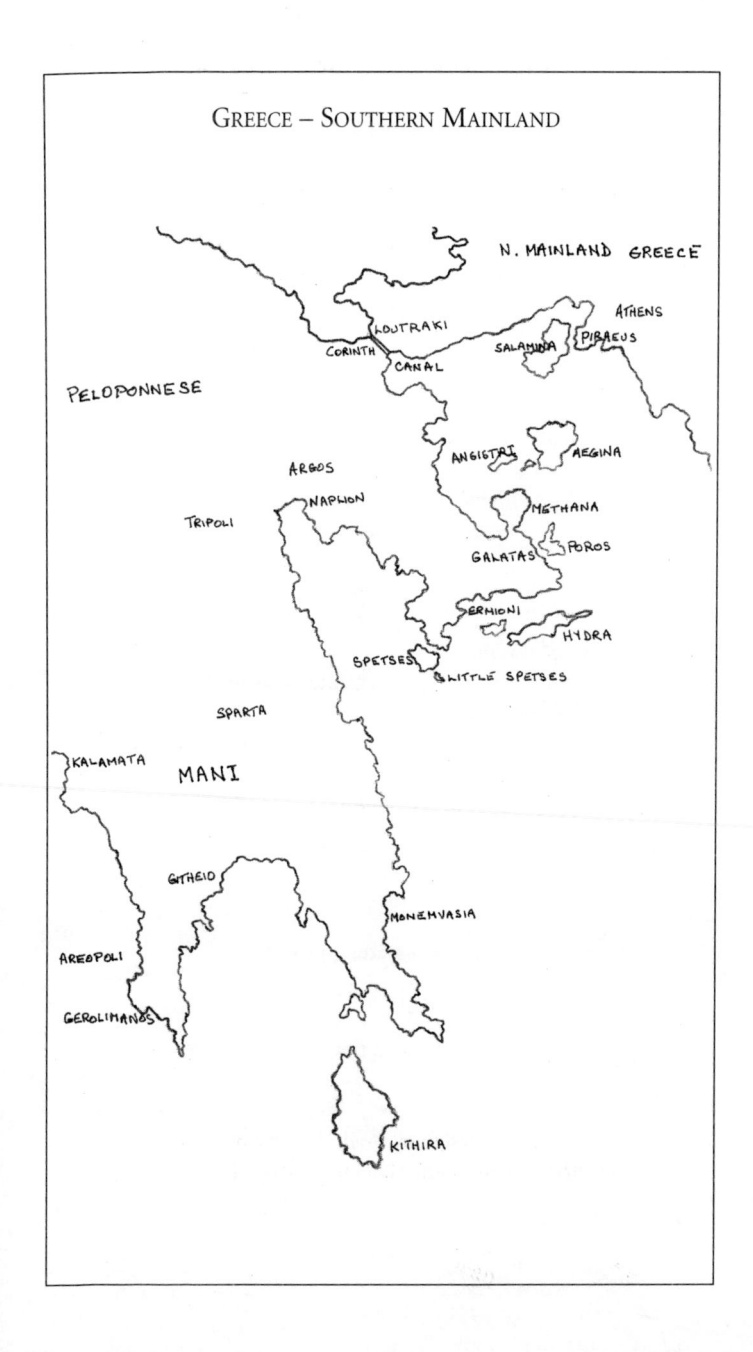

Greece – Southern Mainland

First published in Great Britain by

Ashgrove Publishing
27 John Street
London WC1N 2BX

© Anne Ibbotson 2006

The right of Anne Ibbotson to be identified as the
author of this work has been asserted by her
in accordance with the Copyright Designs
and Patents Act 1988.

All photographs appear courtesy of the author.

No part of this publication may be reproduced, stored
in a retrieval system or transmitted, in any form
or by any means, electronic, mechanical,
photocopying, recording or otherwise,
without the prior permission
of the publisher.

ISBN 1 85398 149 4

First edition

Book design by Brad Thompson
Printed and bound in Malta by Progress Press Ltd